D LEARNING RESC   ENTRE
College, Barnsley

Lynsey Hanley was born   Birmingham in 1976. She has written for newspapers and magazines including the *Guardian*, the *Daily Telegraph* and the *Times Literary Supplement*. She lives in London with her husband and son.

Northern C
Librar

NC302

D1325200

CANCELLED

ESTATES

AN INTIMATE HISTORY

LYNSEY HANLEY

GRANTA

Granta Publications, 12 Addison Avenue, London W11 4QR

First published in Great Britain by Granta Books, 2007
Paperback edition published by Granta Books, 2008
This new edition with preface published by Granta Books, 2012

Copyright © 2007, 2012 Lynsey Hanley

Extracts from Mass-Observation 'Worktown' collection
reproduced with permission of Curtis Brown Group Ltd, London
on behalf of the Trustees of the Mass-Observation Archive.
Copyright © Trustees of the Mass-Observation Archive.

Lynsey Hanley has asserted her moral right under
the Copyright, Designs and Patents Act, 1988,
to be identified as the author of this work.

All rights reserved. No reproduction, copy or transmission
of this publication may be made without written permission.
No paragraph of this publication may be reproduced, copied
or transmitted save with written permission or in accordance
with the provisions of the Copyright Act 1956 (as amended).
Any person who does any unauthorized act in relation to
this publication may be liable to criminal prosecution
and civil claims for damages.

A CIP catalogue record for this book is
available from the British Library.

3 5 7 9 10 8 6 4

ISBN 978 1 84708 702 7

Typeset by M Rules

Printed and bound by CPI Group (UK) Ltd, Croydon, CR0 4YY

MIX
Paper from
responsible sources
FSC® C020471
FSC
www.fsc.org

For Jamie,
and in memory of Lily Payne (1919–2005)

Contents

Preface

Never a driver, I spend a lot of time on buses and trains. It was nearly twenty years ago that I realised I spent most of my time on those journeys – short hops and long hauls alike – looking at the kinds of houses that people in Britain live in. Those who live in the centre of our towns and cities inhabit terraces and low- or medium-rise flats; those towards the periphery tend to live in newer, boxier semis and high-rises. It was on the edge of a city, Birmingham, and in the latter sort of house, late-1960s-built, that I grew up in the 1980s and early 1990s. The deregulation of bus services in the late 1980s had made the service from our estate, Chelmsley Wood, to the city centre, nine miles away, scrappy. There was no hint of serving the public in the service: to travel on one of these buses, you felt, was to do a bus owner a favour rather than to take part in an everyday activity necessary, and sometimes enhancing, to urban life; but without a family car, we relied on them. In Thatcher's eyes our family failed every time we boarded. Yet if the windows were clean enough to see out of, there was always something worth noting to see, and it was always those places on the outskirts – what the poets Paul Farley and Michael Symmons Roberts have termed the Edgelands – that made me reach for the ticket and scribble some commonplace thoughts about them on the back – usually about which bit of the past I was suddenly reminded of. The desolate seesaws and soggy mattresses that tend to furnish the periphery of the periphery didn't get a look-in; it was always about the pitch of the roofs or the measliness of the windows. I collected these written-on stubs and put them away until there was a thick stash in my pockets and on the desk.

I met my husband in 1998, and within a few months he started to note that I was always going on about the same things: complaining about how you can always tell council housing from private housing and about how newspaper journalists are incapable of describing council estates as anything other than 'tough', or wondering aloud why British estates had such a dire reputation, and then going on to answer my own question before anyone else had chance to. (Reputation is about class, I would argue, or at least about what we perceive to 'have class' or not, and class is built into our landscape in the form of housing.) In pubs I would always pipe up with my own version of the Four Yorkshiremen: Yer mum and dad 'ad a car? Luxury! Your school let you take more than one GCSE! Getoutofit! Between them these signs suggested that, of all the things one might choose to do in life, writing a book about council estates could constitute, for me, several years' worthwhile pursuit. I'd enjoy writing it, even if no one would enjoy reading it afterwards.

The phrase 'council estate', I write in the introductory chapter of this book, is a sort of psycho-social bruise: everyone winces when they hear it. It makes us think of dead ends (in terms of lives as well as roads), stereotypes, the absence of escape routes. It makes us think of bad design, identical front doors, windswept grass verges, and the kind of misplaced optimism which, in Britain especially, gives the individualistically inclined an easy way to kick social-democratic values. Council tower blocks had their appalling reputation sealed by the collapse of Ronan Point, a newly built high-rise in east London, in 1968. Large-scale estates such as the one on which I grew up are associated in the folk memory with the break-up of extended families, though also with childhoods spent running free, perhaps too free, in what used to be the green belt.

I wrote the book during the longest period of Labour rule in the party's history. As Prime Minister, Tony Blair made one of his landmark early speeches on the point of New Labour – social justice without sentimentality, it seemed at the time – at the Aylesbury estate in south London, which he announced would be demolished and fully replaced with low-rise housing. He described it as one of the '2,000 worst' estates in the country – worst in the sense that they combined high unemployment and low educational attainment with, apparently, large numbers of families 'known' to social services. Note that he didn't describe them as the 'poorest', only as 'the worst', despite the fact that poverty made the estates hard to live on at the same time that the estates' location and existing unpopularity tended to entrench poverty.

Although I was writing in a spirit of purely personal inquiry – why did I have a thing about estates, and why did there seem to be a thing about estates in the collective consciousness? – it always seemed significant that I was writing about a form of social prejudice which was being reinforced, sometimes unintentionally but not always, by government policy. It became an article of faith, brandished in particular by those ministers with harsh inner-urban constituencies, such as David Blunkett and Hazel Blears, that any government spending on, any attention paid to, people living on council estates was conditional on their behaving well. After 1997, regardless of the true intentions and effects of high public spending, if you were one of 'these people' who lived on an estate, you would still need to 'do the right thing' and 'play by the rules' in order to deserve a Labour government's munificence.

In Gordon Brown's New Year message to the nation in 2010 he stated his belief that 'we can create a new decade of prosperity with opportunities fairly shared amongst those who work hard and play by the rules'. The phrase 'playing by the rules' – born in sentiment during the early New Labour years, later to become one of the Brown government's mantras, alongside 'hard-working families' – referred to anyone believing themselves to be of the respectable lower- or would-be-lower-middle class, convinced as the government was that civilisation has only a thin veneer and that only the righteous actions of the 'silent majority' were keeping the id-fuelled impulses of the masses at bay. The experience of Shannon Matthews, an eight-year-old girl from the Dewsbury Moor estate in West Yorkshire who was hidden in 2008 by her own mother and step-uncle in the hope of convincing the public that she had been kidnapped, was widely inferred to be the inevitable consequence of her having the misfortune to live on a council estate. By the time the Labour party lost power in 2010, after thirteen years in government, both it and society as a whole had grown blind to the fact that the overwhelming majority of people 'play by the rules' regardless of their economic circumstances. Over the years the rhetoric had hardened so much, yet so slowly and subtly, that no one noticed the strangling of compassion. As ever, the 'rules', in so far as there are any in place of unspoken and universal social norms, are made by the privileged and change at the whims of the privileged; this can be observed as much in the content of the BBC's mid-2000s hit 'Little Britain' as by reading Hansard. The 'Little Britain' character Vicky Pollard, a wilfully ignorant, fecund, mouthy teenager, could not have been shown to live anywhere else but on an estate. It never made me comfortable or conspiratorial to watch Matt Lucas, a middle-class man from the affluent south-east of England, play a working-class girl from one of the many wrong parts of Bristol; the only part of the satire that rang true was Vicky's desperation to cleave to her ignorance. Growing up, I could never understand how people – peers, parents – could be so keen on ignorance, to appear to prefer it to knowledge. The problems of choosing ignorance are manifest in a society that now relies on knowledge for jobs and which places a punishingly high premium on self-policing, self-regulating behaviour. Governments seek to criminalise people at the bottom of the pile for making bad decisions without acknowledging the paucity of options available to them, or the policy decisions which led to, or at least exacerbated, that paucity. The French sociologist Loic Wacquant, who has based much of his work on the study of people living in socially marginalised areas such as housing estates, describes this phenomenon as 'punishing the poor'.

'Something is profoundly wrong with the way we live today,' wrote the late historian Tony Judt in his 2010 book *Ill Fares the Land*. His concise account of the building and destruction of social democracy in Britain and Europe reminds us that in the twenty-five years following the war, governments attempted, and to a large extent managed, to establish conditions of material security for the majority. Even then, not all of us benefited: countless individuals grew up in the 1960s and even the 1970s – a period during which there was a surplus of council housing for rent – accustomed to midnight flits and insecure housing. What could be called relative poverty then would look like absolute poverty now. Forty years ago, to buy enough food to feed a household of four for a week took up a third of the family income. Today it's more like 15 per cent for a household on an average gross income of around £480 per week. At the same time, the TUC reports that 'Britain today is a society increasingly divided between the top 40 and the bottom 60 per cent'. In other aspects, however, mass prosperity appears to be receding. A report conducted by the National Housing Federation in 2011 predicted that home ownership would fall within a few years to just under two-thirds of households, from 2001's high-point of nearly three-quarters, taking us back to levels last seen in the mid-1980s, when the privatisation of social housing through the 'right-to-buy' was in its early days and the interest rate, like inflation, was in double figures.

The signs and effects of housing tenure go far beyond simply reflecting a household's economic circumstances. I received many dozens of letters and emails about the book on its publication in 2007 and in the months and years following. It seemed that it had hit some sort of nerve, in that most of the responses were from people who themselves had grown up or lived on estates, and who had also felt that the fact of class segregation in Britain's housing stock had been overlooked. Many described their own experience of 'the wall in the head', which they'd never quite escaped, despite most having experienced upward social mobility, including moves from council to private housing, from flats to houses, and from the struggling North to the genteel South, in adulthood. Some were positive about 'their' estate. One wrote: 'I think there was a little window in the history of the human race when someone in charge believed that ordinary working people like us should be provided with somewhere beautiful to live. It was brief and fleeting.' Others reflected on the downsides of not fitting into an environment in which tall poppies get cut down: 'Success was to get through the school day unnoticed, and get home without being beaten up.' A disproportionate amount of the correspondence, unsurprisingly, came from people who had worked in housing management during the building zenith of the 1960s, and often referred to the appalling state of most private rented housing up to the 1970s, when the abundance of new council housing made such stock all but redundant. Others were more interested in class symbols, of which the council estate has become arguably the most potent in the last forty years, as a general indicator of Britain's social sickness.

At the time of publication some innovative and thoughtful changes were being made to estates to make them less cosmetically distinguishable from private housing and, through redesign and in many cases an increased police presence, safer for tenants to live on. Even so, estates remain disproportionately linked to 'bad' events, one example being the largely urban riots of August 2011. Council estate architecture is still overwhelmingly associated with being trapped, with the disappearance of individual lives and personalities into warren-like structures, where they fall off the radar of mainstream society. Most lives lived on estates are, of course, utterly mainstream, but that fact tends to be circumvented in discussions of 'the broken society', a phrase coined by Brown's Conservative successor, David Cameron, and used regularly by his minister Iain Duncan Smith on one of his regular visits to benighted, and therefore perversely photogenic, estates in Scotland or the north of England. On these occasions it's worth recalling the words of Tariq Jahan, the father of a young man who was run over and killed while trying to prevent local shops being trashed during the 2011 riots: 'I don't see a broken society. I see a minority of people who took advantage of the country when the country was in crisis. They didn't think of the country and only thought about themselves, their own personal greed and satisfaction.' What he's referring to is ignorance manifesting itself, again.

Government inaction on housing is nothing new: announcing generous or radical policies that involve lessening or ameliorating inequality risks simply looking like acting to appease 'scroungers' and 'immigrants'. Public opinion on the workless, whose situation is often conflated with council tenancy, has hardened during the recession which began in 2008, but this is largely because such rhetoric was unchallenged during the credit boom of the New Labour years. Huge investment in social housing took place during New Labour's tenure, but went unremarked upon by the government for fear of appearing to reward fecklessness. The effect was to reinforce the idea that living on an estate was something that only the lazy, unmotivated and hapless did: those too dysfunctional to be counted as full citizens. In 2007 Brown announced a massive programme of house building to counteract short supply and rising prices, promising that three million new homes would be built by 2020. This promise came to nothing, and not only because it was announced on the eve of a huge recession. Much of this new housing was to be built in the form of 'eco-towns' – new satellite developments intended to showcase building methods which would reduce domestic energy use and promote working locally as against commuting – an idea that was derided, while at the same time only piecemeal plans were being made to reintroduce direct government subsidies to local authorities to build council housing, as opposed to funding social house building through housing associations.

Under the Conservative-Lib Dem coalition, government rhetoric on housing has been similarly puffed up when compared with the reality. In 2011 David Cameron announced that he would 'get Britain building'; at the time of this book's original publication in 2007, 175,000 homes a year were being built, whereas at the time of writing this foreword at the start of 2012, it's fewer than 125,000. Nearly five million people, representing 1.8 million households, are on waiting lists for council housing at a time when the coalition plans to cap housing benefit regardless of tenure – a policy designed, it seems, to distance people on low incomes from the service-sector jobs and public transport on which they rely. What social housing remains is threatened by the government's reintroduction of high discounts for tenants wishing to buy their council or housing association home, a practice all but phased out under the previous administration. Shortage of supply in both the private-rented and the owner-occupied sectors keeps rents and property prices disproportionately high at a time of frozen wages and high unemployment, making the situation progressively worse over time. Not enough is ever done to challenge the basic problems of undersupply of housing, unaffordable private property, social stigma and structural unemployment. Something has to give, yet the current situation is stagnant, as is the underlying class structure of Britain.

This was a book written out of anger and a sense of injustice, some of it justified in hindsight, some a clear attempt to disentangle the – perhaps unnecessarily – complicated feelings I had about the place I grew up in. I started out wanting to write about the relationship between class and the built environment, and ended up writing about the internal walls that we build to keep us from collapsing under the weight of that relationship's implications. I'll finish with the words of another letter-writer, who wrote to me in 2009:

'Today is the 20th anniversary of the fall of the Berlin Wall. I sometimes think your wall in the head will be a damn sight more difficult to dismantle!' He was right, and we'd never even met.

Lynsey Hanley
London, February 2012

Introduction

We lived in Area 4. It was on the edge of the Wood – an estate on the periphery of Birmingham – in a row of terraced houses that led into a fistful of dead-ends. Between the house and my primary school there were no more than a few yards of road, the rest being a series of inter-connecting walks and avenues lined with more terraces and maisonettes. You could walk past the school and as far as the shopping centre, a mile away, and only have to cross the road once. From Area 4 into Area 5 (south) – past my Aunty Lil's ground-floor flat, past the tower block where, in 2001, a man in his thirties shot himself in a siege outside my primary school, past the corner shop where, in 2002, another man was mown down by his own van by its getaway drivers – along a predestined pebble-dash strip.

Life wasn't always as dramatic as this, but it had its moments. One day, walking with my mother along this stationary travelator, we reached a whipping wall of wind that prevented us getting any further than another tower block. This one was a hundred yards – if that – from our destination, my school. It was as though it didn't want us ever to get there. It was as though it was trying to scare us away. It wasn't even an especially windy day, merely that what breeze there was raced around each ninety-degree corner and was funnelled through the space between us and a squat row of garages near the front entrance. My mum picked me up and we tried shouldering our way through the forcefield. We had no chance. It threw us back like a magnet repelling another. Within a minute or two there were a dozen of us, infants and juniors, mostly travelling alone, all of us screaming, until a wised-up older girl called Marsha bossed us – even the adults – over to the back wall of the garages.

'Stand with yer backs to it! Down't move!'

A whirlpool of rubbish, by now containing my mum's glasses, sought an absent plughole. We were trapped inside it, assaulted by flying Panda Pops bottles and empty Quavers packets; tiny boys, the kind of boys who never blew their noses or had their noses blown for them, were whiplashed by their parka hoods. It lasted until the monolith relented, after what had seemed like an hour but was probably no longer than ten minutes. The new glasses were snapped in two. We passed through in traumatized silence, with me leading my mum the rest of the way. I don't know how she found her way back home.

It was fine, though: people had jobs, people had families. At least, most of the ones we knew did. It felt as though the estate had always been there, even though it was barely fifteen years old. I remember it having a settled quality: it was, for the most part, deadly quiet except for the rattle of aged buses every twenty minutes or so as they passed the end of our road. We had an almond tree on the front lawn that produced sappy little buds. We lived near a playing field, next to the maternity hospital where I was born and my mother before me. When she was born, my grandad had to cycle from the edge of Birmingham through a thick bluebell wood to reach his wife and newborn daughter. In the same year, a local man wrote a little ode to the Wood when it was still a wood: a place where 'the bluebells were lying in every fold and bracken-green dell among the trees'. The city only reached as far as Lea Village then: fifteen or twenty minutes by bus from the centre. By 1970, from bull's-eye to perimeter and Area 4 would take forty-five on a good day.

The bluebells lay in every fold until 1964, when Richard Crossman, Labour's new Minister for Housing, legislated for Birmingham City Council to purchase green belt land in the borough of Meriden – the geographical centre of England, halfway between the second city and Coventry – on which to build nearly 20,000 flats and houses as part of a massive slum-clearance project. It's easy to groan, What was he thinking? But when cities were still filled with slums at the dawn of the white-hot technological era, when children were still playing on wartime bombsites twenty years after VE Day, in town centres that resembled innards, something had to be done.

The City Architect, one Mr Maudsley, signed off the plan and work commenced. My father, a wages clerk with the corporation water department, was sent down to the site of the new estate with cash wodged into dozens of brown envelopes at the end of every week, to pay the Irish navvies who were laying the pipes. 'They were honest as the day is long,' he tells me. It was completed in 1969, five years after work had begun, and just after my mum – by then aged seventeen – had moved to a brand new end-of-terrace house in Area 6 (south) with my grandparents, who by then had spent nearly two decades on the council's waiting list for housing. At twenty-one, my mum would marry my dad, move a mile away for a couple of years, and move back to the estate shortly after I was born. By then the Wood Estate, as it had come to be known, had bedded in, and had already begun to take on that sometimes glaring, sometimes murky, sometimes solid, sometimes flimsy – but somehow always uniform – look of municipal housing. Nearly 60,000 people lived there, on what was one of the biggest council estates in Europe. And yet it still didn't feel like a town.

The Wood. I was born there, and lived there between the ages of eighteen months and eighteen years. Even though I have lived away from home for over a third of my life now, it continues to shape the way I think about the world outside it. Rather like rappers who continue to talk about the ghetto experience long after they have moved up and out to their own country ranches, it's a lifelong state of mind. Perhaps this is because, even though I live a long way from my original 'hood, I still live on an estate; this time in the inner city, but surrounded once more by tall, inhospitable-looking tower blocks. They sap the spirit, suck out hope and ambition, and draw in apathy and nihilism. It's hard to explain why I feel so strongly about housing in this way, other than that I know I had a lucky escape where others did not, and that too many people will not know what I mean by that. My nan has nothing but wonderful things to say about the Wood, her home and the local council, but that probably has something to do with the fact that she grew up in a falling-down house in the Rhondda valley. If we're to be post-modern about this, it's all relative.

The point is that most people now have a surfeit of choice in their lives at the same time as a large minority of people have none. That large minority tends to live on council estates, whether in cities or outside of them. The 50 per cent of poor people (that is, those whose incomes are less than 60 per cent of the median average) who are homeowners also tend to live on council estates, as beneficiaries of the Right to Buy policy – proof, if any were needed, that a property-owning democracy doesn't necessarily mean an equal one. They too have little choice over where they live, due to the fact that council housing – with the exception of one or two listed buildings in London – is never as desirable, and therefore can never be worth as much, as private.

It's not something you think about when you're growing up. *Wow, I'm really alienated. My school is suffering from its single-class intake. What this estate needs is a decent public-transport infrastructure.* It's more a sense you have. A sense that someone, who lives in a proper house, in a proper town, sat on the floor of an office one day with a box of fancy Lego bricks and laid out, with mathematical precision, a way of housing as many people as possible in as small a space as could be got away with. And, in so doing, forgot that real people aren't inanimate yellow shapes with permanent smiles branded on their plastic bodies. That real people might get lost in such a place.

I wonder if the stigma of coming from a council estate is ever turned to an advantage, and whether that inherent sense of inferiority ever becomes a source of pride. You believe yourself to be proud of having overcome the limitations of your environment – literally, of having escaped a kind of prison – and yet you know that in some ways you will never escape. That's because, to anybody who doesn't live on one (and to some who do), the term 'council estate' means hell on earth.

Council estates are nothing to be scared of, unless you are frightened of inequality. They are a physical reminder that we live in a society that divides people up according to how much money they have to spend on shelter. My heart sags every time it senses the approach of those flat, numbing boxes that prickle the edges of every British town. I feel bad talking about them in this way, as though every house were a human waiting to be hurt.

I don't have a very good relationship with council-owned or council-built housing; yet money, or lack thereof, draws me back to live in it, as it does with anyone in housing need. It ought to be that I feel safer and happier knowing that, unless a major failing or catastrophe befalls us, I'll never be out on the streets due to lack of funds. It could be that I'm a born miseryguts who'll never be happy wherever she fetches up, but I know – no, I *believe* – that not to be the case. I can't think about council estates without having a pronounced emotional reaction to those very words. How much of that can be attributed to the experiences I had while growing up on one, and how much is due to a verging-on-sentimental attachment to the founding principles of the welfare state, it's impossible to tell. But there's something about them that makes me brim over with pain, and a sense of wrongness; even the bits that anyone else would think right. It's not even a feeling of having been hard done by (or is it?). It's more a feeling of having been consigned, contained, delivered to a place, to serve a sentence that may never end.

A more rounded view would take into account the degrading living conditions endured by working-class families in industrial cities, in slums and shanty towns, before council housing provided millions of them with warmth and space for the first time since their ancestors left the fields. Our grandparents – even our parents – do not forget how good it feels to have your own bath and an inside toilet, but then neither do they forget what it's like to live in a place that feels knitted into the fabric of the town or city it forms a part of.

'The modern housing and impressive physical amenities of [the] Wood are appreciated by the families who moved there,' wrote the American journalist Leonard Downie Jr, in a report on the final slum clearances that took place in London and other major cities towards the end of the 1960s, 'but the project is cold and uninviting socially.' The words 'modern' and 'impressive' rub up against 'cold' and 'uninviting' like partners in a forced marriage. You can be as modern as you like, but it will not equate with human warmth. Modern homes, he suggests, do not have hearths, or beating hearts.

Play word association with the term 'council estate'. Estates mean alcoholism, drug addiction, relentless petty stupidity, a kind of stir-craziness induced by chronic poverty and the human mind caged by the rigid bars of class and learned incuriosity. In London, there's an estate at the bottom of almost every gentrified road, a self-contained world signposted by lopsided bollards, DO NOT PLAY BALL signs and standardized double glazing. The privet hedges stop where the sound of shirtless men shouting begins. I don't even have to open the hollow door or big square windows of my ex-council flat in the East End of London to hear a diurnal chorus of drunkards, men and women, who have long since lost the ability to prevent cackles and profanities (more so than vomit) escaping their mouths. If Hogarth were here now, he would paint the capital's grimmest council estates, not its sewagy, gin-soaked back streets.

I walk down the narrow concrete stairwell that leads from my flat to the chip shop below. Six or seven girls, all aged about fourteen, are standing listlessly outside the pub next to it, which acts as a kind of rain shelter to those drunks who have the money to buy pints of beer and cider in glasses rather than cans. One girl is holding a tiny pink smudge in her arms: a baby, whose whitish blanket absorbs the smoke blown out by a circle of mouths. Another girl wears a headscarf, but is otherwise clothed in the uniform of the street: navy tracksuit bottoms with white stripes galloping down the outside of each leg, pristine white trainers and hooded Gap top. She looks mystified at the company she is keeping, as though it's something she's doing under duress, while the rest are dull-eyed and palpably bored. But it's what you do, or rather, what you end up doing. Having a child before you really know what to do with it; sidling up to people (like me, on their way into the newsagent's, where the toothless wife of the fruit-and-veg man takes her daily place by the sweet racks, leaning on the fridge for support and gorging on Chewits all day) and asking them if they'll buy you ten Lambert & Butler; passing round a two-litre bottle of sparkling perry. If you're asked why you do it, you might say 'Dunno,' but defensively, because you know that there's something else in the world you could be doing; it's just that no one has ever told you what those things are or how you can get to do them.

Sometimes, estates feel as though they serve to wilfully deaden or disrupt lives, but they were never intended to. The crushing inevitably of the saddest lives lived on council estates lends itself to a pejorative shorthand used by the rest of the population, who think it's funny, or disgusting, or haven't thought about it at all. When the Wood's local football club plays a team from elsewhere in the borough, they compete to the sound of a terrace chant that goes 'Go back! To your council estate!', sung to the tune of 'Go West' by the Village People. Recidivists are reported in newspapers to live on this or that estate as though it were a matter of course that they would. Any rich or famous person about whom it's discovered that they were brought up in a council house, no matter what else distinguishes them, is understood to have something of the Pygmalion about them.

But although most estates acquire undeservedly bad reputations in this way, there are a few that live up – or down – to an image of incomparable decrepitude. The first time I visited the estate in the East End neighbourhood where I live now was on a canvassing slog against the British National Party in 1994. It struck me as the most depressing place I'd ever seen and I could barely imagine what kind of desperate state I'd have to be in to find myself living there. Five years later, my monthly housing budget eaten up by ever greedier landlords, I moved on to that very estate, into a one-bed-room flat that was leaky with condensation and which overlooked the world's least savoury pub. The rubbly patch of waste concrete outside our block, originally a historic site associated with the suffragist movement, is still one of the grimmest places it is possible to see. Drunks, to a man and woman on crutches, clobber one another with cans of Special Brew on their patch next to a trio of burnt-out Daleks posing as recycling bins. In the summer, the young-but-old girls join them, often with their babies, wandering in circles all day between the off-licence, the pub and, when hungry, the chip shop, spending whatever they have left on cigs and mobile-phone credit. It's a gutting kind of personal squalor, to have nowhere else to go but this terrible square which offers little that may help them, except that which enables them to forget where they are.

It is a reminder that people fight themselves or each other, rather than the system, simply because it's easier and there's an obvious way to do it. Because the secrets of that system have been opened up to me through years of non-compulsory education and the social mobility that comes with it. I do not have to fight to be seen or heard or listened to. Although I'm aware of the monolithic and frustrating nature of the authorities, I have learnt how to deal with them confidently and to get done the things that need to be done. When I read the free newspaper produced by the local authority, not only does it make sense to me, but the telephone numbers, websites and addresses listed in it all have an obvious use, and I take time to store them away for future reference. I have the money and freedom to create a comfortable home in an ex-local authority flat that's prone to damp; indeed, I know whom I must call when that damp threatens to ruin my chest and clothes. All this means that I'm less likely to want to spoil for a scrap outside the chip shop.

One day in 2003, I came across this story in a local news-paper:

A Wood man found himself in hot water after asking his estranged partner to fill up his Pot Noodle. The 30-year-old admitted putting his hands around his partner's neck and pulling out her earring, causing a cut ear and lip and a scratched neck. Colin Doyle, defending, said that his client lived opposite the house where his partner lives with their two children, and he had gone over to ask for some hot water after his own home had been burgled, leaving him with no food.

Perhaps this is why the brand name Pot Noodle – 'the slag of all snacks', the dirty secret of our nominally bourgeois, and therefore nominally food-loving, society – seems so apt an emblem of the council estate. It's synonymous with seaminess, of lives not lived well but eked out joylessly, and, again, used as a fun insult by those who have grown tired of disguising their snobbery. Poor taste, bad grammar, the betrayal of family history beyond that which is conveniently aspirational: all these traits are now deemed 'council estate behaviour'. The collision of Pot Noodles, wife-beating and council estates in a single news clipping seems almost too funny – in that way we now have of laughing at the misfortunes of poor, daft people, because it's their fault for being stupid – to be true. It encourages a kind of forehead-slapping despair in otherwise right-thinking people who wonder how it came to pass that a country with a national health service and universal child benefit could fail to prevent people's lives from turning out so catastrophically.

Broadly, there are two public perceptions of the British council estate. The first is of the dream gone sour. Council homes were once the golden standard for a bright, uncynical working class who had every reason to feel entitled to the best the state had to offer them. To get a council house in the immediate post-war period was to have a full stake in society.

Ownership didn't matter: what did matter was that you had succeeded in persuading those in power that you deserved better than to live in a slum, at the mercy of an exploitative landlord. The dream of holding a fair and equable stake in the collective wealth of the nation – of which good housing formed a part – barely had time to bear fruit before it was punctured, without ceremony, by the idea that the only way to feel fully anchored to society, and therefore to be fully a citizen, was to own the property you lived in. Council homes were never intended to be holding cages for the poor and disenfranchised, but somehow, that's how they ended up.

The second perception of the council estate is bound up in the myth that the poor will always be with us, and that the existence of cheap housing to contain them is a nasty fact of life. You've got to put them somewhere, after all. Preferably somewhere a long way away from the rest of us; somewhere not very nice, so there is always that invisible stick to the backside, with the far-off prospect of escape to a better place as the tantalizing carrot. This fear and hatred of the impoverished, as John Carey's illuminating *The Intellectuals and the Masses* showed us, has existed since ordinary people were first permitted to leave the slums and have their own little patch of pleasant land. Only the rich, it seems, are permitted to nibble away at the green belt, with land-greedy 'executive' estates: ghettoes for those who can choose which type of ghetto they want to live in. The regeneration and rebuilding of once-coveted housing estates, on the other hand, is a waste of taxpayers' money, because 'they' – the dregs, the scum – will only go and have more babies, smoke more fags, fry more chips and set fire to the whole damn place when the lit match hits their shellsuit.

Between the two world wars, about a quarter of working-class people moved from the inner cities out into new outer-urban – the word 'suburban' sounds too middle-class – housing estates. These were built by both local councils and private developers, encouraged by skilled workers and clerks reporting that they would like to own their own homes. Oxford's first motor-car factories were built on its outer edges in the mid-1930s, drawing in migrants from the bigger cities of the Midlands, who would receive a decent and steady wage and who needed to be housed quickly and cheaply. In Cutteslowe, a farming area two miles to the north of the town's centre, a large piece of land was cleaved in two, one half taken by the council for its own housing, the other bought by the deceptively modern-sounding Urban Housing Company for building private homes on. When the adjoining municipal and private estates had been built, you would have been hard pushed to tell the difference between the restrained brown terraces and semis. From the outside, it appeared to be an early exercise in mixed-tenure occupation, where well-paid working-class men could coexist peacefully alongside middle managers and tradesmen. The private developer thought differently. Without recourse to planning permission, the law, or any motive beyond profit and the presumed snobbery of his prospective customers, he built two walls that isolated his own houses from the council ones. The walls crossed roads and gardens, and had no break in them to allow passage of the council-house tenants to local shops and bus stops. They were even capped with barbed wire to prevent members of the forbidden caste – encouraged to sabotage the developer's efforts by Communist students enraged by this act of social apartheid – entering his land.

What is extraordinary about the Cutteslowe Walls is that they stayed up for twenty-five years after their illegal erection in 1934, enduring a world war and the first fifteen years of a welfare state that had been created to destroy pernicious class divisions once and for all. Despite their illegality, the walls seemed to represent something else: the divisions that existed, and continue to exist, *within* a single class. Many of the buyers of the Urban Housing Company's semis were as working-class as the renters who lived on the other side of the wall: clerks or foremen they may have been, but their wages were barely higher. What mattered is that they thought they were better, and were terrified of the calamities that might befall them if the wall were to be knocked down. They had scrimped and saved for a deposit, and they were damned if their postage-stamp gardens were going to be trampled on by barefoot kids who wouldn't know a bar of soap if they slipped on one.

The early working-class home buyers in Britain were often those who would have been considered snobby or different – quiet, preoccupied, distant – by their fellow tenement dwellers in the days when upper and lower working class alike had to share close quarters in the cities. The first estates gave aspirational tenants a chance to get away from people they considered smelly and uncouth. There was suddenly an opportunity to express your displeasure at those whose behaviour and morals you disapproved of. Families who moved from the cities on to new estates such as Cutteslowe, Wythenshawe in Manchester and Speke in Liverpool could place themselves on a new class spectrum according to the poshness of the part of the estate they found themselves seconded to. In interviews similar to those conducted as part of the means test, they were asked by housing officers to reveal how they did their washing, whether they kept noisy or quiet pets, and how – if at all – they budgeted for essential items. If you spent your money as you got it, you would get a rented terrace without a bathroom (the bath in the kitchen would serve as a countertop when lidded with a slab of wood). If you planned and saved for the future, your reward would be an inside toilet. Poorer council-house dwellers suffered accordingly. They could not afford to keep up with the

Joneses, and yet were required for the first time to buy or rent curtains, and to ensure that their children had shoes. Those who could not, or did not, became the ultimate pariahs, and the predecessors of those people we now revile for the degrading circumstances in which they find themselves.

If the lumpen working class is contained in places where no one else dares to venture, their children attending schools that no one else in their right mind would allow their own to attend, there is, surely, no obvious problem. If the poor will always be with us, isn't it best to leave them where they are and condescend, with wringing hands, from afar? Or to suppress the lingering shame of inequality with gallows humour? For today's middle class, contamination is the fear that dare not speak its name.

There is one political quotation that is guaranteed to make me flare my nostrils and mash my right fist into my left hand every time I think of it. It's attributed to Margaret Thatcher. She is widely quoted as saying in 1986 that 'a man who finds himself, beyond the age of 26, on a bus can consider himself a failure'. By that sick logic, every person who takes part in public life, whether by using public transport, living in public-owned housing, educating themselves and their children at state schools, or being treated at NHS hospitals, has failed at the game. The idea of investing in public-owned assets has returned, belatedly, to the top of the political agenda, but the lasting harm of that statement – one of what sociologist Richard Sennett calls 'the hidden injuries of class' – resounds, whether it's apocryphal or otherwise. In newspapers and on television, every reference to a council estate is prefixed with the word 'tough', as though bare-knuckle boxing is the leisure activity of choice for every British person who doesn't own their own home. It does its stigmatizing work as intended. Estates are dangerous, they imply: don't visit them, and whatever you do, work as hard as you can so you don't have to live on them. All the people who live on estates are failures, and failure is not only contagious but morally repugnant. Any connection between the physical, economic and social isolation of council estates and the sometimes desperate behaviour of their tenants is ignored, or dismissed, or laughed at, because that's what they're there for: to contain the undeserving, un-useful poor. If the feckless poor did not exist, neither would council estates. Now, do you see why they're not worth spending money on?

There was a time when I was innocent of all this knowledge. Where I came from was, simply, where I came from. The Wood was the place that I came from, and though I felt lonely and sad for a lot of the time, I didn't know any different. Phrases like 'aspiration', or 'relative deprivation', I wouldn't find out about until many years later. It was only when I left that I learnt that I had been surrounded by drugs, which had started to arrive in larger quantities from the international airport a mile away, and the endemic dealing of which had led to the closure and demolition of the pub nearest my old primary school. Girls from the estates would enter their twenties acting as cocaine runners, rooting around in toilet bowls for something to do and the promise of more cash than they'd ever seen in their lives. None of this I ever knew.

You're not thinking about that at the time. I had other things on my mind then, most of which, though, were caused and influenced by my environment. I didn't even notice what I was doing, which was working out how and when I'd leave. From the age of about twelve, I would sit down with my mum's mail-order catalogues – Kays, Great Universal, Freemans, all the greats – after tea every night and pick out which washing machine I would have, which cooker and which settee, when I had my own flat. Never a house, for some reason, always a flat. Then I'd open the *Evening Mail* at the classifieds section and circle all the jobs I thought I'd be able to do once I reached sixteen. I was already good at typing, so I went for clerical and secretarial work, usually with someone or something called Agy. I had no idea who or what an Agy was, still less that you had to apply through an *agency*. In those moments of imaginary flight, I felt rapturous and unfettered, or rather, rapturous at the thought of being unfettered.

It wasn't even as though I didn't like living there. It was all I knew, and to some extent all I still know of Birmingham. We went in and out of town, ten miles away, by bus, and occasionally to visit my grandad's widowed brother and sister, in the flat they shared in Ward End. On most bank holidays, we went on day trips out to the seaside and other big towns by train and coach, but I still wasn't truly aware that other kinds of houses existed. I still remember the thrill of seeing the higgledy patchwork of London's housing for the first time. It seemed as though every house was different from the others, even the council blocks, which filled every space in a jumble of clashing panels. Now I know London better than the place that was once my home.

But the Wood stays with me like a shadow. In the summer of 1971, when the estate had just been completed, a reporter from the *Birmingham Post* – a newspaper not usually known for reflecting the city council's socialist idealism – visited the estate and concluded that 'When (the children) are grown, they will have little or no affinity to Birmingham . . . The city will seem a million life-miles away.' The fact that, thirty-five years later, we grown children of the Wood still speak like Barry from *Auf Wiedersehen, Pet* and support Birmingham City with fundamentalist vigour puts paid to any idea that the affinity has been altogether lost. But I think what he was referring to was the estate's very self-containedness, the way in which it created a world that, if you were lucky, you could leave, but could never get to leave you. It poured you into its mould, so that you would always carry its shape.

Since 1980, the Wood has been controlled – neatly and effectively, but with the same air of mortification displayed by the archetypal snob Hyacinth Bucket whenever her slovenly brother Onslow comes to visit in the sitcom *Keeping Up Appearances* – by the more affluent Solihull metropolitan borough council. It refers to its unrepentant problem child as 'North Solihull'. A new mayor, himself from one of the four council wards that cover the estate, announces an end to the apartheid, as though he can somehow will equality into existence at the same time as the council's own Director of Public Health admits that his borough 'exhibits the greatest social polarity of any English local authority'. The estate is in the top 5 per cent of deprived wards in England. In 2001, a man could expect to live 71.4 years, and a woman 77.6, in Solihull proper, which was roughly in accordance with the English average at the time. On the Wood, they could expect only to reach 61.8 and 66.1 respectively. Ward unemployment reached 23.3 per cent in 1992, prompting the EU to list it as one of the most disadvantaged estates in western Europe and moving local newspaper the *Solihull Times* to describe the Wood, on its front-page headline in 72-point bold type, as a BLOT ON LANDSCAPE. Thanks for that.

I don't need statistics to tell me that the Wood and the rest of Solihull – the world of the isolated, single-class peripheral council estate, as opposed to the *nouveau riche* commuter belt – have little in common. I went to the local secondary school, which swapped places most years with the estate's other school at the bottom of the local authority's examination league table, not realizing that the education we were being offered was never intended to prepare us for a world in which your potential means little without a university degree to prove it. In any case, education was for dorks: I stuck out not so much like a sore thumb as like a gaping wound, and it felt at least as painful. There is little use in pretending that I ever felt at home, as Morrissey – with echoes of Philip Larkin – put it, with the 'ordinary girls/supermarket clothes/who think it's very clever to be cruel to you'. These days, I know why they were cruel. I saw a way out and clung on to it like you would the sides of a cable car, not having any idea where it was going except that, wherever it was, life would be better there. Today I'm sitting here, able to spell and count well, in a flat I own, writing a book. My life has turned out better than I could ever have imagined. I have had the freedom to choose not to have children yet, or at all, and have the confidence and financial independence not to have to rely on men. Unlike many of those ordinary girls, I had the secret knowledge, so curiously opaque and inaccessible on estates like ours, that life could be free and good.

This book is an attempt to work out how much of the stubborn rigidity of the British class system is down to the fact that class is built into the physical landscape of the country. It began as no more than a hunch: it seemed to me that we are divided not only by income and occupation, but by the types of homes in which we live. Of course, there have always been better and worse parts of town; the rich have always lived up on the hill, away from slurry smells and floods. The first council homes were built in a spirit of something-has-to-be-done paternalism, reflecting the values that defined the Victorian era. They were flats – not ideal living quarters for large families – and yet, by replacing dark, insanitary hovels, their very existence transformed the lives of the people who moved into them. For the first time since the Industrial Revolution swept millions of people into the cramped warrens of the cities, a working man could expect to live long enough to see his children reach adulthood. In the same spirit, the planned garden cities of the Edwardian period integrated workers' cottages into the design of the whole, so that they enjoyed equal access to the amenities of the centre and the green lung of landscaped parks and the nearby countryside.

The interwar years provided the first opportunity for governments to exhibit the political will that would ensure generations to come would not have to endure the stigma of living in visibly inferior housing; the first of many that were to be missed. The first wave of mass council housing was intended to provide 'homes fit for heroes', but in order to qualify, you first had to prove that you were morally upstanding enough to be so considered. When the second war was over and the bombed-out slums were cleared, another chance to build a classless infrastructure – literally, to build social iniquity out of the landscape – was not taken. Instead, following a brief period during which strong and lasting homes were built at a rate at odds with the incoming tide of consumer convenience and disposability, a decision was made to bolt homes together, rather than to build them brick by brick. By the 1970s, the further entrenchment of the class system through housing was complete. You could no longer look at a council house without knowing it was one.

Why does this matter? Why should it matter? There are some areas of society in which the welfare state has worked spectacularly well: you can't, for instance, blame the vast difference in life expectancy between people in affluent areas and those in poorer ones, on the NHS. It treats all those who enter its doors equally (although it helps if you know what treatment to ask for, and believe that you have the right to request it). But you can blame higher incidences of poor health and premature death, to a large extent, on the concentration of poorer people in a single area, where there are fewer fresh food markets, fewer open and green spaces, fewer sports amenities and fewer opportunities to have a social life outside the family. Council estates have the effect of making people feel worse about themselves, and in turn, physically worse than other members of society, because they know that they are in many ways cut off from the mass affluence – the mass middle-classness, if you like – that the rest of the nation enjoys.

There is a further reason why I felt compelled to write about this subject in particular. In literature, broadcasting and newspapers, depictions of working-class life are often either hopelessly sentimental or offensively vilifying. As with any other set of cultural traits that are rarely written about and, by extension, poorly understood, the truth is somewhere in between. In many ways, what defines the state of being working-class is veering between sentimentality and bitterness like a drunk trying to walk down the aisle of a moving bus. I wanted to write about the shades of feeling that are passed on the disorientating trip from one to the other and back. This book, then, is as much about class as it is about estates; it has to be, since the history of council housing is also the history of how the industrial working class was – or should I say is – housed. I started writing it with the plan to give it a snazzier, snappier title – a real nugget like, you know, 'The Estate We're In', or 'I'm So Ghetto' – before realizing that you only have to say the word 'estates' for someone to infer a vast amount of meaning from it. It's a bruise in the form of a word: it hits the nerves that register shame, disgust, fear and, very occasionally, fierce pride.

I won't pretend that my feelings about council estates are any less complicated than they were before I started to search for evidence that would back, or disprove, or illuminate, that early hunch. There is always a voice inside, telling me to be grateful that affordable housing for those in need exists at all. A second, idealist voice responds by saying that there shouldn't be anyone living in need in the first place. A third grinds its teeth at the idea that, today, 'affordable housing' usually means a plasterboard box next to an electricity generator two miles from the nearest bus stop. A fourth wonders aloud whether I am not, in fact, completely delusional. And so on. A multitude of conflicting voices say one thing and then another, but even that chorus cannot drown out a conviction that working-class people are not rabbits, but people, and as such should not be housed in hutches away from the higher, richer orders.

1

This Must Be the Place (I Waited Years to Leave)

The road my parents live on is on the extreme south-eastern border of the estate: a long, boomerang-shaped crescent from which car-free stalks of terrace housing spring out. Everywhere you look there are houses. There are no high-rise flats in this neck of the Wood, only criss-crossing macadamed walks with boxy brown rows set on either side. In the early days, people would regularly get lost looking for their own houses, such was the uniformity of the housing and the complexity of its design.

When I picture my parents' home – its position, its plot, its proximity to this and that – I think of all the other houses it so closely resembles in the immediate area. I keep thinking of the same word: square. Square and solid shapes, 18,000 times over, laid out in lines and curves that lead into each other like a never-ending maze. Their home – the house I lived in from the age of nine until I moved to London aged eighteen – is square and solid, and without embellishment. It's made from

sandy brick, a three-bed semi, with a front lawn about the size
of an adult's armspan and a drive that has never housed a car.
Unlike most of its neighbours, it doesn't have an awning or a
porch, and its windows were free of net curtains until the time
it was burgled twice in a month. Its pitched roof makes it
seem proud, if not handsome (flat-roofed houses look to me
like headless bodies). Inside it has been improved and
improved again, with a knocked-through wall to make the
living room long and lean, a buff-coloured Ikea kitchen, and
a wheat-coloured carpet that shows up every speck of dust.

A peacock chair holds court in one corner next to the
telly, on which a collection of battery-stomached cuddly toys
talk and gurgle on demand. I squash them by sitting on them
and look sideways out of the front window, just as I used to
do when I was waiting for my mum to get back from work
on long afternoons in the holidays. Shrek mumbles something sage about onions into the small of my back. I see a
narrowish road quietened by speed bumps and the deep red
row of two-bed terrace houses, as flat-fronted as pancakes
on a washing line, that sit on the other side of it. This is
the quiet, nice end of the estate; very nearly *rus in urbe*,
backed not by further rows of square semis and two-bed
terraces but by the vast gardens of those whom I only know
as the posh people, whose desire not to be reminded that
they are bordered by a council estate has led them to grow
forty-foot-high walls of coniferous trees that starve my
parents' own plants of light.

The only thing that reminds you of where you are, and how
you came to be there, is the wind. When it blows in the wrong
direction, towards the house, the trickle of the goldfish pond
and the twirrup of the birds gives way to the modern-day roar
of the M6, M42 and M45 motorways, which converge less
than a mile away. Then there is the grating pulse of intercity
trains a further mile from that, and the thrust of engines from

the adjacent airport. They say it's handy for transport links: handy if you've got a car or if you fancy going to Toronto or Cancun, but less so if haven't and you want to visit friends down the road on a Sunday. Neither I, my parents, nor my grandparents have ever owned a car; a doubly strange feat in an area whose main source of skilled employment is the motor industry. Fresh lines of newish Ford Focuses (for the men) and Ford Kas (for the women) seem to crop up on this road every day, making my parents seem ever odder for their complete reliance on public transport. 'I've got better things to spend me money on,' says my dad, meaning that if he were to run a car he would never be able to afford to go on holiday, and to him and my mum (and to me), holidays are sacrosanct.

My nan, who has never strayed beyond England and Wales, lives fifty steps away from my mum and dad, on one of the pedestrianized culs-de-sac, in an end-of-terrace house that is also square and without embellishment. Hers is built with a creamy, lighter tone of brick that matches the dozen in her row, most of which have now been bought from the council and enhanced with brown-paned double-glazed windows and clear-panelled doors with little stained-glass tulips at eye height. Behind, there is a fair patch of garden, about fifteen feet by fifteen, where once she grew strawberries and green beans. I thought my memory had betrayed me when I remembered being able to see out from her garden to the redundant lump of green space on to which a four-sided barrage of back-yard gates opened: her eight-foot-high fence looks pretty old these days. But then my mum reminds me how none of the houses with gardens had their own fences for several years, until the tedium of fetching footballs from one end of the green expanse – now potholed with shrubbery in order to prevent children from playing there – to the other became too much, and tenants were allowed to erect dividing fences.

The strange thing about the Wood is that it's so large, and

yet in the course of my life I feel like I've traversed nearly every one of its roads and 'stalks' at least once. It's warren-like and labyrinthine, and yet so hideously familiar that I want to see if I can take the most complicated walk I can without getting lost. It's still light; I've got nothing to lose but a digital camera which I keep under wraps, not for fear of mugging, but of looking even more of an outsider than I do already.

The estate splashes itself over four pages of the *A to Z*, but I ignore the map and start with a journey I could make blindfolded, even though I haven't covered the route for eighteen years. I'm going to walk to my old primary school. The sky is bright blue and blustery, making the very sharp squareness of everything I see look beautiful and ordered. I smile at an elderly woman walking her rug-like dog and she smiles back; today, the Wood is good. Passing my nan's house, I absent-mindedly close her front gate and note a police sign, the colour of banana skins, stating that car crime in this area is higher than average. Quite what action or emotion this statement is designed to induce, apart from paranoia, is beyond me, but I shuffle on in my metropolitan corduroy jeans and sensible hat, past the broken-down fence and along the side of the now defunct play area. Once, when I was about four, a slightly smaller boy tried to trip me up with his foot while I was riding my first bike along this path, and was rewarded with a right earful from my mum. When I was a child, I used to walk down blind alleys in the gaps between terraces; as an adult, I flash my eyes up and down like danger-detectors. The bright lights flick on one by one in the square windows of the square houses. I have been walking for thirty seconds, and have passed thirty households.

Five minutes later – five turns along short interlocking paths, and a hundred-odd homes, half a dozen terrace houses and a Battenburg-cake layer of one-bedroom flats on either side of the walkway, with a bollard at each end – I come to my first road. I look back at the domino contest I've just passed through and realize exactly what fascinates me about the estate I grew up on: it's all houses. That's what it is: houses everywhere, without a break. That's what it's there for. That's the only reason it's there.

At the beginning of the 1960s, the government began to express alarm at the low rate of slum clearance in the provincial conurbations. Birmingham, the second city of Britain with a population of a million, had already spread as far as its city boundaries would allow. The city had been permitted to double the populations of nearby Redditch, Tamworth and Daventry – market towns in Worcestershire, Staffordshire and Northamptonshire respectively – by building the odd few thousand council houses on their edges, but as Harold Wilson's Labour government entered power in 1964, it was yet projected that Birmingham would have a housing shortfall of 10,000 by 1971 and 30,000 by 1981 if drastic measures were not taken before the end of the decade. This is how the Wood, an estate of 18,000 dwellings built to house 60,000 people, came to be built.

The prolific parliamentary diarist Richard Crossman, Wilson's Minister for Housing, set about the task of rehousing the slum dwellers of the major cities with a pragmatic zeal that would have made him a star of future Labour administrations. He never quite went as far as to say that the green belt was a bourgeois luxury, but the eagerness with which he signed off great tracts of virgin land to local authorities who, only a few years earlier, had had their planning applications refused by the Conservative government suggested that he felt as much. His efforts are the reason why most major towns and cities in Britain wear a ruff of identikit Woods, peripheral council estates whose blank solid swathes, joining earlier waves of outwards building from the Depression

years and the late 1940s, can be dated back to the period
between 1964 and 1971.

The Wood bled into the smaller Kingshurst – a low-rise
estate of 5,000 homes within the city boundaries that had
been built in the late 1950s to accommodate former slum
dwellers from the inner-city wards of Nechells and
Ladywood – but you can tell the difference in age between the
two, just as once it would have been obvious how Castle Vale,
another vast estate on the other side of the M6 and just within
the city boundaries, predated building at the Wood by five
years or so. Crossman allotted land for the former estate
when the wartime airfield at Castle Bromwich in the east of
the city was decommissioned in the early 1960s. Castle Vale,
true to its name, was a thrown-up fortress of thirty-four tower
blocks (of which only a few are still standing following a
scorched-earth regeneration project), built close enough
together for each to cast the next in shadows.

Crossman's attitude to the rehousing of the inner-city poor
was encapsulated by his alleged refusal to allow one of the
former military aircraft hangars on the Castle Vale site to be
used as a community centre. This greatly angered Sir Frank
Price, Birmingham City Council's leader at the time: 'I remember arguing with the then housing minister, that educated idiot
Crossman. I pleaded with him to keep one of the old
hangars . . . he gave me a tongue-lashing for being so old-
fashioned. But it was madness to build estates like that
without proper community facilities.' (Eventually, nearly 4,000
homes were squeezed into an area of one and a half square
miles.) The housing – as much of it as possible – was what
mattered, which was how on 21 December 1964 he came to
dispatch a letter jointly addressed to the Corporation of
Birmingham, Warwickshire County Council and Meriden Rural
District Council, all of whose boundaries would be affected
by the building of a discrete township that would lie outside

the city's borders but would be administered by its council. The building of an estate on the site of the bluebell wood, reported the Centre for Urban and Regional Studies, 'supported a previous Ministerial statement that the right policy was to move people and industry beyond the green belt'.

A public meeting was held in February 1965, at which it was stated that Crossman's aim was to have the first residents of the extra-boundary estate moving into their new homes by September 1966. To give Birmingham's City Architect his credit, the planning of the Wood seemed to have much more thought put into it than many other contemporary estates, which had come to comprise a high proportion of flats in multi-storey blocks. It won architectural awards for its landscaping and for the design of some of its homes, and because the estate was large enough to function as a town in its own right, the provision of schools, a library and shopping areas was planned and costed in considerable detail. As with Castle Vale, however, further community facilities were deemed a less urgent priority, and came only at the behest of frustrated residents, who had to wait two years before they could go for a drink on their own estate.

Virtually everyone on Birmingham's council waiting list was given a house or a flat on the new estate, but my mum's parents were cheeky; they had an 'in' to getting the house of their choice. They had lived in council housing for nearly twenty years, after first being given an inner-city flat opposite a gasworks, and then granted one further out in a split-level flat in Tile Cross – which now borders the Wood on the eastern edge of Birmingham – on account of my mother's pollution-enhanced respiratory illness. Despite being rehoused once, they stayed stubbornly on the list in the hope that one day they might be rewarded with a house and garden of their own. (Their Tile Cross flat was on the fourth floor: they and their neighbours had to haul the coal, which was dumped in the basement shed once a week by the delivery men, up the stairs and along the concrete deck to their front door. It could have been worse, but to my nan, by then in her fifties and fed up of living as though she were still in service, this was no way to live.) Janet, my mum's friend from school, worked for the Housing Department, which is how the family came, one day in 1970, to be lent a handful of keys on the quiet and told to pick out a new house of their own.

'We looked at a few of them,' said Mum. 'I don't know why, we just liked this one. And it had a garden, whereas some of them didn't. The thing was, they'd built so many houses that they'd pretty much housed everyone who had a young family, and the old ones they put in the bungalows, who'd been on the list for years. So then they started asking people like my mum and dad who didn't have children or who only had one child.' Her cousin, who'd recently had her first child but had only just joined the waiting list, was housed on the top floor of one of the tower blocks, where the breeze whistled through the fresh-painted corridors and you could feel the whole building rock when the wind got up. My grandparents' house in Area 6 – the creamy-bricked end-of-terrace where my nan still lives in pristine, gloss-painted, late-1960s functionality – was one of the last to be built on the estate. It was completed in 1970, almost five years after work began on its earliest homes on the very borders of Birmingham. Two miles further east and they were still building, as far as the motorway borders would allow.

What my mum remembers most is how every day she would be stopped by someone who needed directions to their new home, or to the home of a relative or friend recently deposited in this strange, clean, faraway place, where the corporation buses refused to go and the only way of getting there was on a specially timetabled Midland Red coach that you had to catch from the city bus station. It made the journey feel like an intrepid excursion. My mum was courting my dad by then, and she would go and pick him up from the bus terminus at the end of the estate and its ten-mile trip. The end of the world. A few years later, they would have their own home here, another squat, square mid-terrace, this time with dark-brown tongue-and-groove panelling covering the front and scratchy pebble-dashing on the garage, which they filled with old paint pots and my bike. There were council laws saying what you could and couldn't do, as my mum remembers: 'None of the gardens had a fence around. You know those very low fences round the open areas? That's all they used to have around the gardens, because they were meant to be open to everybody. But the thing was, all the dogs and the balls used to go into the gardens, and there was no privacy. So everybody started building fences and walls, but you weren't supposed to build over eighteen inches. There was a height restriction to building fences, which they don't have now. People used to play ball in the green bit behind your nan's house, but the balls kept hitting the windows, so they put the restriction notices up, but they still did, which is why they put up those planted areas to stop them. That's the problem now though because the kids have got nowhere to play.

'I think it's because people had been brought there from all over the place that they decided they had to have a go at making their own community,' she said, thinking back to the time when an annual carnival trickled along its main roads and seemed to attract the whole estate to its grass verges. 'It must have been like manna from heaven for a lot of people who were really stuck for a long time where they didn't want to be, because I guess everyone who was on the housing list, especially on this side of Birmingham, must have managed to get what they wanted. Virtually all of us got a house when we only had flats before. It's a shame. People tend to be more concerned with getting things these days rather than being part of a community. They don't need it so much now. They're more interested in getting all this stuff.' She gestured at imaginary cars and televisions, and sighed, silently.

Jenny and Charlie, a retired couple from over the walkway who seemed to love their house and yet left it in their late sixties to move to north Wales, were waiting with cups of tea the day my mum and her parents moved into their house, just as they would pop over with an ice-cream or cake when I'd visit my nan and grandad as a small child. They became firm friends, but because no pubs had yet been built, Charlie and my grandad would have to take a half-hour bus journey to the British Legion in east Birmingham if they wanted a pint. It would be comforting to state that these car-free walks – they're all called one kind of Walk or another – helped people to get to know one another, but it could just be that, with sparkly new houses and a sense that, for once, the powers-that-be had done right by working people and given them somewhere as decent to live as their characters deserved, the early residents of the Wood made that extra bit of effort to bring themselves together with other people. It was either that or spend the rest of their lives as lost as the day they arrived.

That's not quite how I remember it, I reflect as I cross the road, having negotiated a hundred houses and one friendly stranger. I come to that half wood-panelled, half pebble-dashed house where I lived with my parents until I was nine, and wonder whether to take a photo. I decide against it and realize that the tiny garden, where we had the little almond tree, has been paved over and parked with a car that obscures the entire front window. I used to look out of this window and wait for the sweetie man to come: a big grey shop on wheels that turned up every teatime to sell us a pudding of cola chews and jelly wriggle-worms. The children would run out of their houses, form a line, the coppers in their hand toxic with metallic sweat, disappear through the door of the silver Tardis and emerge with a 10p mix-up bag full of teeth-rotting jewels. On Fridays, the chip man would hulk up on to the kerb and sell fish and chips from the back door of his van, and the pop man would collect his Corona cherryade bottles and give you 10p for each one, which went towards the following week's supply of fizz. If you weren't fussed about veg or vitamins, you wouldn't even have to go to the shops; the shops would come to you if you waited long enough.

Here I reach a cul-de-sac, a crescent of privately owned houses that seemed insanely posh and exotic when I was small, with their own wrought-iron gates and privet hedges. The Wood was built to contain just over 80 per cent council houses for rent, with around 18 per cent built by private developers for people to buy with mortgages lent by the corporation. Even in those days, when about half the population of England lived in homes they owned, this represented a significant imbalance in favour of rented local-authority housing. Thirty-five years later, these figures are now almost completely inverse to the national rate of home ownership (72 per cent) compared with council-rented homes.

Over a hundred houses on the estate were held over for policemen, around ten in each numbered area, so that there would be local officers on hand to deal with the social problems expected on a municipal estate of this scale and population. Additionally, rows of terrace houses were rented out or sold cheaply to teachers, who would have easy access to the new schools. My only friend from the Wood – though we didn't meet until we'd left our respective schools and gone to college – was the daughter of a local teacher, and recalls how her entire street was made up of newly qualified teachers who had been offered cheap loans by the council. Most of them, with the exception of her own family and a few others, moved away as they inched up the social and economic scale. It tickles me to think of middle-class people living here, because I certainly don't remember ever meeting any who were not my own teachers, doctors or dentists. There must have been a few, but they would have owned cars and the means and the know-how to get their children bussed out to other schools. I was offered a scholarship to a grammar school in Birmingham in my last year of primary school, but didn't take it because I thought it would probably be best to go where everyone else was going. I don't know why I thought this. I didn't know what it could have meant.

I pass what I used to know as the AA man's house – no longer any sign of an AA van, but still the same white tongue-and-groove panelling – a few rows away from my old home, and dodge a sweatshirted girl riding a mountain bike along the finger-narrow pavement, a feat akin to crossing Niagara Falls on a thread of wire. Everything seems miniaturized; pretend house-boxes built for people whose very spirits, surely, are larger than this. Doesn't everyone feel squashed? I know I did, and yet at the time I didn't think it was the physical size of the houses that crushed me. It was the anonymity and conformity of the estate as a whole that threatened to consume me. It felt as though the identikit homes produced identikit people. I'm ashamed to reduce people like this, for I know that every one of them has a story far more fascinating than the flat face of their house would ever reveal. But there, somehow, I never felt free to be the person I knew I was inside.

Turning out of the cul-de-sac, I hop over a bollard and direct myself towards the path that will take me all the way to my old primary school. I have no chance of getting run over by a car here, because there is nothing except walkways for the next half a mile. Each grey path is stubby and zig-zaggy, now only long enough to hold four houses on either side. The security door on either end of each terrace is a new feature: in their place used to be white-painted gates with nothing more secure than a latch keeping the tenants from whoever it was they ought to have been scared of. The one nearest to me is bottle green. It's where my Aunty Lil, my nan's sister, used to live until she moved into a municipal nursing home three years before she died. I remember her back yard: it had a shed that smelled of damp like nowhere else on the estate (which had a dry smoky smell about it from the motorways and farms). It was made entirely of concrete, apart from a two-foot oblong of soil where she had rose bushes and the occasional strawberry plant, grown from a tendril my nan had snipped off her own. If I stood on my Aunty Lil's doorstep, I could stretch out and touch that of her neighbour opposite. Their close quarters were the nearest I can think of to how back-to-back houses must have been, and yet inside, the flats were large L-shaped palaces with kitchen-dining rooms and two big bedrooms. I was dying to go in and see how it had changed, but the great silent slab of the security door put me off. I don't think she would have liked that door, my Aunty Lil. She had too many friends in that flat to keep having to let them in, rather than leave the front door on the latch as she always did. She grew up with cerebral palsy after being starved of oxygen at birth, in the cellar where her parents lived; for her, having left the Rhondda Valley aged fifty, coming to the Wood was like the beginning of her life. She joined the Fellowship of the Handicapped – the estate had a larger-than-average proportion of disabled people who were moved from unsuitable housing in the inner city to ground-floor flats here – and got piecework at home, assembling the plastic masks that promise to drop down in plane crashes. She had parties all the time; she loved how she suddenly knew so many people. When we went back to the Rhondda to visit, I would climb over the slagheaps and wonder at its hilliness, but the way the local kids stared at us, mud-smeared and uncomprehending, wasn't new at all. It was just the same at home. My Aunty Lil's experience wasn't that of leaving a close-knit community to live in isolation and loneliness a long way from the place she knew and loved: it was the exact opposite. I remember what she said about her cousins and neighbours in the valleys, where she looked after her elderly mother alone until, eventually, Lil had a breakdown: 'They just didn't want to know.' And this was in the 1960s. *Plus ça change*. She left that insular world and never looked back.

The door is the biggest thing about these terraces, where the front gardens get smaller and scrubbier and the back gardens wither into nothing. These little house-hives, still barely 500 yards from my parents' relatively spacious semi, are more claustrophobic; laid out, cynically I think, to maximize the number of dwellings in the minimum space. Crossman crosses my mind again. I wonder what the point was of moving people ten miles away from the city they knew only to put them in hutches that were barely any bigger than the slums they left. The nearby shopping parade, which used to house a dressmaking shop, a 'fancy goods' shop, a chandler's and a greengrocer's, is now less of a parade than a lie-in. All that remains is the chippy and the newsagent's. Another hundred houses pass, and I don't see a single person until a couple of young blokes in Blues shirts and baggy pants slip out of the first tower block I come to, fifty yards or so on from my aunt's flat. One of them tells the other he's got to start work at four o'fookin' clock the next morning. A small boy, with the same ginger hair as his dad, kicks a ball between their legs and I wait for them to pass so I can take a picture of the Elim Pentecostal church, built opposite the tower block on a spare patch of grass where the kids who lived there used to play. It's twenty-odd years old now and has seen better days. The reedy grass it was built on seems to want to reclaim the space and take the building – square, squat, red-bricked, but in a distinctively early-1980s style, less form-and-function than an attempt at copying the vernacular in Lego – with it. I remember that when it was built, dawdling kids taking themselves to school would gather round it and stare at the builders, as though they hadn't realized how buildings came into existence until then: layer by layer, brick by brick. It seemed like an attempt at urban renewal at the time – not, of course, that I would have had the means to describe it that way then. Now it lies here, prematurely old, begging to be renewed itself. What it needs is for its pastors to exercise the Right to Buy, to cover it with awnings and install brown-paned double glazing with diamond-shaped leading in the windows.

I come to the primary school that I began attending in 1980. The building then was only a few years older than I was. It is a long snake of a school, open-plan, with no stairs for little legs to exhaust themselves climbing. Although it looks friendly, it is fenced in high and surrounded by endless terraces. The terraces are getting boring now: I trudge on along the straight-backed narrow pathway, depressed at how something so boring can have become such a fixation when I could be thinking about something far more interesting. I find myself wishing I'd come from a real place, with proper, chimneyed houses instead of endless tragic boxes with people in them. The terrible thing is, I've only been out of the house ten minutes.

Seeing my primary school provokes a curiously nothingy sensation. I was expecting a Proustian rush of nostalgia for the littleness of childhood, but it looks so flat and tiny I can't believe I ever fitted in there. Instead of trying to will a feeling into existence, I carry on, meeting another cul-de-sac and a rash of creamy-bricked houses that look a lot like my nan's. The main road just beyond it is empty enough to cross without walking to one of the too-few pedestrian crossings, so I skip across it and, arriving on the other side, admire the way someone has splodged the name and number of their flat across its entire side wall in magnolia paint, should a visitor, or the postman, fail to find it. Here there is a rare hill: the rest of the estate is entirely flat. It gives the landscape the variety of texture I realize I have been craving, and I force myself up the steep gradient as though it were a mountain I had always wanted to climb. I almost get excited when I notice that even the houses are a bit different here. They are little terraced pixie-huts with steep roofs that stagger up and down in the dark blue air, like log cabins pulled out of their rugged context and dropped on to a smooth grassy knoll.

At the top of this sort-of hill, I can see the centre of the estate. Here there is a large patch with no houses (though more pale terraces border it on every edge); instead there is the drive-through McDonald's, the shopping precinct – a vast concrete pallet that can only be entered via ramps and foot-bridges – and the traffic roundabout, in the middle of which stands a sole pine tree that stays put from one Christmas to the next. It was supposed to be the beating heart, I can tell: the focal point of a vast people-locker that would otherwise have none. A burger bar and two branches of KwikSave are the prizes that await you if you can negotiate your way through the maze without first going crackers.

I now exit the first part of the estate riddle – Areas 4 to 6 – by taking a short-cut towards the shops through a row of hag-gard garages detached from the households to which they belong. Again, I feel momentarily worried because I've never been here before. Not this exact place, anyway. I could trick my mind into believing that I had: there are hundreds of these garage-terraces strewn across the estate in odd little patches where they couldn't fit more houses in. More terraces, more garages. The sameness drives me half mad. Isn't it strange how this act of civic socialism – the state sequestering large tracts of virgin land so that it might house its poorest in the clean, wide-open countryside – ends up feeling like a boot on the face? But of course, it's not socialism: it's a kind of ghettoization. It's a clean, wide-open prison for those who had little choice in the shape, the age or the location of the house they were given. I ask myself, under my breath, why I'm so angry. I could shout this as I cross the silent road and no one would hear. A generation's worth of council leaders, architects and engineers were handed these great green playgrounds to draw us in like numbers. What was their problem? Did they not see us?

There are few things less radiant than the shopping precinct here, which was opened by the Queen – the Queen! – and Prince Philip in 1971. I reach it by finding a narrow alley off the garages and walking across a footbridge that lasts 300 yards and stretches over three roads and a derelict petrol station. It drops me off down a zig-zag of steps that lie between two twelve-storey tower blocks directly opposite the Gala Bingo hall. It feels like a machine, this place: it carries me from dwelling to amenity on a concrete magic carpet. How can you fight something as concrete, as concretey, as this? You would have to be as strong as nature not to shrink back from it.

I turn away from the pale-grey wasteland of empty shopfronts and Tannoys that growl out a tinny facsimile of pop music for no reason. I can visualize it anyway: an open-plan, open-air platform of concrete slabs, broken up by loud Woolies signs and an indoor market where you can buy goldfish and get your ears pierced. I have spent years in there, sitting in a corner of the betting shop while my grandad put 50p each way on the third-from-favourite, reading Barbapapa books in the children's library downstairs, buying potatoes and bread and meat and putting them in the trolley, sitting in the red plastic booth at the supermarket entrance with my mum while she sat knitting booties and waiting for pensioners to buy scratchcards from her at 25p or five for a pound.

Or eating chips with sausage in batter on a Thursday lunchtime and going down the slide in the concrete playground. Or waiting to have my eyes tested, or waiting for the bus. I did all of those things, but it isn't the things I did but the feelings I felt that I don't want to remember. I head back on to the concrete carpet, and up towards the hill.

From here, where there are shops and its own drive-thru McDonald's, the Wood almost does seem like a proper place, albeit one of those nowhere towns that gets voted 'most nondescript place in the country'. Yes, it's spiritless, and it fails to inspire when compared with the handsome, special house I dream of living in one day, but it's a place I know intimately. This strange place is like my blood family: I didn't choose it, but somehow I'm bound up in it. That in itself is as much of a comfort as it is a torture. You have to come from somewhere.

I've reached the first part of the estate that I have no recollection of ever visiting. There would be no reason to: I don't know anyone here, at the top of this hillock of mock log cabins made of chocolate-coloured brick and UPVC panels. This is the 'Scandinavian' bit my mum told me about (although I couldn't quite get over it), where yard-square patches of alpine trees stop dead as soon as the houses turn to square-cream-sand again. If they could be so imaginative here, I wonder, why not everywhere else? Why give up and resort to boxes of brick? This miniature oasis – still free of people, still blank-seeming, but with a leavening hint of elegance about it – reminds me of the Byker Wall in Newcastle. (I once walked around that, too, but since its tenants have had serious-looking people inspecting their primary-coloured wooden benches, bright green awnings and soft-edged communal areas for the last twenty-five years, no one took any notice.)

I take a sharp right and confuse myself, mildly, just for a second. I've reached a walkway I don't recognize, which leads off in four directions. All around me, at a distance of eight feet or so, are peach-brick terraces with plain wooden porches and patches of white tongue-and-groove under the three front windows. There is no road for at least a hundred yards: I know that from the vague echo of each car as it gravels past. Each house has a stamp of grass in front of it, growing out and showing limp roots like a bad haircut. Every few doors along, an oily motorbike treads on the tufty blades. Shiny but unused, in direct contrast to the house behind it, which is lived-in and scraggily painted. I could *ratatat* the letterbox of sixty houses in sixty seconds, then run fifty yards up the walkway and find another two hundred stacked like a pile of unpaid bills in two grey tower blocks. Everyone is inside or out, but there is no one merely out and about. The doors to the housing cabinet have been locked for the day. Now I'm forty minutes from home.

In *The Road to Wigan Pier*, George Orwell fails miserably to hide his disdain for what he calls 'the Corporation estate', wondering why on earth the working man of the 1930s insisted on wanting a house of his own five or more miles from the city in preference to a newly built flat closer to his place of work. 'Apparently a house in the middle of an unbroken block of houses a hundred yards long seems to them more their own than a flat situated in mid-air,' he writes, having spent several years living on the continent, where flats are the norm rather than the exception. The houses I walk past here, as I hurry to beat the encroaching dark (the walkways are well lit, but so empty and suddenly unfamiliar that I find myself wanting to run to the nearest place where there are passing cars, passing life), seem no cheerier than flats; they are so closely packed that they have no gardens, only yards. I feel the chill of Orwell's words again: 'In a Corporation estate there is an uncomfortable, almost prison-like atmosphere, and the people who live there are perfectly aware of it.'

A police car, the prison governor, sits with its engine off, its uniformed driver catching up on printed titbits. It's six o'clock; time for lights-out. The two tower blocks, casting oblong shadows across the car, act like radio speakers, providing the only music I have heard since getting lost in the maze. When I was a kid it was always reggae you would hear anywhere within earshot of the blocks: the ricochet of dub, lovers' rock, lots of UB40. Now it's the thump and grind of American rap and R'n'B. Both these forms are minimal and bass-driven, as tough and angular as the buildings these sounds inhabit. You never hear The Eagles here. I wonder what the policeman is doing, waiting in his car, the only living soul around apart from me. It's so long since I saw human life – getting on for an hour – I almost want to go over and hug him. I find myself imagining that I've strayed into a secure, monitored part of the estate not amenable to the wandering pedestrian.

I have walked round and round this place for thirty years without ever making a lasting friend or wearing my home like a happy skin. I think back to Aunty Lil's self-created community around her open-plan flat and realize that it's probably me who's the problem: too insular, too much of a daydreamer, too much of an only child. Why else would you walk around a council estate for fun? But there is something in its endless pattern that compels me. The walkways seem like fractals, each leading from one to the other in a self-generating whirl, first numbing then dulling the mind with their similarity. You could easily go mad here, if you didn't have enough to do, if there were few opportunities to leave. I know of those who have.

I pass a row of houses that were originally rented to nurses: key-worker housing, rented or sold at a lower cost than on the open market to workers in essential services, is nothing new. The city architects encouraged this type of housing to be grouped together, 'so that people of similar interests would be living in the same area. It was said that teachers, nurses, social workers and even policemen . . . might have something in common (and) might form communities of their own.'

I like that bit, 'even policemen', as though the other three groups would be sitting around each other's kitchen tables plotting the permissive revolution over cups of Bovril while the policemen sat to one side complaining that their efforts would send us all to hell in a handcart.

Across the road there is a cul-de-sac of semi-detached houses – bright orange brick, pitched roofs and a distinct, though distinctly relative, sense of solidity and comfort – notable for the white vans that sit on their driveways. Here live plumbers, roofers, pavers, window replacers, plasterers and builders. These are the self-build houses, homes built with the sweated labour of those who were to live in them and, accordingly, sold cheaper. The self-builders of Area 13 helped each other with supplies and skills, and after completing their homes formed a residents' association. I have barely seen a single soul. I feel as though the estate has been put on show for me; as though it has been placed in stasis for my inspection. Could a residents' association even exist here? I can hardly believe that people would know each other well enough to go around to each other's houses for meetings. At the last Girl Guide meeting I ever attended, the group leader dressed us down, saying that if we couldn't be bothered to come to meetings or to wear the proper uniform, how could we expect to make useful members of society? She used the word 'deflated' to describe how she felt. She couldn't find a replacement, so we were no longer Girl Guides.

There must be good news here somewhere: there must be
something worth seeking out and celebrating. There must be
another area to find new things in, to break the dead weight
of over-familiarity. There must be. I cross the main road,
which is full of parked cars but none that are moving,
towards a closed corner shop surrounded by grass-tufted bollards and prised-up paving slabs. There is a Range Rover
outside that dwarfs the shop. Taking a sharp left, I leave the
sight of cars again and find another walkway to plough
along.

I did go mad here, when I was seventeen. This walkway
leads to the doctor's surgery, where – by then old enough to
articulate this feeling I had had for half my life – I told the
doctor I was depressed, and he said, 'Don't be silly, you're not
depressed.' It's smell-less and dark grey, and surrounded by
tiny flats that pile on top of garages last painted in teal, in
1970. Security gates poke into the corners, of which there are
too many to count as each yard of paving seems to lead off into
another dead-end square. It is horrible and hostile, designed by
a cyborg, or someone who has yet to see what bad housing
can do to people. It has insanity designed into it. As if by
order, a woman, the first I have seen for nearly an hour,
bundles a snowman-sized Argos bag through the gate to her
brown maisonette and tells her toddler son to fucking move,
or she'll fucking kill him.

The shorthand for proletarian hell used by those who don't
live on them is 'council estate', and this is what they mean.
Yes, it exists, and this is why. You are a poor person, living at
such close quarters with other poor people that you could
take each other's faces (if you ever saw them) and rub them
into the patch of dirt that separates one dwelling from the next.
You are twenty minutes' walk from the nearest bus stop. You
are sewn into rows of houses that are all inhabited, and yet
you don't see anyone to whom you are not related for days at

a time. You were put here and you don't know why. Your environment makes as little sense as your life.

I carry on walking towards the surgery. This is where they give the drugs to the people who live in the ghost-ship houses. A strip of bungalows look as small as Wendy houses, and as vulnerable as children, at the end of the walkway, lorded over by another pair of sky-grey tower blocks fenced in with new dark green railings. I'm getting nearer to the motorway, but first there is a dual carriageway whose traffic screams bounce off the surgery walls.

'It's like being slashed with a machete, isn't it, having that road running through it like that,' my dad says later when I tell him where I've been. The cars and lorries rage through it endlessly, parallel to the motorway that also rages a few hundred yards away. The environment here gets ever more inhospitable, louder and fumier, with every new car that is bought and driven. So that's where all the people are. They're all in cars.

To get to the other side of the estate, the part sliced off by the machete-road, you have to walk under a long subway with a parade of declining shops at its mouth. There is no other way of crossing: all along the road, on either side, is a metal fence as tall as high hurdles. The subway entrance eats into the ground with twenty steep steps and no ramp. I gulp, muttering to myself not to be stupid, nothing's going to happen down there, and walk down under the road, feeling every car bump above my head, and almost leaping in shock when I see two women, in Blues away shirts, enter the other end with a pram, talking about someone they knew they couldn't trust because they hadn't seen them in the area before. Their eyes trace me casually; mine must have traced theirs.

I exit into Woodbine Walk, a long concrete pathway – as if there was any reason why the estate would change its pattern on the other side of the road – that sneaks along the side of a primary school. Its high green railings shield empty crisp packets and pop bottles in the corners. The other side of the walk is all terrace houses with identical doors, meaning that they haven't been bought from the council. I turn 360 degrees: here again there is no one to be seen, only hundreds and hundreds of houses which jut and snake at every angle, the better to sandwich them in. I take a sneaky picture of the street name and another one of the houses, forcing my finger over the flash in case anyone sees. They won't; there is no one here to see me.

The prospect of being mentally overtaken by the uniformity of the Wood doesn't immediately come to mind when I ask my parents if they have anything to say about the place in which they live.

'It's a friendly place, you know,' says my dad, slightly defensively, perhaps aware of the times, frustrated and bored, he might have dismissed his neighbours as dull and indifferent. 'I only have to go up the shops and I see someone I know.' Not well, perhaps, but at least faces he recognizes and can acknowledge, in this sea of people cut adrift from Birmingham.

What doesn't he like about it?

'I worry about the kids, the sixteen-year-olds who've left school and they've got nothing to do, so they stand there in these silly baseball caps. They've got nothing to do, they've got no money, so they can't go anywhere, so they just stand there intimidating people like me.'

Not the layout of the estate itself?

'No. You see some of these godforsaken estates and you're glad you live here. I mean, I've never seen a used needle or anything like that. I can get to where I want to go on the bus. It's not a problem.'

Family and Kinship in East London, a famous sociological

study of the effects on family and community life of a vast slum-clearance project that moved thousands of east Londoners from Bethnal Green out to new estates in the Essex countryside in the early 1950s, portrays Greenleigh – not its real name – as a deadly quiet, if orderly, alien landscape that contrasts with the smelly but vitality-filled streets of the East End. Its writers, Michael Young and Peter Willmott, detail row upon row of practically identical houses, each beside a concrete road, each with expansive front windows. They interview a housewife, Mrs Sandeman, who, upon moving out to the estate, 'cried for weeks, I was so lonely. It was a shock to see such a deep hill going up to the shops.' After Bethnal Green, she says, Greenleigh had seemed 'like paradise' until she realized that open space could also mean emptiness and desolation. The verdict of her neighbour, Mrs Harper, is that 'It's like being in a box to die out here.' Tenants on the Watling Estate, built out on the north-western corner of London by the London County Council in the late 1920s, told as much to their vicar, who reported: 'The loneliness of the people here in the first months after their removal to Watling is extreme. The women are mostly affected by that desperate loneliness. They feel as though they have moved to the desert. I hear it again and again.'

Notice that he uses the word 'removal'; they were removed from the place they knew, to materialize in a place so alien that the desire to go back often overtook their relief at being given a new house. In Watling, as in Greenleigh, most families stuck it out in the belief that the fresh air and space would give their children a better chance of a healthy life, but many couldn't hack it and moved back into the city murk, believing the closeness of family and friends to be more important than having a larger house and their own toilet. The *Birmingham Post* journalist sent to interview new arrivals to the Wood in 1971 found the same emotions a hundred miles from north

London and Essex: 'You can go for days without speaking to any of your neighbours, but you know they're there because their curtains move as you go past,' he reports Mrs Joan Burne of Area 4 as saying. He sniffs: 'It is an ideal place to live (so the planners say) because it offers a physical, if not now a total spiritual attachment to Birmingham, while, at the same time, bringing the countryside to within walking distance of the front door. (But Mecca will build a nightclub and bingo hall before the youngsters get adequate play areas.)'

For the migrants to Watling, Greenleigh and the Wood, the experience of living on the new estate was bare and unfriendly compared with their old life lived at close quarters with each other; a story that echoes with the fragments of memory my mum has thrown up, casually, over my lifetime. I've picked up the scraps and pieced together a sense that no time was ever as good as the time she was growing up, in the inner city, with teeming houses and parties that lasted all night with no one complaining. The adults would pile back from the pub on a Saturday and carry on singing until their voices went. When she compares the present with the past, she wears a heavy crown of disappointment. Her eyes melt without her even seeming to notice. I ask her – later, when my feet have gone numb and my nose red and all the bad or blank memories have piled on top of me like a falling bookcase – where all the people are.

'People are always working these days, so they don't get together with each other. You don't see the same people around during the day, they're all out somewhere and doing their own thing, aren't they? So you don't really get a chance to become a community like that. And people move around a lot more, so you don't know people from when they're born to when they get old.'

I ask her if she minds; she shrugs. She shrugs and sighs and looks down instead; she won't talk. Something, inevitably, changed when I left the Wood's sharp boundaries for a city so vast it has no shape. I remember coming home from London for the weekend in my first term at university and telling her how depressed seeing the Wood – its boxes, its man-made hillocks, its hidden-away people – made me feel. It was a tactless thing to say, and it upset her, but I had this idea that telling the truth as I saw it would one day make things better. I doubt very much that it did.

Seeing the estate still has the same effect now, but whether that's because it induces too many of the old feelings – 'the type of memories that turn your bones to glass', to appropriate a favourite song of mine – of loneliness and alienation that drove me towards another life, or because this cold grey outpost, full of houses but devoid of people, might depress anybody with a brain and a heart, I just don't know. They give away so many drugs for both at that doctor's surgery. I reach the end of Woodbine Walk and find a strange little mole-hole for humans at the bottom of a cul-de-sac, from which you can see the heads of Dutch lorries heading north. There is a twenty-foot fence here that was intended to block the noise from the M6. It doesn't: all it does is tell you that here there is a wall you cannot climb. I walk closer to the mole-hole to inspect it: it's muddy and riven with the wheel marks of our old friend, the abandoned supermarket trolley. It opens out to a tunnel that burrows under the motorway, and on the other side of it is open country.

2

The End of the Slums: The Rise of the Council Estate

There are four photographs propped up on a bookshelf to the left of my desk, evidence of my preoccupation with public housing of one kind or another. One shows a slum, the others three examples of how working-class people have been housed in Europe over the course of the last century, as the idea of mass public housing grew from a just-right-of-Bolshevik folly to the means by which the vast majority of non-homeowners found a place to live. By turns grand, ugly and plain, between them they illustrate the paradox of council housing: that it exists at all in a society dedicated to the acquisition of wealth and property induces pride; that it has to exist at all, because that society excludes so many from the wealth and property that the rest of us enjoy, is a source of shame. What began as a nineteenth-century crusade to house the urban poor in clean and comfortable surroundings eventually turned into just another industry, co-opted by large building firms who received state subsidies to build quickly and carelessly, and encouraged by the short-term thinking of governments whose votes relied on quick solutions to visible problems.

In between, however, there was a sustained and glorious period of renewal, during which time two generations of slum dwellers were lifted from cellars and tenements into seemingly vast new houses that lengthened their lives and transformed those of their children. The battle that was undertaken – to house the nation fairly and equably – cannot be underestimated. Hundreds of thousands of council homes were built in the midst of the Depression, giving work, as well as housing, to the workless. The population of Britain grew by a million in the very years – 1939 to 1945 – in which nearly four million homes were destroyed or damaged beyond repair by aerial bombardment; and yet somehow, eventually, we managed to house them all. The enlightened self-interest that characterized the building of workers' villages – Port Sunlight next to the Lever factory in Merseyside, Bournville at the Cadbury factory in Birmingham – was swelled and amplified by two world wars into a central, life-changing pillar of the new Welfare State. For a few decades, there was a sense that society could be transformed for the better on the strength of the living conditions of its people.

The first picture on my shelf was taken by my mother, in the yard of the house in which my nan and her sisters grew up in south Wales. I say house: it looks more like a shack from here. You can see a narrow stack of misaligned bricks piled up in rough approximation of a wall, against which sloping banks of corrugated iron form a makeshift parlour and outside toilet, the result of successive Housing of the Working Classes Acts, which legislated for such things in the latter years of the Victorian era. A bin and a mop fight the once white-, now brown- and grey-wash, and fail. Grime is ingrained into the bitty paving like coaldust on a Maerdy miner's face. There's a single window, open, its wooden frame rotting, with a mournful tray of flower bulbs on the sill just above a clump of soggy Bonio and New Zealand Butter grocer's boxes. Damp invades the scene despite the fact you can tell that, on this rare day in July 1967, the sun is shining on the valleys.

What makes this sad sight a little bit funny is the way my mum's two teenage cousins, visiting from America, stand amidst this squalor in pristine outfits: one in mauve, one in navy, hairbands matching dresses, their struggling smiles failing to mask a deep horror of the surroundings in which their own mother – my great-aunt, Ivy – grew up. Aunty Ivy escaped from here to El Paso, Texas, and air-conditioning; her sisters to domestic service in the south-east of England, then to Cardiff, then to Birmingham and the promise of newly built council housing. This is the first house in the picture-story: the slum, the dark harbourer of miasma and cholera, whose hideous conditions arose from Britain's rapid industrialization two hundred years ago, when teeming cities were created overnight.

The first subsidized rented homes, like the workers' housing built by Titus Salt in West Yorkshire and by the Cadbury family at Bournville in the mid-nineteenth century, were encouraged and funded by philanthropists terrified of the consequences for society that the bubbling tension of inner-city slums seemed to predict. Visitors to the crowded honeycombs of London's East End invariably came away describing the populace as 'vicious, mostly criminal' and incapable of self-improvement, while Engels' horror at the living conditions of workers in Salford informed his contribution to the *Communist Manifesto*. The Royal Commission into the living conditions of Britain's poorest people in 1885, which followed the Artisans' Dwelling Act of 1875, recommended programmes of slum clearance that would replace the dank back-to-back terraces in which filth reigned and families of twelve or more crammed themselves into single, rat-infested rooms. Despite the late-Victorian surge of interest in civic pride, public health and disease prevention, the life expectancy of mechanics, servants and labourers in Bethnal Green was sixteen. Yes, sixteen. Tradesmen, on average, reached the age of twenty-six before keeling over, while the outlying professional classes generally made it to forty-five.

Andrew Mearns' 1883 book *The Bitter Cry of Outcast London: An Inquiry into the Condition of the Abject Poor* warned that 'We shall be pointed to the fact that without State interference nothing effectual can be accomplished upon any large scale ... These wretched people must live somewhere.' The early social scientist Charles Booth's *Inquiry into the Life and Labour of the People in London* came to the same conclusion. His report represented an exhaustive seven-year

(1886–93) study of the living conditions of these degraded East Enders, just as the first council estate in Britain was being built by the London County Council on the border of Shoreditch and Bethnal Green. The first bricks of the Boundary Street Estate were laid in 1893, replacing the grotesque cellars of the Friars Mount, or Old Nichol, slums fictionalized by the locally raised author Arthur Morrison in his grim semi-autobiographical novel *A Child of the Jago*. Thousands were packed away into the underground warrens of the Old Nichol, rat-like and miserable, only exiting to visit what Booth called 'the curse of the district': late-night drinking clubs where men and women would bash each other to bits in mutual hatred of their predicament. In 1863, the *Illustrated London News* had reported that the slum was 'but one painful and monotonous round of vice, filth and poverty, huddled in dark cellars, ruined garrets, bare and blackened rooms, reeking with disease and death, and without the means, even if there were the inclination, for the most ordinary observations of decency and cleanliness'.

It was, Booth noted, by far the poorest slum in London, housing – if you can call it that – pieceworkers who scrabbled together a living making matchboxes and clothes pegs. Under the pressure of working upwards of twelve hours a day for pennies, few families stayed together. Teenage children were often left to raise their younger brothers and sisters. His detailed recording of their plight, abetted by the activities of Old Nichol's campaigning vicar, the Rev. Osborne Jay, persuaded the LCC that the decrepit slum should be the site of its first attempt at planning and administering its own housing for the poor. Due to the constantly moving and self-replacing population of the Jago, what had been a mostly white, if mongrelly, slum comprising few conventional nuclear families became a rebuilt tenement housing only families, mostly those of Jewish recent immigrants from eastern Europe.

To describe the new estate at Boundary Street as a tenement is broadly accurate, but at the same time does a great injustice to the careful layout and the beautifying Arts and Crafts-influenced design of the 1,069 dwellings, which were positioned to maximize the amount of light that streamed through each window. The twenty-three blocks of the new settlement were planned in a star formation, with solid dark-red brickwork, handsome peaked roofs, and communal areas large enough to play in and even to house a bandstand in its centrepiece at Arnold Circus. The designs, which came straight from the drawing boards of LCC architects Owen Fleming, Rowland Plumb and T. Blashill, predated the dignifying Arts and Crafts cottages of the garden-city movement by a couple of years, achieving what we would now call 'high density' – that is, housing a large number of people within a relatively small area – without sacrificing health-improving amenities such as the communal laundry and nearly 200 shopfronts. While the Old Nichol squashed 381 people into each acre, mainly below street level, the new estate still managed to house 359 per acre, but with access to daylight.

Anyone who was lucky enough to migrate directly from the hovels of the Old Nichol – whose inhabitants were shorter, weaker and more likely to die young than any of their Bethnal Green neighbours – to these new, attractive flats would have found the effect on both their perceived and actual health to be transformative. Children would have unfurled like sun-starved flowers, their bones suddenly solidifying with exposure to Vitamin D. However, in an ironic twist that imprinted itself on every major development in council housing in the century that followed, the rents were set at just high enough a level – three shillings per week – that would put off all but the best-paid working people, attracting instead small businessmen, clerks and artisans whose habits and behaviour were already considered a cut above the rest. Respectable Jewish families were encouraged to move into the new development in the hope that it would speed up the process of assimilation, and also because they were less likely to mind that the twelve pubs which once added to the chaos and violence of the Old Nichol slum had been demolished, never to be replaced.

The blocks at Boundary Street constituted the first proper council housing, built by a local authority which both received rent payments and administered repairs, thus taking vital trade away from exploitative slum landlords and acknowledging the need for consistent, sanitary and fairly priced housing among the poor. That's not to say that the undeserving poor of the Old Nichol, too poor or deemed too feckless to be rewarded with an LCC flat, did not continue to suffer slum conditions and exploitation for many years to come. Then, as now, it was only the respectable-seeming, the literate and those who could fathom the system – those who could talk to and reason with the authorities in question – who would have benefited, while the worst-off were left at the back of the queue.

The LCC's actions would still have lasting significance in that it was the first example of the state, operating at a local level, stepping in to do what once only charities, the Church and philanthropists had been prepared to do. The council showed that it was prepared to act in a way that would improve quickly and directly the lives of poor (though not the poorest) people. Not only that, but it was an early example of power-holding authorities acknowledging, and then acting upon, abundant evidence of the link between poor living conditions, social immobility and early mortality – which, it has come to be argued, is key to understanding the persistence of premature death in apparently affluent societies.

Peter Hall's *Cities of Tomorrow*, an absorbing study of the twentieth-century struggle to house the huddled masses in the world's great cities, holds Ebenezer Howard, creator of the

first garden city at Letchworth in 1903, to be 'the most important single character' in the story of progressive housing for
the working classes. His only book, *To-morrow: A Peaceful
Path to Real Reform*, published in 1898, was renamed
Garden Cities of To-morrow in 1902, forging a lasting
impression of the eccentric inventor and – to Hall, at least –
'social visionary', as a mere town planner. But his radical
plan to dismantle capitalism through the creation of self-
governing, self-sustaining cities in the country made him
more like a cross between Karl Marx and William Morris.

Howard's Letchworth was the culmination of several years
of planning, persuasion and hard fund-raising to realize his
vision of a clean and green city in which small townships of
10,000 people or so would flourish in clean air, privacy and
space, eventually growing into a vast network of co-operative
communities in which every citizen had an equal stake.
Greenery would be preserved in the form of a huge town-
centre park, from which Haussmannesque spokes of roads led
out into miniature suburbs of terrace houses for workers,
artisans and clerks. It's the sort of thing that made Olympian
literary types such as H. G. Wells – and later J. B. Priestley, on
his *English Journey*, and even Orwell, in *The Road to Wigan
Pier* and his aspidistra-loathing novels – squirm with horror
at the thought of thousands of these mimsy no-marks, with
their gardening tools and uninspired habits, encroaching on
England's virgin land. However, the depressing outcreep of
suburbia wasn't quite the thing that Howard had in mind
when he painstakingly set out his diagram of accessible, inter-
dependent sociable cities, each buffered by a legally
impenetrable ring of green belt.

The original edition of *To-morrow* featured Howard's
'Three Magnets': a sort of well-organized brainstorm, in
which the various attributes of 'Town', 'Country' and 'Town-
Country' are represented as magnets to which 'The People'

are drawn. To Howard's mind, the worst aspects of 'Town' and 'Country' – 'Foul Air', 'Deserted Villages' – vanish when *urbs* is conjoined with *rus*. The 'Town-Country' magnet lists the qualities that might form the basis of his imagined Utopia: 'Low Rents . . . Low Rates . . . No Sweating . . . Pure Air and Water . . . Freedom . . . Co-Operation'. Once freed from exploitation by landlords and given their own piece of land to use, both for subsistence and for enterprise, 'Town-Country' dwellers would no longer be at the mercy of capital. Eccentric Howard may have been, but hare-brained he was not. The appropriation of his book in the decades to come, by governments and local authorities, as a kind of prettifying town-planning manual absorbed what was essentially a revolutionary tract into a policy intended to hold back that very revolution.

The birth of the garden city and the municipal estate coincided with the birth of the Labour Representation Committee, later to become the Labour Party, which committed itself to working-class representation at the highest level by joining, rather than combating, the existing legislative system. Just as Howard's eloquent treatise on the causes of persistent inequality, and his proposal to eradicate it by ensuring that each citizen had an equal physical stake in the land on which they lived, was co-opted by government, so the workers' movement – represented by trade unions but, in some areas such as the mining villages or 'Little Moscows' of south Wales, susceptible to dreams of overthrowing the ruling class – underwent the same process. As Russia stumbled, then fell, to the Bolsheviks, the need to fulfil the basic needs of the working class and thereby dampen their desire for revolt became ever more urgent. You could say that, between them, council housing and the Labour Party would avert revolution; or that the revolution did take place, in the form of bricks, mortar and concrete.

*

There was still a long way to go in Bethnal Green alone, given that the district had another 18,000 dwellings within its boundaries, but the first step had been taken towards the state's acceptance of its responsibility to house, and house well, its people. Beginning with the Boundary Street Estate, the London County Council was instrumental in finding new and humane ways of housing the capital's full-to-bursting population. The LCC had its own political group, the Fabian-influenced Progressive Party, which had dominated the Housing Committee since as early as 1890, pressing success-fully for the right to build good-quality housing for working-class renters both within and outside its own bound-aries. Despite a shift in power to the Conservatives in 1900, whole council-owned estates of vernacular cottages – popular with workers who believed flats to be barely an improvement on their former slum conditions – went up on the southern borders of London in Tooting and Norbury, at the Watling estate at Mill Hill in the north, and out west in Old Oak, Acton. Once again, these attractive, health-improving homes were open only to those whose earnings were higher than those of the average worker. The LCC experienced difficulties in letting out flats they had built in parts of the East End, for instance, due to the casual nature of working patterns in the docks industry: dockers could neither afford to move away from their source of work, because of its unpredictability, nor to pay the rent on a three-room council flat. Instead, they stayed within the private sector, crowding cheap two-room flats with their young families. A pattern was thus set from there, it seems, to eternity: the poorest endured, and continue to endure, the poorest conditions. But let's look on the bright side. With every passing year several thousand more cramped, unhealthy households were given the chance to decamp from their condemned inner-city quarters to the new suburbs: to Becontree in Essex, where 120,000 were to reside without a single pub, causing near-riots among its settlers; to sprawling Wythenshawe in Manchester; to the Joseph Rowntree-funded New Earswick in York; to new estates in Birmingham that aped Bournville's chocolate-factory village; and to Cutteslowe, the walled-off Oxford council estate.

The First World War begat the first large-scale state funding for council housing, after the Liberal Prime Minister David Lloyd George announced that the returning troops deserved nothing less than 'homes fit for heroes'. Such a policy, the virulently anti-Bolshevik Prime Minister deduced, would have the added benefit of nipping revolutionary stirrings in the bud. Amidst the horror of the First World War, there was an attendant horror at the thought of Britain's working class following the Bolsheviks and electing for revolution over the slow drip-feed of putative social democracy. Lloyd George's promise may have rung with moral zeal, but behind the rhetoric lay his fear that Great Britain would hold out against the alarming spread of Communism only if the people were given a sense of confidence, and only if they were made to believe that things were being done to improve their post-war lives.

It had been a national scandal at the beginning of the war that nearly a tenth of all conscripts had to be barred from service because of poor health: what good is a nation if its people are not fighting fit at all times? Now the Minister for Health, Dr Christopher Addison, conducted an inquiry into housing need and estimated that 500,000 council houses would have to be built at pace in order to clear the most insanitary slums, and another 100,000 per year would be required to replenish a rented-housing stock which had fallen stagnant over four years of war. The Housing and Town Planning Act (more commonly known as the Addison Act), the 1919 piece of legislation that allowed this state-sponsored building campaign to begin, was never fully carried through. Though it was revised in 1924, further extending the state's powers and responsibility to provide adequate housing for the poor, only 213,000 council homes had been built by then. Had half a million homes materialized in this short period, there may never have been another housing shortage of the kind that, to this day, regularly sends newspaper reporters into paroxysms; there may never have been a situation in which demand for housing outstripped supply, sending the price of owner-occupied houses ever upwards; but those houses would not have been built to last. Quantity takes time and money, but quality takes more of both.

Addison's inquiry surmised that the only homes that were truly fit for heroes were houses with private gardens, which could only be built outside city boundaries where restrictive green belt laws had yet to be enforced. The suburbanization of the working classes was aided by improvements in public transport, and the apparent desire on the part of early council-estate dwellers to lift themselves, bootstrap by bootstrap, into a respectable and unthreatening new lower middle class. Councils were helped by the fact that the upper echelons of the working classes were also beginning to express a preference for owner-occupation, taking some of the burden of rehousing the poor away from the slums. Nevertheless, the rate of council-house occupation increased rapidly, from under 1 per cent of Britain's housing stock in 1914 to 10 per cent in 1938. Over 90 per cent of this new housing was on the new suburban estates, where first-time council tenants – under pressure from housing officers to strive for respectability, and from neighbours to keep up with the Joneses – scrimped to buy net curtains and antimacassars. The quiet conformity of the new suburbs was reinforced by the lack of social amenities; in particular, pubs and social clubs. In part, these essential pieces of social Velcro were left out of town plans in the rush to build houses, but a precedent had been set by the Quaker values of the early housing philanthropists –

such as the Cadbury family – who believed that temperance, like cleanliness, was next to godliness.

In the midst of the Depression came a genuine uplift in the fortunes of many ordinary people as a result of Addison's legacy. Among the many thousands who joined the exodus from the cities were my great-grandparents, who moved from the inner-city Birmingham ward of Ladywood to a new council house in Lea Village in the mid-1930s. It's strange to think how Lea Village was regarded as 'the back of beyond', when these days, positioned halfway between the centre of Birmingham and the Wood on its outskirts, the village-cum-suburb's green spaces have long since been swallowed up by McDonald's and Texaco.

Its houses are pretty, white-painted and large, still solid and strong after seventy years. To me they look like an English version of what the Red Viennese were trying to create at Karl Marx-Hof: a self-sufficient village of working people in attractive homes that no outsider could despoil. This is the second picture on my shelf. I took it in Vienna on a mid-holiday pilgrimage to the great social-housing monuments of Europe: the vast estates of southern Prague, the Communist statue park outside Budapest – full of public art depicting The Happy, Proud, Strong Workers and Their Struggle – and the tower-block Stonehenge of Petrzalka, in which nearly half the population of Bratislava lives. You would be surprised at the number of tourists you find lurking around places like these, at how many people are interested in looking at such monuments to banality: I like to think it's not so much a case of rich Westerners dipping their toes into other people's misery as a sort of atavism, a primordial memory of man as social animal and his desire to live in close (but not too close) proximity to his neighbours. Or perhaps they dream of social-ism, and come to these places in order to ask themselves what went wrong with it.

The photograph shows a narrow slice of the Karl Marx-Hof, a kilometre-long edifice in cream and claret containing 1,325 flats for rent, built between 1927 and 1930, in the years when the name 'Vienna' was prefixed with 'Red'. It is six storeys high, with the same pretty pitched roofs of the Boundary Street blocks, but in place of Arts and Crafts flourishes the building combines the clean angles of Modernist architecture with what the Viennese local government – then controlled by the Social Democratic Workers' Party – called *Schmuckbedürfnis des Wiener Volkes*, or, as translated by the art historian Philip Ward-Jackson, 'the Viennese thirst for ornament'. Stone cherubs dance at the top of stairwells, knot-like gardens punctuate the vast courtyard, and a chain of large plain windows is matched on either side with a big pink balcony, over which even pinker geraniums tumble from narrow troughs – like Iced Gems falling off a child's birthday cake.

KARL MARX-HOF, it shouts in claret capitals from the highest storey. Its name has never been changed, unlike those of so many residual monuments to socialism: there may as well be a subheading that reads FOR WORKERS AND DIE-HARD SOCIALIST ROMANTICS ONLY. It's the kind of model estate that moves architecture critics to compare it to a mighty 'workers' fortress', immune to the destructive influence of the ruling class. That it was besieged by Fascists during the 1934 putsch, which threw the Red Viennese out of the local government seat, doesn't reduce its power to induce a sense of pride and optimism. When it was built, Karl Marx-Hof didn't contain a single private bathroom, instead modelling itself on an idea of wholly communal living which, for good reasons, never really caught on.

In Britain, however, neither the communal living experiment of Karl Marx-Hof, nor the more thoughtful Modernist principles that informed the design of Önkel Toms Hütte and Mies van der Rohe's Afrikanische Strasse – both products of the progressive Weimar era that still stand in Berlin – took hold. The interwar period saw a focus on projects that were characteristically, well, British. While in Europe a certain ease with semi-communal living – through large complexes of flats with balconies and shared gardens – was manifested in banks of solid, centrally located blocks for all classes of tenant, in Britain there continued the vast and concerted push outwards from the cities to their edges, where neat estates of houses with gardens – both privately owned and rented from councils – would begin to munch greedily at the countryside.

An explosion in the number of houses provided by local councils – from almost none in 1900 to over a million on the eve of the Second World War – didn't, at least to begin with, mean a sudden decrease in the quality of the new housing offered. There was a noticeable emphasis on the values behind Lloyd George's slogan, if not the money to back it up. It is often said of the post-1945 welfare state that Britain intended to build a 'New Jerusalem'; this was also the case in the years that followed the 1918 armistice. Not only could revolution be averted through the provision of a decent lifestyle for working men and their families, but council housing was seen as an investment: a national asset. The Victorian ethos of civic pride cast a long, stubborn shadow; there had been no lasting damage caused to the status quo by war, and news of the Russian uprising (touch wood, as long as we got those houses built); council housing was still novel enough to have to prove that it was a superior option to cheaper private rented accommodation. It had to be so good that tenants – who had never before had the state as their landlord, and who had good cause to be suspicious of its new-found magnanimity – would trust the local authority, and would rush to fill the new houses in their thousands. Addison's inquiry concentrated on the socially palliative qualities of giving the people what they wanted. That's not to be cynical – providing the mass of people with what they need and deserve is nothing more than pragmatic socialism – but one wonders if the state's commitment to public housing between the wars would have had quite such sweeping intentions if not for the looming spectre of Communism.

The period between the two world wars, in particular, was a time in which there were fewer cosmetic differences between outer-urban houses built for renting from the council and those built for owner-occupation. From the mid-1960s onwards you could tell council estates from a mile off, giving you the chance to avoid them, to duck out and treat them with the suspicion that their reputations seemed to warrant. But to be given a council house in the 1930s was, in many ways, comparable to winning the lottery. Your living conditions were raised and protected by something called the Tudor Walters standards, named after a 1918 commission set up and chaired by Sir John Tudor Walters to investigate the needs of would-be estate dwellers and to set a basic standard for the proposed new homes. These conditions, which included provisions for minimum room sizes, the number of windows (containing up to twenty-four small panes each, with metal frames that wouldn't rot like wood did) and the density of homes per acre, were developed in part by Raymond Unwin, the architect of Letchworth Garden City. Tudor Walters recommended that houses should not be built at a rate of more than twelve per acre, with six good-sized rooms and large windows to maximize the penetration of daylight. Minimum floor space was set at 760 square feet, using three standardized types of house design which, Unwin recommended, should be used to break up the monotony of an otherwise uniform landscape. On Unwin's advice, the suburban council estates replicated the greenery-saturated, spacious feel of the garden city as far as possible.

It's hard to overstate the importance of the Tudor Walters standards: backed by the state, they expressed a commitment to building mass council housing of the highest quality. They did not extend to the two million private homes built by speculative builders between the wars, meaning that council houses built around this time were likely to be larger and of a higher quality than many of the suburban homes you could buy. The cottage estates were handsome, self-contained and meticulously planned, but despite their palace-like size and low density, were not immune from criticism. They were often far from decent public transport, lacked churches, pubs and community halls, and sent families far away from their extended network of friends and relatives. Lea Villagers, like thousands of new estate dwellers, were stuck miles from their work- and meeting places, reliant on bikes to get into work in Birmingham's legion factories, just as thirty-five years later the new citizens of the Wood were transported ten miles from the city centre without a decent bus service. The price for a superior home with a decent patch of garden was, at worst, submitting to that prison-like atmosphere noted by Orwell. But then again, I wonder how my grandad and his brothers and sisters might have prospered – survived, even – without that childhood lifeline out of the hellish city grime.

The results of the first push towards mass council housing were mixed. By 1939, the LCC alone had rehoused 258,126 of its slum dwellers in new estates on its outskirts, the vast majority in houses, for fewer than 3 per cent of residents expressed a desire to live in flats. Gladdening examples of working-class housing could be seen in the model communities at Bournville and Port Sunlight (Lord Leverhulme's similar estate for his soap-factory workers on the Wirral peninsula), which provided invaluable prototypes in how to create successful new communities. The photographer Bill Brandt followed the work of the Bournville Trust in Birmingham as it recommended to the council ways of rehousing its inner-city population in the style to which Cadbury workers had become accustomed. An illustrated pamphlet with the pride-swelling title 'When We Build Again' was co-produced by the Bournville Trust and Birmingham City Council in 1941 and featured Brandt's clear-eyed photography. It presents a dispiriting portrait of domestic life during wartime: dirty tenement forecourts, filled with grubby toddlers and their harassed-looking mothers, whose inadequate homes the council – aided by the wisdom and experience of the Bournville Trust – promises to do away with as soon as war is over. Two years later, 'Our Birmingham', another book based on findings sponsored by the trust, promises a post-war city of plenty: 'When we build again we must not repeat our old mistakes – no more playgrounds like this' (under a dour scene of small children clambering over rotting iron bars), 'no more congested streets, no more overcrowding, no more dingy courts, no more drab districts, no more huddled houses . . .' The next page continues: 'but create a city of which our grandchildren will be proud with more green play parks, with healthier houses, with sunny airy schoolrooms, with fine hospitals, with better factories, with good gardens'.

Brandt's unsentimental portraits show young families swapping back-to-backs in Ladywood and Small Heath for new homes on the 1930s estates of Weoley Castle and Kingstanding, and the process by which their domestic habits, their complexion, their gait and their clothing are transformed by the move to municipal housing. Chocolate-funded propaganda it may have been, but there is little in the fresh and delighted faces of his subjects that looks faked from here. When *We* Build Again. *Our* Birmingham. The council homes of the interwar period were part of a contract: we will give you a good home if you look after it.

That's not to say that every long-suffering slum tenant was rewarded with a comfortable house between the wars. Many inner-city families were moved from one slum to another, newer slum, in tenements designed as cynically as those they replaced. The first experiments with great barracks of low-rise apartment blocks took place in the mid-1930s, with the kind of disastrous results we have come to associate with the mass experiments in tower-block building of the 1950s and 1960s. An intriguing book I found in the deepest recesses of a town-planning library reports on the fate of an outer-city estate of twenty-seven tenement blocks. 'Tenement Town' was built in 1933 to house slum dwellers from 'three dock and riverside boroughs' in a city that I suspect, but can't be sure, is London. The estate is described as 'an island, bounded on three sides by railway banks, high enough to isolate it completely from the surrounding neighbourhood, and on the fourth by a cemetery'. An instant ghetto, then. The full horror unfurls thus: 'We find that no provision whatsoever was made for the social needs of the people. There was no Community Centre, no Church, no cinema, no post office; there was not even a public house.' Tenants who are dumped here without a minute's consultation complain of kitchens in which the only shelf is seven feet from the ground, where there are no sheds for prams and bikes, and where the headmaster of the local school dismisses their short, pallid children for standing out 'like red pillar boxes' among his well-fed suburban charges. The high standards of the garden-city ideal had been ignored here in the rush to build nothing more solid and effective than a pile of cardboard boxes.

The psychological effects of decanting inner-city populations to remote suburban areas began to be analysed, beginning with the army of Mass-Observation volunteers that was corralled by socio-anthropologist Tom Harrisson in the late 1930s. Families interviewed by Mass-Observation just before the war are at first surprised to be asked what they like and dislike about their new estate homes, largely because they have had no choice in where they were sent to live and, as with all other aspects of their still-harsh lives, see no other option but to put up with it. But when given the time to consider their feelings, they come up again and again with the same answers: they hate flats and prefer houses, but only when they have a sufficient number of rooms and a garden. They need to feel part of a community, but not to live so close together that they can hear each other's thoughts. A woman cries as she admits how much she misses the whelk stalls and fried-fish shops of her old stamping ground: smells and noises that no one had thought to recreate out in this strange people-depot.

Mass-Observation's extended study of Bolton, which it renamed Worktown to preserve the anonymity of its subjects, took place between 1937 and 1941, at a time when large numbers of miners and millworkers were settling into new corporation houses on the outskirts of the industrial town.

Many of its volunteer anthropologist-snoops chose to report on the social and psychological effects of moving from a crowded slum to a spacious new estate. They reflected on the changes, sometimes radical, sometimes subtle, that commonly took place in family life once men were removed from proximity to their downtown 'boozing partners', their wives from the back-to-back bush telegraph of gossip in the yard and at the market, and their children from the close quarters of the street they never strayed from.

One keen observer writes reams on this subject, focusing on the tensions between the 'village atmosphere' created by most families upon their removal to a remote moorside estate only accessible by bus, and the inevitable sense of isolation brought about by this change in geographical circumstances. He describes the prevailing mood on the estate as 'jovial', but, tellingly, links this to a collective feeling among the new estate dwellers that they are in this faraway boat together, and have been forced to make the best of it. The unpretentious majority, he writes, seem 'amused' by the petit-bourgeois pretensions of those mover-outers who, also considering themselves mover-uppers, 'would dearly love to label their home The Laurels'. But the only real outlet for this collective jolliness remains the town, to which they flock on the bus that winds its way, every weekend, back from the distant-seeming moors to the heart of the action:

> This spirit of good humour . . . is particularly marked on the late Saturday night buses, when hilarity and noise reach their peak. Several of the passengers of these late buses have provided themselves with 'liveners' for the morrow, in the shape of pint bottles of beer or stout which advertise themselves by a passenger's difficulty in passing down the gangway owing to numerous mysterious bulges in the pockets of the men . . .

The bus appears to be the connecting link between two worlds as typified by the town and the estate, and is the scene of more exchanged intimacies than any other place. In this respect, it partially takes the place of the absent pub. It is the 'meeting place' of the estate, and the 'bus stop' at the shopping centre becomes to a limited degree, the centre around which the estate revolves. Generally speaking, it is as if the sociability of the estate is hurled into the town at week-ends, to drift back into the estate, bus load by bus load, to take up its routine until the following week-end, when the process is repeated.

In later dispatches the volunteer – an unemployed miner like many of his neighbours – paints at times bucolic, but at others competitive and tension-ridden, vignettes of the Top o' the Moor estate, claiming that the most hated individual on any of the new streets is 'the man who allows his plot to run to weeds'. Since moving to the estate, gardening has quickly become not so much a pastime as an obsession among the menfolk, who are to be witnessed on summer evenings discussing with each other over the fence the best way to nurture cuttings. Women are excluded from this new club: having formed the chatty centre of street-dwelling life, they are now closed off, from the life of the estate and from each other, by the very lack of informal places to meet. In the nuclear family, spurred into being by suburbanization and the building of single-family homes, it is women – deprived of the old-girl network of casual friendships, matriarchs and daughters living near by – who suffer the most.

Not wholly impervious to tittle-tattle himself, it seems, our Mass-Observation man notes that women who take the evening buses into town are the talk of the estate, and not, he claims, 'above suspicion' of having boredom-relieving affairs: 'I can vouch for 4 cases in my immediate vicinity where quarrels due to jealousy are of frequent occurrence, and in each of the 4 cases it is the woman who regularly goes to town. In regard to this point, an interesting statement by one of my men friends here was as follows: "I don't know how a woman stands the deadly monotony of this estate without going nuts."'

In their turn, the largely unemployed men of the estate, newly green-fingered and apparently content to live without the weekday pull of the pub, lose the political teeth they once sharpened on work-related grievances. Trade-union memberships are allowed to lapse, and a distinct apathy with regard to improving the quality of life on the estate soon settles in: 'This lack of organisational effort is peculiar. "Everyone" knows that the shopping centre facilities would be improved by a little judicious competition, but whilst the knowledge is common, no one does anything about it. "Everyone" knows that the bus service is inadequate, but this only results in continuous railing against the corporation.'

Mass-Observation's prolific volunteers, whether in Bolton or on the LCC estates in London, highlighted the unintended effects of moving people from one environment to another that is entirely different. A lot of these effects were contradictory: the 'village atmosphere' on the Worktown estate is tempered by cruel gossip, and a sense that its people only really start living when they head into town on a Friday night. Women are given the space and the labour-saving devices to enjoy a less back-breaking domestic life, only to find that boredom fills the free time. Men remain unemployed for years at a time, at least partly because of the physical inaccessibility of work. It's as though rehousing were a pill that could provide only a partial cure for the manifold ills of the working class, and one that was shown to have painful side effects.

Tenement Town, alas, proved not to be an early,

experimental one-off: minimum standards, little by little, came to be thrown out in favour of building flats at high volume and low quality. This was not to happen for another twenty years, however: although the generous recommendations of the Tudor Walters standards were endangered by a further inquiry into 'The High Cost of Building Working Class Dwellings' in 1921, most large local authorities pressed ahead with a scheme of building mostly cottage-style estates on suburban land long designated for housing. Only the outbreak of another world war could stop the biscuit-cutter stamp of new homes imprinting themselves on the landscape: where 5.9 per cent of Britain was taken up with urban development in 1919, 8.6 per cent was covered by the time war commenced in 1939.

The third picture on my shelf is of a beige-ish council semi, sprinkled with shadows from a tall tree in blossom, painted with photo-realist precision by the artist George Shaw, whose pictures depict silent scenes from the Coventry estate on which he was brought up. Tile Hill was a post-war 'Bevan estate', conceived and built by the first fully realized Labour government in history, whose leaders had been thrown out of power by the time its homes were occupied in January 1952. These homes were named for Aneurin Bevan: Welsh, loud, extremely proud, the socialist-atheist's deity, and a powerful advocate for the right of working-class people to live in comfortable and, crucially, socially integrated surroundings. The founder of the National Health Service, who, despite bragging that he only spent five minutes a week on the housing brief that was then attached to his duties as the first post-war minister for health, was so passionate about the subject that his involvement can be credited with prolonging a creed of quality over quantity in council house provision in the years following the Allied victory. He was to impose his personality

on Britain's muddled, but broadly successful, push to increase
the national stock of council housing more forcefully than any
politician before or since.

From 1941 onwards, there was already a focus on winning
the peace through high-quality council housing. The liberal
civil servant and economist William Beveridge was handed the
brief for creating Britain's first classless society, through the
formation of a cradle-to-grave web of state provision.
Beveridge was a meticulous Old Etonian, who, reports the
biographer of the welfare state Nicholas Timmins, was
instructed by the master of his Oxford college, Balliol, to 'go
and discover why, with so much wealth in Britain, there continues to be so much poverty and how poverty can be cured'.
His report combined Bevan's vision for health and housing
provision with a tightly woven net of social-insurance support
for council tenants and homeowners alike. The report sold
600,000 copies while Britain was still at war; it's hard to
imagine an offical inquiry into poverty and inequality stirring
up so much interest today. Beveridge used rhetoric effectively,
naming 'Five Giants' that stood in the way of creating a more
equal society: Want, Ignorance, Disease, Idleness and Squalor.
The wartime coalition government prepared itself to assault
all five as soon as the conflict was over. Upon its inception,
the welfare state seemed to promise the world to anyone who
wanted to try and reach for it.

In 1945, as the war staggered to an end, the need for housing – any housing, private, council, sublet, prefabricated, you
name it, as long as it had a roof – was so desperate that homeless ex-servicemen and their families, encouraged by
Communist Party activists, were storming disused army barracks and squatting them in their thousands. Many future
residents of Tile Hill were to be found living in a makeshift
shanty town of old caravans and converted buses on a piece
of wasteland outside the half-destroyed city centre, only to be

hauled up by the local courts for failing to ensure that they had access to proper sanitation.

As Timmins notes, the wartime coalition had committed itself, months before VE Day, to providing 'a separate dwelling for every family desiring to have one'. A government White Paper, produced along the lines of the Addison Inquiry a quarter of a century earlier, threw up figures of three to four million new homes that needed to be built before 1957 in order to achieve that aim. At that early juncture, too, it was impossible to predict how the incidence of births, marriages and divorces would explode in the freeing first days of peace-time, creating thousands of new family-cells in need of a discrete home. Relationships held in limbo during wartime were legitimized, annulled, fixed and broken, putting the official figures even further out of joint. Bevan's insistence on putting brick-built cottages ahead of 'jerry-built' flats only set the government further behind in its quest to rehouse the nation, but his rhetoric was rooted in a strong belief that the people who returned Labour to power in 1945 – war-battered but optimistic, convinced of nothing if not that the events of the previous six years must never be repeated – deserved the kind of house that he and his fellow ministers would them-selves be happy to live in.

The post-war town planner Thomas Sharp examined the successes and failures of the vast interwar estates in his 1946 book *Town Planning* – which, along with the LCC's 1943 *County of London Plan*, written by Sharp's contemporary Patrick Abercrombie, served as the blueprint for the first wave of New Towns. These centrally planned settlements were intended to prevent Britain's major cities from sprawling ever outwards in endless suburb-ribbons. It was hoped that, if orchestrated carefully enough, the New Towns would not act as mere dormitories for the cities they were built to relieve, but would have their own economic infrastructure and their own amenities, providing the benefits of city life for millions of people on a more manageable, town-sized scale. This progressive-seeming development in housing policy was indebted to the garden-city movement, except that the element of social engineering encouraged in Ebenezer Howard's original vision was, in true Bevanite spirit, skewed in favour of the urban work-ing class. Thus, hundreds of thousands of East Enders and north Londoners were moved out to the New Towns of Harlow, Hemel Hempstead and Stevenage, three of the eight satellites that were built twenty or so miles outside the capital in the late 1940s.

Sharp's book on planning, along with the *Housing Manual* that the government produced in 1949, could have been designed with the phrase 'Never again' in mind. This was a chance to create a new and more equal society, and to learn from the mistakes of the past; not just in war and economics and diplomacy, but in providing for the basic requirements of life in an industrial society. Sharp warned of the dangers of segregating the working classes from the wider population by shipping them en masse to vast municipal townships:

> To-day there is a large scale physical segregation of the various social classes of the community that is almost as effective at stopping intercourse as the electric-charged barbed-wire barriers of a concentration camp. And that is in fact what many of our towns and suburbs largely are to-day: social concentration camps: places in which one social class is concentrated to the exclusion of all others ... Around the great cities we have enormous one-class communities (if they can be called communities) the like of which the world has never seen before; Becontree, where no less than 120,000 working-class people live in one enormous concentration: Norris Green, one of many Liverpool Corporation Estates, housing 50,000 working-class inhabitants.

Sharp's ideal, to have all classes living alongside each other and interacting on a daily basis to breed out snobbery and to give all members of society an equal sense of pride in their home, was shared by the victorious Labour government, with Bevan providing the money – and the mouthpiece – for this social democratic plan to build equality into the fabric of the national landscape.

Such great optimism! The 1951 Festival of Britain showcased the new Lansbury Estate in the East End of London, named after the legendary Labour MP for Poplar, and the most comprehensive example yet of what Bevan called 'the living tapestry of a mixed community', where well-designed homes of differing sizes mixed with shops, vibrant markets and public-transport routes to ensure that the grievous mistakes of Tenement Town were not repeated. It was a shining example of how ministers, architects and planners could work to design out the potential for well-intentioned housing to end up as the 'social concentration camps' of Sharp's nightmares. As a young man, Prime Minister Clement Attlee's working residence at Toynbee Hall – a campaigning settlement in Spitalfields, not far from the Lansbury Estate, dedicated to improving living conditions for the poor – had enlightened him to the sense of mixing up social classes to promote social mobility and the cohesion on which the success of the welfare state relied.

'On this ground,' hailed the Festival of Britain guidebook, 'so recently a derelict and bomb-scarred wilderness, has arisen not a tangle of jerry-built and pokey dwellings, but a new urban landscape in which the buildings are growing together as a community.'

Prior to the war, Mass-Observation volunteers had carried out surveys on the nearby Ocean Street Estate in Stepney Green; the results, needless to say, stated that families hated living in flats. (An estate composed as thoughtfully and carefully as the Lansbury, then, ought to have escaped the spell of Modernism that was, from the 1950s onwards, to compel so many local-authority architects to build upwards. It was not to be. Later stages of the estate's development included plans for tower blocks that had never featured in the original plans drawn up by LCC.) Their findings were fed into the plan for the Lansbury Estate, where maisonettes and terrace houses mingled with low-rise blocks of flats intended for single and elderly occupants. Even the furniture was designed especially for these comfortably large new homes:

'The three-piece is of entirely new design, consisting of a settee, one armchair, intended for the man – comfort being the key note – and the other for the woman, which gives firm support to the back and ample elbow room for sewing, knitting and the other spare-time occupations which fall to the lot of the housewife.' Hurrah!

It's exhilarating to think that the 1945–51 government seriously considered nationalizing the entire stock of rented housing, as Timmins reports in *Five Giants*, his exhaustive study of the welfare state. Had this been carried through, the 1958 riots at Notting Hill – caused, at least in part, by competition among poor people of different races for private housing at the exploitative bottom end of the market – would never have happened, and nor would there be 100,000 families today existing in bed-and-breakfast rooms while waiting for a council house. But that's another story. The idea didn't stick around for long: Bevan eventually settled for placing a restriction on the construction of private houses, so that for every new owner-occupied home, four would be built by local councils. I think his assumption was that his red-brick palaces (three large bedrooms, a garden in the front and at the back, and two toilets) would appeal to every sector of society, whether rich or poor, on the up-escalator or stuck in poverty. The late critic and memoirist Lorna Sage confirmed this in her account of growing up in an isolated row of new council homes in a rural village on the Welsh borders in the early 1950s, commenting that 'at the time, council house people were socially mobile – upwardly in most cases, although not in ours. We all shared a sense of being out of place, on the move.'

What, for Bevan, made a good council home? A large terraced or semi-detached house that recalled the Tudor Walters standards of the interwar period, but with an even greater floor space – at minimum 900 square feet – and the guarantee of a garden. He preferred aesthetically harmonious designs, built from expensive local stone where possible, that would emphasize the similarity, the quality, the equality, of his council homes compared to the ones they would exist alongside. For him, the issue of well-built housing was connected with his desire to create 'modern villages and towns . . . where the doctor, the grocer, the butcher and the farm labourer all lived in the street'. Why ought the farm labourer to live in worse conditions than the doctor? Does he work any less hard? Not at all, he reasoned, which is why he deserves a house fit for a labourer and a doctor alike. A former mineworker whose father, also a miner, died prematurely of the pit disease pneumoconiosis, Bevan's overriding preoccupation was with the health and dignity of the working man. This was manifested in his idea of the solid, attractive, spacious home to which each Labour voter should return every night. But he had real and imagined enemies every step of the way to building his socialist paradise, from the small matter of suitable materials (most of which had been used up in the war, or had been left fallow as energies were diverted to the war effort) to civil servants who, time and again, tried to get him to compromise his vision. He held firm, dismissing proposed cuts in standards to raise productivity as 'the coward's way out . . . if we wait a little longer, that will be far better than doing ugly things now and regretting them for the rest of our lives'.

Within a few years, Bevan's warning would be discarded like so much chip paper in the scramble for votes. In the general election campaigns of 1950 and 1951, the Conservative Party seized on the government's house-completion record, which peaked at 227,000 a year in 1948, pledging to build 300,000 new homes a year and to bring an end to the mood of incipient crisis caused by the slow materialization of Labour's New Jerusalem. Hundreds of thousands of families, including my own parents', remained crammed into private digs until the early 1950s, and even then supply could not meet demand.

But for this brief period, nothing – not two toilets, not a spare bedroom, not a shed, not hand-cut local sandstone – was considered too good for the workers. Bevan and Sharp together envisaged a post-war policy that took into account

the disadvantages, as well as the benefits, of the first generation of suburban cottage estates. 'We shall be judged for a
year or two by the *number* of houses we build,' said Bevan, an
early master of the soundbite. 'We shall be judged in ten years'
time by the *type* of houses we build.'

One stinging failure of interwar council housing, it had
already become clear by 1945, was that the Tudor Walters
standards gave estates a dully self-similar appearance that was
easy to stigmatize. No matter that Raymond Unwin had
painstakingly drawn three versions of his standard cottage in
order to prevent this happening: snobbery is snobbery, and
council estates, no matter how pleasing they were to the eye,
offended homeowners purely because they housed large numbers of poor people, and did so visibly.

This stigma would persist through the decades. A 1994
report by Anne Power and Rebecca Tunstall on behalf of the
Joseph Rowntree Foundation into the success or failure of
several interwar cottage estates holds municipal planners
to account for creating single-class areas of housing that
were too easily distinguishable from owner-occupied homes.
Speculative builders between the wars largely ignored the
Tudor Walters standards, believing them to be too rigid and
too closely associated with council housing to be popular with
the first generation of working- and lower-middle-class house
buyers. The irony is stunning: Power and Tunstall's findings,
taken from repeated visits to cottage estates in declining areas
of the north and north-east, show that all the back gardens
and spacious front rooms in the world cannot compensate for
access to work and education. That these estates – shown to
be among the twenty most 'hard to let' and manage in the
country when the researchers arrived in 1981 – remained as
economically and socially isolated from mainstream society as
when they were built proved that the garden-city model could
only work if council housing, of any standard, was linked to

an infrastructure that guaranteed jobs and good schooling. Large areas of social housing with their own postal code were, and always have been, easy targets to identify for those with a fixed, and unflattering, view of the 'feckless' poor. The 1930s council estates – not only the tenement towns, but also the miniature garden cities that were built according to Unwin's rigorous standards – were considered too plain, too monotonous and prone to stigmatization by residents of the surrounding areas. It wasn't so much the case that working-class people were unwelcome wherever they went – one might argue that this problem is as stubborn as poverty itself – but that their social betters didn't appreciate the idea of having vast, unprepossessing dormitories built at the end of their gardens.

The very fact that Tudor Walters designs became the unmistakable blueprint of interwar council housing, while speculatively built private housing – so hated by Bevan – escaped such regulations, suggests that it was the policy of housing different social classes separately, in identifiably separate housing, which gave council estates the poor reputation that has persisted throughout their existence. There is a terrible paradox here: the cottage estates were built outside cities in order to give the urban poor a chance to live in single-family homes amid greenness and light and, in so doing, ameliorate the huge inequalities in health and social status that existed between the classes in pre-war Britain. Yet it was their very estate-ness – the fact that they were built for a specific purpose, rather than growing organically within an existing community – that would, at least in part, cause estate dwellers so many problems. Not only were they sent to where they were not wanted, but it was often to a place where it was expensive and difficult to travel to somewhere they *were* wanted: to places of work, to pubs and social clubs, to the old streets where their friends and family remained. For all the great intentions that lay behind the massive movement of working-class people from one collective residence to another, the price – literally, socially and psychologically – paid by those who moved was high.

The Labour government managed to build around a million homes during its first five years in power. The party scraped a second election victory in 1950, but the government only lasted a year before collapsing, handing power to the Conservatives for the next thirteen years. Bevan's instructions to build for posterity, rather than for popularity, had caused builders and local authorities to lag behind with plans to rebuild on bombed-out sites, which led to the government's reluctant (extremely reluctant, in Bevan's case) acceptance of prefabricated building methods to ease at least a fraction of the housing shortage. Prefab homes could be built in around five days by local authorities, mostly in clear urban spaces created by bomb damage, using aluminium and concrete which, from 1944 onwards, were the only readily available alternatives to steel and brick. Wartime aircraft factories suddenly became prefab factories, turning out 125,000 units by 1948 and unexpectedly becoming some of the most treasured housing of the last sixty years. Although their intended life was ten years, a few still exist and are often visited as evidence of Britain's post-war architectural heritage. Most of those that remain have been Artex-clad and double-glazed beyond recognition, but are so beloved of their now elderly inhabitants that hunger strikes to avoid their demolition are not unheard of. The obvious reason for the popularity of these squat little boxes is that although they were small ('rabbit hutches', Bevan called them) they were detached, and self-contained, and had gardens at the front and rear: every Englishman's dream rendered in flat-pack slabs.

Houses were built for all, everyone got a garden, and the British people lived happily ever after in a state of blissful parity with each other. Except they weren't, they didn't, and – this is Britain, after all – no, they didn't. To have built sufficient council houses to Bevan's exacting standards all over the country would have used more money, time and resources than either the incoming Conservative government or an impatient voting public would allow. The 900-square-foot, three-bedroom semi of the immediate post-war years – expensive and slow to build – would become a thing of the past, to be replaced by smaller terrace houses and, increasingly, the very kind of low-rise 'barracks' that Labour's 1945 election manifesto had pledged to avoid. But there was a whole new way of living just around the corner. Streets would no longer be on the ground, but in the sky, saving precious space, thrusting city skylines upwards, allowing engineers to take the place of builders and concrete to take the place of brick. Tower blocks would be the future.

That Britain, a country with little experience of apartment-dwelling, whether low- or high-rise (with the exception of Scotland, which had thousands of walk-up tenements), and with flats whose tenants complained endlessly of their lack of privacy or a garden, would see fit to transform the thrust of its public house-building policy over the course of a decade, is a testament to the persuasive powers of three parties. The first were large building companies, who poured money and effort into persuading local authorities to invest their council housing budgets in 'off-the-peg' packages of prefabricated apartment blocks instead of houses made of brick. The second were local-authority town planners and leaders, the former having found a quick and easy way of housing large numbers of people without busting city boundaries; the latter thrilled by the prospect of putting their city on the map with its ambitious futurism. The third were architects who, as the American architect Philip Johnson recalled to Alice Coleman in her 1985 book *Utopia on Trial*, 'really believed, in a quasi-religious sense, in the perfectibility of human nature, in the role of architecture as a weapon of social reform ... the coming Utopia when everyone would live in cheap prefabricated flat-roofed multiple dwellings – heaven on earth'.

In 1947, the men charged with replacing Glasgow's notorious tenements sought inspiration for its slum-clearance programme, centred around 'comprehensive redevelopment areas' where high-density blocks of flats would encircle the city centre, while the overspill population would be carted far out of the city into a combination of peripheral housing schemes and New Towns. A contingent of architects employed by the council travelled to Marseille, where the Swiss architect and theorist Le Corbusier had completed the first of his near-identical Unité d'habitation mass housing blocks, which represented the realization of his theory that homes were nothing more nor less than machines for living in.

Le Corbusier envisaged that, in the blankness of the collective machine-home, people would turn away from thoughts of individual improvement and instead concentrate on mutual improvement; that, in the absence of opportunities to assert superiority to one's neighbour, man's spiritual nourishment would start to come from within, rather than from without. Like his Czech contemporary Karel Teige, designer of the hive-like 'minimum dwelling', he believed in the revolutionary potential of domestic architecture. Both believed that bourgeois society would wither and collapse if that seat of bourgeois life, the family home, were subverted or replaced by identical communal dwellings with minimal individualizing features. 'Judiciously industrialised,' wrote François de Pierrefeu in *The Home of Man*, his book-length collaboration with Le Corbusier, [kitchens] might attain that economic point where luxury simply displaces in one step the horror of slums, were one foolish enough to by-pass the intermediate stages and not allow proletarian families – or for that matter families from a more stable class – time to accustom themselves to a better way of living, to homes made worthy of men who have achieved victory over, and control of, the machine.

Teige's manifesto went a step further: 'Merely including a common laundry and bath by no means makes for proletarian or socialist housing,' he wrote in reference to his idea for entirely communal flat-blocks. 'Much more important is to liberate women from kitchen work and to relieve them from the supervision of children by establishing common dining facilities and children's homes.'

What the Glasgow contingent saw in the immense slab of the Unité d'habitation impressed them, not least because its simplicity and density gave them an answer to how they would fulfil radical plans drawn up by the city's chief engineer, Robert Bruce, to transform Glasgow's urban landscape by demolishing and rebuilding 170,000 of its 280,000 homes. The council would build 300 high-rise blocks in the twenty years that followed, making it the British city with the most tower-block dwellings per head. (At one point in the 1970s, 70 per cent of all Scottish housing was rented from the council.) Its council planners and architects were early adopters of Le Corbusier's vision, with results that, in the main, could only be described as disastrous. They were the first to find out the danger of falling for the idea that families with children could be housed hundreds of feet from the ground, but they would not be the last.

Which brings me to the fourth photograph. It's the only black and white one in my small collection, taken, I would say, in about 1966, judging by my mum's pubescent figure and demure white dress. She is standing in a recreation ground behind the first tower blocks that were built in Birmingham: based on a template produced by the construction company Wimpey, they were Y-shaped identical sextuplets with a communal playground that lies, in the photograph, just behind my mum's shoulder. The flats, situated at Tile Cross, where the city crept east towards the soon-to-be-deflowered virgin bluebell wood, were just over a decade old at that point and showing no signs of decay beyond the dirt that had nestled itself into the pale pebble-dashing.

Birmingham City Council, which needed to house a million people within its tight city boundaries, proved itself to be just as eager as Glasgow's to build upwards from the mid-1950s onwards, but both my parents – just – escaped the fate of being housed a hundred feet from the ground. My mum's parents got their fourth-storey walk-up flat in the early 1950s, just as my dad was removed with his family from the inner city to a brand-new estate of Bevan-sanctioned council semis at Longbridge, south of Birmingham. As he remembers, 'they were building them like billy-o just after the war'.

The new house was a revelation to his Irish father, who had become miserably accustomed to the limited range of digs at the grotty bottom end of the private rented market which had hitherto been available to him, his growing family and a succession of lodgers. The estate, says my dad, teemed with six-year-olds like him who at last had been given room to grow, to play, and even to start thinking about the 11-plus. In their old back-to-back, he couldn't focus on his homework, such was the lack of space and privacy. Not only did he pass his exams in the spacious environment of their new home, but he was able to run or cycle out to the nearby countryside and snaffle rare eggs from birds' nests (he feels pretty bad about this now). What was good for him wasn't necessarily so good for his parents. The increase in rent forced his father to work night shifts to earn the extra money, which made home life fractious and, eventually, argument-riven. But his family's move came at the beginning of the end for an era when council homes were built and bequeathed by a state that had seemed genuinely to communicate with – rather than for, or on behalf of – its citizens.

The Conservative Party entered power in 1951, having committed itself to increasing Britain's housing stock by 300,000 homes a year. Received opinion says that a consensus between the two main political parties had developed in the years immediately following the war. Indeed, there was no peep from the Tories about their predecessors' establishment of a free health service, a 'cradle-to-grave' insurance system, and a house-building programme that prioritized council housing over private properties. In practice, however, the Tories' version of consensus had more to do with ruthless pragmatism than with having converted to social democracy.

Labour's million new homes had evidently not been enough to satisfy voters who had become impatient with the promise of jam endlessly deferred, their achievements in establishing the rest of the welfare state overshadowed by the heavy criticism they endured for not fully meeting the electorate's ravenous demand for housing. While it would be hard to argue with those who had been forced by the slowness of Labour's rebuilding programme to live in overcrowded or half-ruined accommodation, it was partly in this transfer of power, and the shift in world-view from Bevanite idealism to Conservative pragmatism – which held that renting a home was a means to an end rather than the end in itself – that the seeds of council housing's eventual infamy were sown.

'Housing is not a question of Conservatism or Socialism. It is a question of humanity.' This was said by Harold Macmillan, the founding Minister for Housing and the future prime minister, who stole Bevan's thunder solely on the basis that he managed to get more houses built in his time at the newly formed ministry (until 1951, housing was the responsibility of the Ministry of Health). He promised and delivered 300,000 homes in each year of the 1950s. Two-thirds of that figure comprised council housing, reaching a peak of 220,000 built in 1953. Like Bevan, he made an ideology out of being pragmatic. Bevan saw socialism as the work of a Labour government in action. Despite his adherence to Marx, he didn't hold with the ideological left or right of his party, preferring to go with what worked best, both in principle and in practice rather than in principle alone. But Macmillan took this view a crucial step further. He may have equated housing with human decency, but took an entirely different approach to his predecessor, viewing the swiftness with which slum dwellers were rehoused as more important than the quality of the houses they were moved to: the practice without the principle.

Macmillan's great brainwave as Minister for Housing was the 'Great Housing Crusade', which he announced in 1951 at the beginning of his tenure. Known to his Cabinet colleagues as his 'grand strategy for housing', it was based on the rapid building of many small houses – two-bedroom terraces, with 20 per cent less floor space than Bevan's palaces, which Macmillan launched as 'the People's House' in November of that year – and an increasing number of flats, which would meet demand but would not necessarily lay the foundations of the kind of mixed-tenure utopia envisioned by Bevan and the New Town planners. Whether the so-called 'crusade' did its bit to keep Labour out of power until 1964 is unclear, although successive elections during this period were fought by the two parties on the grounds that each promised to build more houses than the other. The 700-square-foot 'People's House' also had to compete with the increasingly affordable private house: while Labour in the 1940s had built two council houses to every private home, the Conservatives, aided by an economy that was starting to gain strength a decade after the end of the war, encouraged private house-building as a preferable tenure for the newly affluent masses. Not only that, but its small size and quality-skimping construction – internal walls made of plasterboard rather than brick, smaller and fewer windows, yards rather than gardens – showed that Macmillan's policy was dangerously preoccupied with short-term results at the expense of the long-term health of both the housing stock and, ultimately, society as a whole.

Macmillan described the operation of his new housing ministry – which was hived off from the Ministry of Health in order to make house-building a government priority – as being 'like cricket, you could see the runs stacking up on the chalkboard'. In other words, throughout the 1950s, new homes went up at a rate that exceeded any previous house-building drive. With post-war rationing and materials shortages finally at an end, the private sector went back to the kind of speculative building so loathed and restricted by Bevan, while local authorities experimented with untested construction methods in order to meet the government's 300,000-per-year target. Macmillan wanted to prove his commitment to the new social democratic consensus by doing even more to house the poor than his Labour predecessor. Unit for unit he succeeded, but at the expense of treating homes as boxes that could somehow be stacked up willy-nilly rather than planned carefully: the curse of Tenement Town. In terms of its diminishing emphasis on quality and its discarding of Bevan's 'modern village' blueprint once the New Towns of the 1946 Act had been planned and built, his 'great crusade' was, in practice, merely a mission to be seen to get things done. Bevan feared building quickly in case he built new slums. Macmillan seemed less bothered by this prospect, and passed this crucial lack of foresight into the very fabric of the council-housing landscape.

While the incumbent government had taken to treating housing policy like a pile 'em high, build 'em cheap super-market – squandering the chance for municipal homes to be considered as desirable as those in the private sector – Labour in opposition diverted its attention to the millions of private tenants, mostly poor, who were still being exploited by unscrupulous 'Rachmanite' landlords (named after the noto-rious Notting Hill slum-lord of the 1950s). They called for the mass municipalization of all privately rented homes, which would have raised the total national stock of council housing, in proportion to private housing, to 60 per cent. It could have wiped out exploitation, and the modern-day phenomenon of 'buying to let', at a stroke; but then, all proposals made in opposition are, by their nature, merely academic. In any case, it was Labour's way of playing the housing-numbers game that had seized the nation.

That council housing, for all its flaws, formed such a significant part of Macmillan's crusade, when his ultimate aim was to achieve 'a property-owning democracy' (a phrase commonly attributed to Thatcher), shows how much had changed in half a century. While Bevan would quite happily have housed everybody in council houses if he could – even if he'd had to resort to stuffing the mouths of the professional classes with gold, as he had paid off private physicians when creating the NHS – Macmillan saw council housing as a stepping stone to home ownership. The result was that quality didn't matter to him so much, because he envisaged that, once he had successfully got the working classes out of the slums and into his People's Houses, they would soon set their minds to the task of saving for a home of their own. That is where Labour and the Conservatives, for all the lip service paid to the idea of consensus, differed crucially: one side believed in sufficiency for all, the other in self-sufficiency. The rise of the council house, you might say, ended at this point, where it became a place of transience on the way to a better life, as opposed to being the magic key itself. The long decline of the council house was triggered by nothing more solid than a change of perspective, from one that saw public housing as providing the nation with a collective legacy to one that saw it as a brief stop on the path towards acquiring an individual legacy. When it came to housing, the post-war consensus between the parties was rarely more shallow, and never more at cross-purposes.

First, in order to hit impossibly high building targets and to save on building materials, Macmillan created his 'People's Houses', so-called because the rent was a few shillings cheaper, and anyway, it sounded nice and democratic. Then, the threat to the green belt collided with the emergent influence of *Towards a New Architecture*, Le Corbusier's paean to mass-produced machine-homes, which had spread slowly down from Glasgow through to Birmingham and the architecture departments of other major city councils. New, industrialized forms of construction, known as system-building – in which concrete panels were manufactured in a distant factory before being shipped to the construction site and bolted together – gained in popularity: partly in homage to Le Corbusier, partly in response to the shortage of bricks that had held up the progress of house-building in the decade after 1945, and partly because of the city-throttling effects of the green belt.

Later still, the 1956 Housing Subsidy Act offered local authorities a greater government subsidy the higher they were prepared to build. Blocks of flats with four floors would bag the council £20 per flat, while blocks over six storeys would receive £38, with a further £1.15s. for every floor above the sixth. Nicholas Timmins writes how Birmingham's Labour council leader, Harry 'Little Caesar' Watton, visited one of the earliest system-built estates, a glass of whisky in his hand, and – recalled the city's then Chief Architect A. G. Sheppard Fidler – ordered five identical blocks 'just as if he was buying bags of sweets'.

In a way, that's exactly what Watton and other council leaders of similar mind were doing: the higher, the faster, the more efficient they were prepared to build, the more money Macmillan's successor, Duncan Sandys, threw at them, as though he were pressing them with ten-bob notes to buy toffees. Large-scale construction companies such as Wimpey and Bryant knew that tower blocks offered their local-authority clients an apparently simple, prestige-building solution to the problem of rehousing slum dwellers within city boundaries (this was important because not only were they compelled to do so by the green belt, they literally could not afford to lose thousands of ratepayers to neighbouring councils). The fact that industrialized building was new and therefore glamorous, and seemed to fulfil a genuine post-war desire among planners and architects to find – or impose – new ways of living, only added to the allure of building skywards. The next two decades would pass in a flood of concrete and walkways.

The four pictures on my shelf tell the story of a half-century in which council housing grew from a single block in the East End of London to something like a national industry, with industrial methods to match. The movement to rid the nation of the shame of slums took different forms, and had different motivations, depending on the very different individuals who led us through the building of millions of homes in the sixty-year rise of the council house. There was Ebenezer Howard, who sought to unify town and country so that all of us would enjoy the benefits of each without exploitation; then there was David Lloyd George, an intensely political beast who knew that 'homes fit for heroes' would also be fit for keeping would-be Bolsheviks quiet; then Nye Bevan, whose refusal to accept anything but the best for long-suffering workers still causes many to genuflect at his altar, despite the knowledge that many of his post-war cottage estates suffered from many of the same ails of isolation and class segregation as the pre-war estates he sought to learn from; and then Harold Macmillan, whose 'People's House' and whose myopic, though broadly accurate, comment that most Britons had 'never had it so good' than in the 1950s summed up the short-sightedness of a housing policy which condemned council tenants to the knowledge that they were of a lower priority than homeowners.

Council houses were not the only homes that were built in the first half of the twentieth century: although the state had embraced its duty to house a large proportion of its population, there was an equally huge movement of upper-working-class and lower-middle-class people towards homes that they owned themselves. The great loser in this demographic shift was the private landlord, whose livelihood was squeezed from the 1930s onwards by the flight of aspirational families to places with green lungs and light. For that we have partly to thank Howard, who saw how the benefits of town and country could be combined effectively, and without whose ideas the democratizing New Towns of the late 1940s would never have been built. It's no exaggeration to say that the generosity of the Tudor Walters standards, reinforced by Bevan after the war, gave millions of working-class people their only chance to stretch out and live healthily after generations spent grinding through life in conditions that nobody deserved to endure. There was, it seems, a cost to this good health, in the form of a prolonged period spent adjusting to the strange silence and raised expectations of the out-of-town estate. But these homes gave children, at least, a better chance of growing up to live fulfilling and physically healthy adult lives.

It's not so much what was taken heed of as what was ignored that was decisive in causing the long decline of council housing that was to follow its rapid rise. Once the Bevanite concepts of quality and dignity in council-house building were downgraded, in the 1950s, housing ministers and local-authority planners had an excuse to ignore the findings of reports which were beginning to suggest that flats were bad for families and even worse for communities. Sir Keith Joseph, the influential Conservative politician who was made Minister for Housing in 1962, recalls going to bed at night and practically rubbing his hands together at the thought of how many bargain-bucket council flats had been thrown up that day by private builders in the pay of the state. Unsurprisingly, he later cringed at this lack of foresight. The Macmillan government egged on councils and architects, who saw the bomb-stripped landscape as a blank canvas on which to project their own versions of Le Corbusier's 'Radiant City' of giant urban towers

and low-rise suburban satellites; the stance of each was
expedient for the other. You would expect them to be opposed:
warm beer and village halls against cold steel and communal
parks. Money and intellectual arrogance got in the way,
leaving the poorest, once again, to endure the consequences.

3

Slums in the Sky: The Fall of the Council Estate

There is one phrase in the English language that has come to be larded with even more negative meaning than 'council estate', and that is 'tower block'. There has to be some reason why people who waited years for a coveted home from 'the Corpy' wouldn't wish the same for their own grandchildren; some reason why the word 'council' has become a pejorative term, which can be used to ridicule people's clothing, their hairstyles, their ways of speaking, the brands of cigarette they smoke and the alcohol they imbibe. Housing seems to have been the one great failure of the welfare state. It is the one area where public investment intended to narrow the gap between rich and poor eventually served to create a firm and visible wall between them. Chris Holmes, former director of the housing charity Shelter, has said that 'Housing poverty is now the most extreme form of social inequality in Britain.' It's hard not to agree. Slums may no longer truly exist in absolute terms, but there is no word that is better suited to describing some of the very worst local-authority housing – some of it seventy years old, some of it built in the 1980s – which fails to provide even the basic necessities of dryness and warmth. Tower blocks, in the public mind, represent all that is worst about the welfare state: the failure to provide the kind of housing that most people regard as a prerequisite for a happy family life; lack of choice; dependence and isolation; bureaucracy prioritized over standards; individuals placed at the mercy of a faceless local authority that seems to maintain or leave to rot its housing on a whim. And concrete. Ugly concrete.

By 1979, around a third of the British population lived in council housing. A generation later, only 12 per cent are housed by their local authority, with another 6 per cent living in houses and flats owned and managed by housing associations or co-operatives. A further 10 per cent of the population rents privately – mostly those in professional occupations, in direct reversal of the pre-war years, when the poorest were forced into landlord-owned slums. The remaining 72 per cent own their own homes, either outright or with the aid of a mortgage. In 2004, 92,000 council tenants exercised their Right to Buy from the local authority: on the Wood, which started life with 82 per cent of its residents as council tenants and the rest as mortgages to the council, the proportion of homeowners now stands at around half.

A great deal has changed in a relatively short period of time. We talk about housing just as much as we always did, but now as property owners, concerned with equity and investment, rather than as tenants hopeful of a chance to escape cramped surroundings. Macmillan's dream of a property-owning democracy, revived and extended by Thatcher, came true for a majority of people. Home ownership is now so widespread that you can't tell a person's class just from their housing tenure. For that, you have to probe deeper: if they bought their home from the council, you can be fairly sure that they will be less well paid and in a lower-status job than someone who bought privately. Someone who rents from the council, as opposed to renting from a private landlord, will almost certainly qualify for some sort of means-tested benefit, whether they are in work or otherwise. You can take this social stratification further, by looking at the height of the council property they rent: if they live above the fifth floor of a local-authority block in England and Wales, they are more likely not only to be working class, but also to be from an ethnic minority. The welfare state and the property-owning democracy have, between them, created neither a classless nor a racially equal society.

Nor, apparently, has the sixty-year drive to clear the slums and replace the millions of homes damaged in the Second World War. Instead, in a sustained period of growth that has benefited a majority – though not the whole – of the population, almost all housing wealth has been disseminated from private landlords to individual property owners. Particularly in the last twenty-five years, this has benefited working-class people as much as it did originally the middle classes. The effect of this spreading-out of wealth through private ownership rather than state-led redistribution, however, has been to make the poorest suffer most, and to perpetuate a situation in which the worst-off are also the worst housed.

The graph on the next page shows the annual rate of house-building in Britain between the end of the war and the beginning of this century. The graph jags like a Toblerone, stabbing the heights in times of prosperity and the new-broom sweep of incoming governments. Post-war council housing enjoyed a boost in numbers whenever there was something to prove, but all the while, more private homes were being built per annum than homes for rent. The first uphill dash corresponds with Macmillan's Great Housing Crusade of the early 1950s, when the Tories ran Labour out of power on the

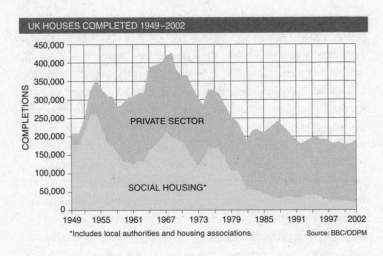

UK HOUSES COMPLETED 1949–2002

PRIVATE SECTOR

SOCIAL HOUSING*

1949 1955 1961 1967 1973 1979 1985 1991 1997 2002
*Includes local authorities and housing associations.   Source: BBC/ODPM

promise of building in excess of 300,000 homes a year. It slopes back quickly following that first rush, leaping again from 1964 onwards as the party-political see-saw tipped from blue to red. One thing you notice here is the astonishing number of homes, both for sale and for rent, that were built in the late 1960s; the annual rate of house-building nudged 450,000 at its 1968 peak, matching the boom decade's drive towards mass affluence. That's where much of the green belt went. Then the juts become less pronounced. You can see that council-house building enjoyed a last brief splurge in the mid-1970s before tailing off in the 1980s, never to recover. In 1980, as a deeply iniquitous condition of the Right to Buy policy, local authorities were encouraged to sell their stock of council homes to individuals, but were banned from using the income from those sales to build replacements. In the two decades between the mid-1980s and 2005, fewer than 50,000 (half of that in the years between 1997 and 2002) socially rented homes were built, and most of those were by housing associations and trusts.

The national housing stock is now topsy-turvy, reflecting

the devastating effects of deindustrialization in the north and the buoyancy of the service economy in the south. A dearth of demand for rented housing exists north of Birmingham, where it is cheaper to live but where there are fewer jobs, and a dearth of supply in the expensive megalopolis that extends throughout London and the south-east. At the same time that the Labour government has proposed a programme of selective demolition of homes in low-demand areas of the Midlands, Merseyside, Greater Manchester, Hull and Newcastle, it has encouraged the building of homes from prefabricated flat-packs, and on the once-polluted floodplains of the eastern Thames. This is intended to make up for the fact that barely any affordable housing has been built in the south-east of England – the seat of the Right to Buy revolution – since the late 1970s. One and a half million people are currently on the waiting list for a council home nationwide, many of whom are unwilling or unable to move to an area of lower housing demand. There is, after all, a reason why there are homes empty in such areas: there aren't enough good jobs to support them. Demand for affordable rented housing has not been met with supply where it is most needed, forcing families into bed-and-breakfast accommodation when there exists a net surplus of housing across the country. Almost all this surplus is privately owned.

Looking at the graph, you might easily assume that the vast supply of private homes built up in the thirty years following the war simply drove council housing out of business. Although council housing comprised over a third of the total housing stock by the late 1970s, levels of building could not match the supply of new, relatively cheap private dwellings which became more and more accessible to well-paid manual workers who believed they had a job for life. In that sense, it is strange that mass home ownership among the working class didn't occur earlier, but the post-war generation's lasting trust in the state extended to housing provision – at least until it became clear that the homes provided from the early 1950s onwards were, in many cases, not only inappropriate but materially inadequate.

One could see the stark differences between the approach to council housing taken by the 1945–51 governments and the methods pursued by Macmillan and his successors most visibly in Birkenhead, where the cream rendering and pointy-roofed terraces of the Woodchurch Estate, built in 1950, contrasted with the hideous early Brutalism of the high-rise Oak and Eldon Gardens, completed in 1959. Each highlighted the other's affectations: the clumsy cosiness of the terraced houses looked even more twee against the allegedly brave Modernism of the flats. A contemporary picture of Oak and Eldon Gardens shows an ant-sized woman walking towards a matchbox-sized pub, both not so much overshadowed as overwhelmed by the King Kong-like scale of the new buildings. Within two years of their completion, the ten-storey blocks, a hundred yards wide, had fallen into dangerous disrepair. (They were knocked down in 1979, eventually to be replaced by a multiplex cinema and a car park.) The Woodchurch cottages, by contrast, were bought in their hundreds by satisfied long-term tenants when they were given permission to buy them in the early 1980s.

Not every tower block in Britain suffered from the same poor building and misguided planning that made Oak and Eldon Gardens so disastrous, especially in the early years: the Y-shaped high-rises in my fourth photograph are still standing, as is the Alton Estate on the edge of Richmond Park in south-west London, which combines well-built low-rise blocks with a carefully designed approximation of Le Corbusier's vast Unité d'habitation. These are exceptions, built to the same exacting standards promised by Bevan in his post-war compact with voters, but at a vastly higher cost.

Because of the large swathes of communal green space that surrounded them, they housed barely more people than would have inhabited an estate of terraced houses built on the same plot. It makes you wonder why high-rise building ever seemed such an economical and space-saving option in the first place.

In the decade between 1955 and 1965, council homes went from being the crowning glory of the new welfare state to mass-produced barracks. They weren't intended to be so: it was hoped that high-rise blocks would confer prestige on a town as much as provide housing for its workers. It wasn't only the thought of subsidies and concrete that excited those who were in charge of designing and implementing housing policy on the ground. There was a desire to create a more European, less Pooterish future for Britain. It was as though the proponents of Modernism had taken every city architect in Britain and hypnotized him, without first investigating the possible consequences, or even querying the logic of his preference for public parks over private gardens when applied to the fortress-like mind of the average Englishman. A retired architect for Liverpool Council, who trained at the city's school of architecture in the years immediately following the Second World War, suggests that may have been the case. He recalls the impact of a visit by Le Corbusier on students who, like Philip Johnson, believed that the devastation of the post-war cities offered a unique chance to build a New Jerusalem: 'All of the students looked up to him as a kind of idol. We saw what he was doing as a way of changing society. We wanted everything to be of very good quality, you see, so Le Corbusier's Unité d'habitation seemed to be a great idea to begin with, but you're going to have an awful lot of people living way up there [he pointed upwards], and most people don't want to live way up there. It's a psychological thing. Also, the psychology of having great glass

windows in these blocks is drastic for some people. They
don't feel safe.'

He told me this as he leafed through the collected written
works of Charles-Édouard Jeanneret – Le Corbusier's real
name – in his study with reverent tenderness. He expressed
disappointment that women, in particular, felt unsafe in
homes where every fourth wall was made of glass, and that
the railings that were put there to make them feel safe
destroyed the purity of the view. The pictures he showed me
were exquisite. Every straight line was to savour; every right-
angle was suggestive of a brave and powerful future. Le
Corbusier's vision was powerfully seductive: it offered a
cleaner slate than any that had gone before. It offered architects the chance to design their way out of the mess of the
organically evolved city.

The 1950s and 1960s offered local authorities a monumental chance to show off to their voters: these
futuristic-looking tower blocks were visible signs of progress,
signalling the death of the slums and the final victory of the
worker, who not only had work for life, but a penthouse flat
overlooking the city he helped to make prosperous. That was
the idea, anyway. In practice, the needs and desires of ordinary people – who, for all their post-war optimism and
education, believed that flats were bad for children and that
homes with gardens of their own would make them happi-
est – were thrown out of the equation, just as they had been
dismissed by suburb-hating writers a generation earlier. The
people who were in charge of rehousing them caught on to
the clean concrete lines of Modernist architecture at a time
when Britain had neither the economic strength nor the political will to fight it off. It was like an intellectual flu,
disseminated from on high by those who thought a strong
dose of it would do the weakest the most good. No one
stopped to think that they might be wrong. In any case, it was

too late: by 1960, as one critic has put it, 'Modernism had become the official architecture of the welfare state.'

It's improbable, isn't it, how a building – a solid thing that won't fall over if pushed – can fail, but it does. All it takes is a loose bolt, a ball of newspaper where there ought to be concrete, an absent building regulation, or an architect's flight of fancy. A government minister determined to do whatever it takes to make good an impossible promise. A building contractor who takes short-cuts so that he can deliver on time. A local authority encouraged by the government to sell its housing stock to tenants, but forbidden to build new homes in their place. A nation convinced that property ownership is the only way to achieve respectability. A working-class and immigrant population blamed for its own second-class status. A wrecking ball engaged before a coherent thought. Whether literally or in spirit, it doesn't take much to knock a building down.

The problem with buildings is that, like anything man-made, they are subject to our desire to experiment. Experimenting with new building techniques in the 1950s and 1960s – a time of fecund optimism and a pervasive belief that science and technology would solve the problems inherent in trying to feed and shelter the world's growing population – was tantamount to experimenting with lives, but the time was ripe for taking such risks. We were, after all, intending to create a new society, not just a new housing stock. Indeed, we were creating a new society precisely *through* rebuilding, whether in the form of universal council housing, as Bevan envisioned, or mass home ownership, in the eyes of Macmillan and his successors. The solution to the problem of how to build all these homes lay in mass production. Industrialized building – which takes much of the building process away from the construction site and into the factory, where prefabricated frames and walls are mass-produced before being transported to the site for relatively quick and simple assembly – solved at a stroke the dearth of skilled bricklayers and other tradesmen at a time when the demand for new homes had never been higher. It enabled concrete – the wonder-material of the post-war age, which was already helping to transform many of Britain's pock-marked city centres into road-ringed, multi-storey-car-parked, giant grey precincts – to replace brick, whether it was pre-cast into wall-shaped slabs at the factory or manufactured on-site, where it could be used to complete buildings and create walkways and playgrounds. Concrete had no shape until you told it where to go and when to set, at which point it became so hard that it would crack your head open if you fell against it. It was strong enough to build with when reinforced by steel bars, yet malleable enough to enable new, apparently non-porous and waterproof, types to be produced.

The mass production of concrete, and the slabs that were cast from it, enabled system building – a type of industrialized building in which large wall panels were bolted, rather than cemented, together – to take place without the need for construction workers to have the range of skills they would have once needed to complete a conventional brick-built house. Both architects, admiring of its austere blankness, and large-scale building businesses – who had the money to try out new techniques and to fashion from them uninspired, but useful, housing kits that they could sell in bulk to local authorities – saw that concrete had the potential to revolutionize the way in which we were housed. What they didn't foresee, and what they ought to have foreseen, was how concrete homes behaved once they were built, and how the people who lived in them behaved in response to this unforgiving and easily abused material.

On 25 July 1966, construction began on a twenty-two-storey block of flats in Clever Road, Canning Town, where the inner-city East End merges into the unending eastern out-skirts of London. It was built using the Danish Larsen-Nielsen method, which involved bolting together large pre-cast concrete panels, and was completed and handed to the borough of Newham for use twenty months later, on 11 March 1968, at a total cost of £500,000. It was called Ronan Point, and its 110 flats – sixty-six one-bedroom, forty-four two-bedroom, five dwellings to a floor – were to be populated by East Enders whose back-to-back terraces and tenements had been either destroyed or damaged beyond repair in the war, and many of whom had waited twenty years to be rehoused permanently. Newham, for its part, was a local authority in its infancy, created by merging the old borough councils of East Ham and West Ham. Newham, in all its new-ness, needed to consolidate the trust and approval of its tenants if the merger was to be successful.

The rapidity of the Larsen-Nielsen building method was useful to the council in many ways: it provided visible results quickly, it was compact (the entire building had a ground-level footprint of only eighty feet by sixty), and it didn't need skilled construction workers to put it together. This last point would prove to be fatal. There had been a stampede of skilled manual workers away from heavy to light industry during the 1960s, moving on to the production lines of car factories, where they would be paid well and not put at risk of injury simply by turn-ing up for work. Many of the men who put together Ronan Point were unfamiliar not only with system building, but with the rigorous checks of architects and independent structural engineers. The building contractors, Taylor Woodrow-Anglian, had insisted on employing their own subsidiary, Philips Consultant Engineers – who, argues Patrick Dunleavy of the London School of Economics, were less likely to voice objective complaints about the soundness of the structure.

By May 1968, Ronan Point was slowly filling up with people – lots of newlywed couples, elderly people and single dwellers. At a quarter to six on the morning of 16 May, Ivy Hodge, a fifty-six-year-old cake decorator whose flat was on the eighteenth floor, lit a match for her stove-top kettle to make a cup of tea. The match inflamed the gas, which, unbeknown to her, had been building up like a secret poison since the supply was installed. In an instant, the two south-east-facing walls of her flat blew out, quick and clean, taking every load-bearing panel above and below with it, as if it had been programmed to do so. Flippity-flip they went down, taking the lives of four people as they fell. Ivy Hodge survived, as did seventeen others who sustained injuries. The only reason that more people didn't die was because the collapse took place on a side of the block where all the living rooms were, at a time when most tenants were still asleep in their bedrooms. One of the injured had walked into her lounge minutes before the blast, only to become lodged in the hallway overlooking two hundred feet of fresh air. Her husband, still in their bedroom, had to hold on to one of her arms while using his other hand to clear the debris that trapped her. For weeks, people came from all over London to see the wound, disbelieving of how a clean chunk could be taken out of a building that was two months old, and how modern construction methods could lead to deaths.

On the day of the disaster, the managing director of Taylor Woodrow-Anglian denied that the collapse of Ronan Point had been caused by poor building standards. But a public inquiry into the explosion revealed that standards had been ignored at crucial stages in its construction. For a start, the gas explosion had been caused by the substitution of inferior materials for high-quality ones. A substandard nut had been used to attach the gas supply to the stove, which probably cracked on installation due to over-tightening. Each of the

wall panels rested on just two bolts – with no mortar to bol-
ster them – which started to rust almost instantaneously on
contact with the rainwater that seeped between them. Tests
showed how the south-eastern side of the building had col-
lapsed at frighteningly low pressure, due to the fact that there
was no solid structure for the panels to rest on, only flimsy
bolts and pegs. Sixteen-year-old recommendations on the
amount of wind pressure that could be withstood by system-
built tower blocks had not been updated to take account of
the fact that high-rise buildings were getting higher and
higher. In fact, the Larsen-Nielsen method was not designed to
be used for any buildings higher than six storeys. Ronan
Point, a building 22 floors and 200 feet tall, was held together
with little else but pins: like a house of cards, but one to which
people had entrusted their lives.

The missing corner of the tower block was rebuilt and the
whole building was reinforced, although it's hard to imagine
who would have chosen to live there in the knowledge of
what had happened. The use of gas cookers in Ronan Point
was banned – implying that the disaster had a chance of being
repeated. In 1984, two years before the building was finally
razed and replaced with two-storey terraced homes, engineers
reported that the gaps between the panels made the whole
block a fire risk and a cause of noise pollution, as tenants
could hear each other's conversations, music and television
through them. A local architect, Sam Webb, had stepped in to
examine the joints that still stood in Ronan Point, and found
that the spaces between the load-bearing bolts had been filled
with newspaper, rather than with concrete as they ought to
have been. He tested the size of the gaps between the floor
and wall panels by dropping coins and pieces of paper
through them: they fell, he said, 'as if going into a slot
machine'. By this time, all that prevented the edifice from collapsing were the 'blast angles' fitted in 1968 to improve its

resistance to trauma; two decades of high winds had done their damage, and the entire block was falling to pieces.

Webb went on to campaign against the use of system-building methods that used large prefabricated panels, leading to the demolition of six other Larsen-Nielsen tower blocks – which he called 'death traps' – that had been built around the country. A public inquiry into the disaster caused building regulations to be changed throughout the world, so that tower blocks built from large panels would no longer have load-bearing walls that risked popping out under the force of a relatively light explosion.

A tenant of Ronan Point who was offered temporary accommodation in the home of a neighbour after the explosion told the BBC: 'I wouldn't live there rent-free.' In his book *The Politics of Mass Housing in Britain*, Patrick Dunleavy reports how Newham residents collected 700 signatures on a petition that read: 'Under present conditions we will flatly refuse to leave our present slums to enter modern slums.' The reply from the Town Clerk read as follows: 'Whether the blocks become slums or not will depend on the people who live in them.' Ronan Point now forms the layer of hardcore that lies under the runway of London City Airport.

After a failure on this scale, one might have expected every tower block in the land to become empty overnight, whether their tenants had other homes to go to or not. And yet the cult of the tower block didn't die out overnight. It didn't help that so many of these prefabricated, pre-cast building kits had been ordered from the big building companies by local authorities in the few years that led up to the Ronan Point explosion: they couldn't simply un-order them, or redraw master-plans so that tower blocks would have no place in the continued expansion of the public housing stock. My mother's cousin did as she was told and went to live on the top floor of one of the thirty-two blocks that were being built on the Wood at the same time that Ronan Point was falling down. She would hang on to the kitchen counter every time the wind got up, and used the television and sofa to pin down the resolutely unmagical flying carpet. A horror of what had happened at Ronan Point may have diminished people's trust in the authorities to house them safely and properly, but it was not expected of local councils or the government to respond by demolishing every high-rise block in the country. If they had, this book may have told a slightly different story. In the years that followed, high-rise homes became the enemy of the population for an entirely different reason. They seemed to be killing off communities, and replacing them with collections of alienated, unhappy individuals.

There is an urban myth about the Hungarian architect Ernö Goldfinger, whose name is one of those most strongly associated with the transformation of public-housing architecture from sprawling cottage estates to industrial concrete monoliths. It is said that he paid a visit to the thirty-one-storey Trellick Tower in west London, his most infamous building, some years after its completion in 1972. Upon witnessing the drug-ridden, socially destructive chaos the block had fallen into, they say, he threw himself off the roof in a fit of self-immolating anguish. This isn't at all true: Goldfinger died in 1987 in the home he designed himself, at 2 Willow Road in Hampstead, north-west London. Number 2 is in the middle of three terraced townhouses, which look like nothing more than generously proportioned, superior-quality versions of most council houses built in the 1960s. Built in 1939, however, the Willow Road houses were somewhat ahead of their time. Large rectangular windows alternate with slices of light brown brick, almost giving the impression that one floor of the house is levitating over the other. (It has now been bequeathed to the National Trust for public viewing. The house is elegant, but more because of the exquisitely tasteful furnishings, parquet flooring and wooden bookshelves inside it, all chosen or designed by the architect himself, than because of the endless right angles that constitute its exterior appearance. Such was the influence of pure Modernism.) It's interesting how Goldfinger built flats for other people to live in, but chose to live in a house himself. Actually, that's not strictly the case. He lived for a short while on the top floor of another of his designs, Balfron Tower in the East End, built in 1968 and which, apart from being four floors shorter, is almost identical to Trellick.

Goldfinger moved into Flat 130 on the twenty-sixth floor of Balfron Tower with his wife, the Crosse & Blackwell heiress Ursula Blackwell, in order to show that he was as happy to live in the sky as the rehoused East Enders he described as 'my tenants'. He invited all of the tenants up to the flat, floor by floor, for convivial champagne parties during his stay. Nigel Warburton's defensive biography of Goldfinger claims that the architect's council-flat sojourn (he only stayed there for two months) wasn't a condescending publicity stunt, but a genuine attempt to show solidarity with his temporary neighbours. I can't help thinking that this is gubbins. If he had really wanted to live among the people who had been housed in his creation, would he not have ditched the house in far-away Hampstead and moved full-time to Balfron Tower, with its unbroken views of industrial east London, the docks and the Blackwall Tunnel? Living in a high-rise block can be a great deal of fun when you have no children and you have the means to treat it like a penthouse suite. Ask anyone who has chosen to live in the Barbican complex of high-specification tower blocks in central London. But for most people tower blocks are far from ideal. My husband lived in Carradale House – the shorter, wider Goldfinger block attached to Balfron by means of a concrete walkway – for two years. Our early trysts were characterized by the need to wear earplugs at

night in order to sleep, because of the noise of the endless traffic approaching the Blackwall Tunnel, from which the flat's
enormous, ill-fitting windows failed to shield us. One night
we heard blood-thickening screams coming from one of the
floors below, which seemed to go on for hours despite our
calling the police, and which sounded like an animal dying
slowly. A couple of days later, we heard that a resident –
whose name or face neither of us recognized – had been
charged with murder.

It wasn't a terrible way for my then-boyfriend and his flatmate to live: the flat was large and easy to maintain, although
the communal walkways and sand-blasted concrete corridors
were grimness itself. In order to leave the block, entire families had to squeeze into the one working lift while the other
was being replaced – a job that took nine months. There
seemed to be something quite wrong about making children
live in machines, next to roads clogged with lorries, the acrid
smell of riverside industry filling their lungs every day, their
noses rubbed into other people's wealth by the gleaming
Docklands skyscrapers on their doorstep. Warburton claims
that Goldfinger never gave up his socialist ideals, but if
that were the case, why did he consent for working-class
people to be housed in such an unprepossessing place? The
architect was not truly to blame for the crime and ignominy
that blighted Trellick Tower, in particular, in the late 1970s
and early 1980s. Indeed, his attempts to persuade the
Greater London Council to employ concierges at Trellick
and Balfron were ignored until the former building, by then
known as 'the Tower of Terror' because of its high rate of
violent crime, was experiencing near-total social breakdown.

Warburton tries to let the architect off the hook, implying
that Goldfinger couldn't help it if the tenants who came to
live in his buildings were undesirables to start with. It is

undoubtedly true that Trellick became 'hard to let' soon after its completion in 1972, and that its lack of manageability was exacerbated by the GLC's policy of filling the empty flats with homeless single people, the drug-addicted and the mentally ill, and those with a poor record of paying their rent. Nevertheless, this statement suggests that there are certain classes of people who can't be trusted to live in any building that was designed by a great man of socialist ideals and spectacular taste in interior design. Of Balfron Tower and Trellick Tower, Warburton writes: 'Viewed from outside, they are incredibly muscular, masculine, abstract structures, with no concession to an architecture of domesticity.' After all, domesticity is the last thing you need when you have a family to raise. He continues: 'Indeed, [the architect] James Dunnett's analysis of Balfron Tower makes much of its warlike symbolism, describing the building as inspiring "a delicate sense of terror".'

Quite how this is intended to be a good thing in the context of housing provision, I'm not sure. Both Warburton and Dunnett seem to fall for the idea that housing should be art. It ought to be beautiful, yes, but not at the expense of the people who have to live in it. Or is living in a council flat *supposed* to be delicately terrifying? When tenants on the higher floors of Balfron Tower can feel the block wobbling in the wind, it may seem as though that is the case.

By the end of the 1970s, 4,500 tower blocks had been built in Britain, each with a complex schedule of needs brought about by the poor execution of new building techniques (which included failing to mix wet concrete thoroughly before pouring it, causing it to set in a way that made it porous and susceptible to crumbling), expensive lifts and the kind of general maintenance problems that could only be solved by highly paid engineers, as opposed to a handyman with a stepladder. Local authorities, encouraged – bribed, effectively –

by lucrative state subsidies, had turned to high-rise building precisely to save time, money and expertise: they were now faced with thousands of high-rise blocks that stubbornly refused to look after themselves in the way that houses seemed to.

In 1980, the year following the demolition of Oak and Eldon Gardens in Birkenhead, the German architect Walter Segal wrote about the effects, on both communities and individuals, of building housing on a mass scale. 'To humanise huge structures by architectural means is an unrewarding task,' he commented. 'The loss of identity, the divorce from the ground and the collectivisation of open space pose dilemmas that cannot be disguised by shape, texture, colour and proportion. A good view over landscaped spaces compensates only a few. The human animal does not appreciate being reduced to the scale of a termite.' Oak and Eldon Gardens, which replaced an area of back-to-back terraces in the dockside north end of Birkenhead, suffered from their size and scale, as well as their poor design: the dank stairwells leading up to each floor invited vandalism and required a level of maintenance that was unplanned for, either by the council or the architects themselves, therefore help and repairs were not always available when needed. Tenants were, indeed, 'divorced from the ground' by means of stilts, under which their cars would be parked and passers-by would thread through on their way to other destinations. The flats showed English council tenants how it felt to live like bees in a honeycomb: as nuclear families in isolated, identical modules, collected together in a building that overwhelmed them with its size. Its scale, and the principles behind it, suggested an experiment in communal living, but people were not truly living together. At the same time that they sensed a loss of control over their private identity, tenants also had to deal with the consequences of communal services – such as lifts, postboxes and rubbish chutes – being damaged or put out of service by individuals whom they could rarely identify.

It was with equal elegance that Segal pointed out that Britain's targets for housing density — that is, the number of households on each hectare of land – could just as easily have been met by building two-storey terraced houses, and that the cost of planning, building and maintaining two flats in an average tower block was roughly equal to that for three or four houses. Time and again council planners were warned of the difficulty and expense of creating new communities from scratch, by sociologists who had studied the effects of slum clearance on the interwar generation, when close-knit towns-people were first 'decanted' from back-to-backs into suburban cottages. Such flats seemed to divide and rule over, and to make faceless, the people who lived there.

The Park Hill estate, completed in 1962 in Sheffield – a city that prospered because of the central role of steel production in the post-war reconstruction of Britain and Europe – is a good example of the public largesse that caused local authorities to ignore such warnings. Park Hill still looms over the city like a giant reminder of what municipal socialism was supposed to look like: a thirteen-storey Meccano snake at its highest point, a giant wall of shoeboxes exposed to the harshest of south Yorkshire winds. Heating and hot-water provision for the flats came from an on-site incinerator, which burned the residents' household rubbish. The concrete walkways that connected each block and provided the 'deck' by which each tenant accessed their front door were wide, so that milk floats could putter up and down them; it was hoped that the sight of the Unigate man might help to create a sense of continuity with the days when people still lived on the ground. (Sir Basil Spence made the same fatal act of condescension when talking about his design for the Queen Elizabeth complex of tower blocks in Glasgow's Gorbals area. He imagined the tenants' clothes fluttering white on the towering balconies like the sails of a ship every washday, an echo of the shipbuilding industry that, at the time, still operated on the banks of the Clyde. His vision didn't wash, and the damp-riddled blocks were demolished in 1993.)

Park Hill and its sister estate, Hyde Park, may have lorded it over the city, but their brave façades masked a swift descent into physical and social disintegration. This was in part caused by the catastrophic decline of the steel industry – 40,000 jobs were lost in Sheffield, a city of 200,000 people, in the decade between 1979 and 1989 – but was exacerbated by their design. Although the 1,000 flats at Park Hill were located less than a mile from Sheffield city centre, it was hard to leave and even harder to get to. Residents were cut off from the city by the same steep hill that gave the estate its commanding views. Its snake-like design was believed by its architects Ivor Smith and Jack Lynn to have harnessed the aesthetic benefits of Modernism's clean lines to the social benefits of living on streets where you could see your neighbours' front doors. In practice, however, the estate felt claustrophobic. The zig-zag pattern of the walkways that connected each block induced a kind of horizontal vertigo in tenants, and provided easy escape routes for muggers and burglars. There developed a vicious circle common to poorly functioning estates, with aspirational families moving away only to be replaced by transient tenants whose behaviour – quite apart from their very transience – made the estate even less desirable to live on. Those who bailed out, and some who remained, nicknamed Park Hill 'San Quentin', after the tough-nut California jail where Johnny Cash once played to toothless brawlers in overalls. The population of Park Hill now stands at 1,500, fewer than two people per dwelling, suggesting that the estate mainly houses single adults, rather than families, who tend to stay in their homes for longer and whose social interaction helps communities to cohere.

Since 1998, when English Heritage conferred Grade II listed status on the estate – partially empty and infested with pigeons, but deemed to have significant architectural value in terms of its contribution to British Modernism – the only way that Sheffield City Council has been able to raise sufficient money for its renovation is to turn the project over to Urban Splash, a property-development company associated with the conversion of disused industrial buildings into loft apartments for private buyers. The council estimates that the cost of repairing the damage caused to the concrete infrastructure by wind, rain, infestation and structural weaknesses to be in excess of £30,000 per flat, half as much again as it costs to repair and refurbish a council house in the city, yet such is the local authority's belief in Park Hill's architectural importance – bolstered by English Heritage, who claim that it has the potential to 'become again the castle on the horizon of the city centre' – that it is seen as a price worth paying. Even so, Sheffield Council's Executive Director of Housing has questioned the rigidity of the estate's listed status, arguing that '[English Heritage] need to respect that Park Hill is not a monument, it's people's homes.' The council has subsequently been permitted by English Heritage to demolish a number of flats on the estate and replace them with houses.

English Heritage's decision to list Park Hill was among the most controversial that the conservation body has made. It legitimized the creed of Modernism, despite its association with bleak, damp-prone, deeply unpopular experiments in council housing and with 1960s shopping centres such as the Tricorn in Portsmouth, voted 'the worst building in Britain' by BBC radio listeners in 2001 (it was demolished three years later). Park Hill, for its part, was among the twelve most hated examples of architecture in the country, as decided by viewers of a 2005 Channel 4 series called *Demolition*. Modernism and Brutalism – a later form that made use of

stark, 'raw' poured or sand-blasted concrete as an architectural feature, and epitomized by Park Hill and the Tricorn –
are emphatically seen as enemies of the people's will, of their
desire not to be dictated to by aloof architects and their
hideous buildings. They remind people of a kind of socialism
that is imposed, rather than agreed: the very opposite of consensus.

There are many good reasons for people to dislike most
examples of Modernist architecture. Concrete is a harsh and
unfriendly-looking material, especially when used 'raw' and
left unpainted or unplastered. If is not washed and attended
to, it quickly turns grey, ugly and dull, even if it gleamed to
begin with. Some types of concrete are tricky to mix and set,
particularly if not worked by experts; they become porous
and lock damp into otherwise sound buildings. Rusting bolts
and reinforcing-bars streak it with brown, making it look
even worse, and corroding the concrete that surrounds them
until it falls off in chunks. There are few council estates built
using concrete that have been maintained to the standards
envisaged and expected by the architects who designed them
and the engineers who put them together. Even fewer were
designed with the consultation of residents; in fact, the only
council estate to be built in response to a direct request by
tenants for new housing was Peterlee in County Durham, a
New Town founded in the late 1960s to house the families of
miners working at Easington Colliery. Peterlee still exists;
unlike the colliery, which closed in 1993. The future of the
Brutalist pavilion in the centre of Peterlee, designed by British
artist Victor Pasmore, is uncertain, despite its having been nicknamed 'the monstrosity' by locals.

You often hear the word 'concrete' next to 'monstrosity'
when referring to British Modernist architecture. The least
loved examples are either inherently monstrous – the dank
and uninviting Central Library in Birmingham, a big brown

sandwich loaf of sand-blasted concrete, was likened to 'a place for burning books, rather than reading them' by Prince Charles – or have been made hideous through lack of maintenance. Stanley Kubrick chose the newly built Thamesmead estate in south-east London as the setting for his film *A Clockwork Orange*: anonymous, empty expanses of concrete ringed by walkways and made labyrinthine by subways. The estate was brand-new, but already looked sufficiently dystopic to resemble the kind of environment that would create and house the amoral boot-boys of Anthony Burgess's novel. All but the most sympathetic experiments in concrete (Louis Kahn's radiant assembly building in Dhaka, Bangladesh, comes to mind, but that was not built for living in) have a coldness about them that seems to seep into the bones. Home life requires a sense of warmth that we, in Britain at least, associate with brick.

Phil Jones of the University of Birmingham suggests that local-authority planning departments, encouraged by council leaders, used slum clearance as an excuse to experiment with Modernist housing design when, even in the 1960s, all research pointed to the efficiency and sensitivity of refurbishing and upgrading – rather than destroying – slum accommodation: 'Most local authorities preferred the opportunity to thoroughly modernize their towns as a symbol of power and prestige. Had the resources been available to them, cities like Birmingham would have continued (slum) clearances until ... areas like Selly Oak disappeared under a sea of cheaply built municipal dwellings.'

However, Patrick Dunleavy of the LSE argues that private building companies, such as Wimpey and Taylor Woodrow-Anglian (the contractors at Ronan Point), lobbied local authorities so heavily to buy their prefabricated tower-block 'kits' that their offers could not be refused. Under pressure to finish the job of slum clearance and offered a quick and easy method to achieve this, councils bought them en masse. A 1955 symposium on high-rise buildings held by the Royal Institute of British Architects provoked local-authority architects effectively to lead a revolution in housing design, pushing an agenda skewed towards prefabricated and high-rise building with such force that RIBA, rather than shaping the opinions of its membership, was forced to fall in line with it. RIBA's preference was to retain the idea of high-rise only as a desirable – and, by definition, exclusive – architectural form with all the abundant theoretical potential that the Modernists assigned to it, but such (literal) high-mindedness was quashed by the greater influence of business and housing statistics. This is why there are relatively few examples of residential tower blocks, particularly in the public sector, that have been designed by individual architects rather than construction engineers. Pre-cast building kits could only be tinkered with once ordered, which is why so many tower blocks up and down the country not only look more or less identical, but are also devoid of architectural merit.

Birmingham City Council commissioned and completed 429 such tower blocks in its inner city and on its outskirts before running out of money. All of them underwent inspections following the collapse of Ronan Point in 1968, which revealed that many of the blocks, none of them more than fifteen years old, had already begun to shed concrete and leak in poor weather. By this time, the Treasury had begun to lose patience with the idea of high-rise building for the sake of modernity and space-saving efficiency. Richard Crossman, who was in charge of housing between 1964 and 1966, began to ask local authorities why they were still building high-rise flats when it had been established that, in most cases, an equal number of terrace houses with small private gardens could be erected on the same plot of land. 'If any of them think they can run up tall blocks just to enlarge their egos and

improve their kudos, they will not get a loan sanction,' he
barked, puncturing their visions for the 'Radiant City' with a
peculiarly English distaste for showiness. This explains why
the Wood, despite having twenty-nine tower blocks (there
were thirty-two, until three were blown up in a demolition
ceremony attended by most of the estate one cold Sunday
morning in 1989), is composed mainly of houses, low-rise
flats and maisonettes.

As damaging as the collision of Modernism and industrialized
building was in determining the overwhelmingly negative
view we now have of council housing, the social malaise we
have come to associate with estates wasn't caused solely by
tower blocks. They didn't help, but neither did the deindustrialization of the post-war economy: the very reverse of the
movement towards the industrialization of housing. Perversely,
the prefabrication of homes was welcomed because of a
lack of skilled workers, who had begun to move into light-
industrial assembly work as Britain's heavy industries became
less competitive. That same lack of skilled work, on the other
hand, came to mean that the skilled manual workers who
remained – the hard-working, rent-paying backbone of the
welfare state and, by extension, the post-war party-political
consensus – began to lose their jobs.

An unflattering portrait of council-housing policy at the
turn of the 1970s would contain the following elements:
thoughtlessness; the hard sell of building contractors; poor
workmanship; Brutalist concrete designs; lack of maintenance; the well-meant but dippy optimism of local-authority
planners and architects; a fetish for quantity over quality;
power-crazed council leadership. Then came the world oil
crisis in 1973, and the gradual breaking-down of the social
democratic consensus that followed in its destabilizing wake.
There were quickening signs of the death of heavy industry and

of the manual job for life; rising unemployment and inflation; huge local-authority debts; the British government applying for loans from the International Monetary Fund to stay afloat; a growing immigrant population forced into the cheapest housing by poor-paying jobs; and a deepening cleft within the working class – between the majority who had benefited from twenty-five years of peacetime social democracy, and a stricken minority that had not.

Of the wartime Beveridge Report's Five Giants, Want had been reduced by a combination of well-directed taxation, universal benefits and the widespread prosperity that came with twenty years of post-war full employment. Ignorance, depending on whether you passed the 11-plus exam for grammar school, or failed and were consigned to a secondary modern, was either cured or unwittingly entrenched. Disease – well, the NHS took care of that, although charges for non-essential work began to whittle away at the principle of free treatment from the 1960s onwards. Idleness was seen off, at least until the 1970s, by the abundant availability of work. Squalor had proven to be the hardest of the giants to slay. Slum clearance, in a period of population growth and a demographic movement towards smaller families, would take until the mid-1970s to complete. During that time, such short-lived disasters as the Oak and Eldon Gardens blocks were revealed to be no better than the slums they replaced. The peripheral estates on the edges of the major cities did relieve squalor, in the sense that they gave inner-city people a chance to live in sanitary conditions in green surroundings, but there remained another kind, which, despite Bevan's early efforts to mute it, refused to die: the moral squalor of stigma.

Britain in the 1970s, then, was not a pretty sight, but things would get far worse in the 1980s. The dealing and use of hard drugs – first heroin, then crack cocaine – took hold on the most neglected estates, where support and maintenance was most needed and least provided by councils. Local-authority housing officers would start to concentrate 'problem families' – the poorest households who found it hardest to cope – together in an attempt to contain their disruptiveness: a policy that would only cause further alienation and, eventually, nihilism and a creeping sense of lawlessness. When Anne Power and Rebecca Tunstall of the LSE investigated the 'twenty worst' estates in Britain – according to their desirability, reputation and levels of social and economic exclusion from the mainstream – in 1981 and again in 1991, they found that the proportion of lone-parent families on the estates had doubled from 9 per cent to 18 per cent in the intervening decade, compared to 4 per cent in Britain as a whole. (Households with one parent are almost invariably among the poorest.) Concentrations of unemployment and tenants without qualifications or skills increased vastly disproportionately on these estates to the rest of society, and, according to their findings, 'were far more disadvantaged' by the end of the 1980s than they had been at the beginning of the decade. On such estates, workless adults, cut off from society by their lack of skills, would pass on their worklessness to their children, who would have children when they were still children who would also be workless. The worst-off communities would start to disintegrate under the strain, and would become ripe for picking apart and selling off as proof that the council-housing experiment had been a failure.

Since the two world wars of the last century – when the British population first exploded, then stabilized, then atomized – there has been a need to find reasons for why poor people, when concentrated into a small space in flats and houses miles from the nearest job or bus or shop, behave in a way that shocks the people who put them there. There is a name for this, the way in which one's mental landscape is moulded by one's physical environment: psychogeography.

The discipline was popularized by the Situationists – a small but influential group of philosophical mischief makers, led by the French writer Guy Debord and given to memorably subversive pronouncements such as 'Never work' – who came up with an idea so obvious that it seems extraordinary that no one got there before them. Debord sought a way of taxonomizing urban spaces, of classifying the feelings that walking through them induces. Some environments, for example, make you feel good, free and open: they give you access to the widest possible view of the sky and don't have dark corners of 'perpetual night' that are difficult to negotiate without a heart-leap of fear. You can't drift easily in this way around many council estates – particularly the mass-produced blocks of the early 1960s, which rely on walkways and subways that direct pedestrians from home to shop and back as a funnel directs liquid into a bottle. They are too channelled, too labyrinthine, to make wandering an enjoyable experience. There's the risk of looking like an intruder, an outsider or, more likely, a wally. You can't be a *flâneur* of the estate, though you are welcome to try.

The Broadwater Farm estate in Tottenham, north London, was one such place, where a series of buildings whose design and layout discouraged communal activity further deteriorated when exposed to the harsh economic and social environment of the 1970s and 1980s. Its twelve system-built blocks were connected by three miles of walkways: not because of an architect's 'streets in the sky' fantasy, but because the estate was sited on poorly drained allotment land that remained a flood risk. Broadwater Farm didn't so much stand out from the rest of Tottenham as create its own force-field. There was no tube station near to the estate and its 1,500 homes were managed remotely from a housing office over two miles away.

Haringey local authority had almost finished clearing its

slums, and was beginning to acquire a surplus of council housing, meaning that there wasn't a waiting list of applicants ready to move into Broadwater Farm upon its completion in 1971. The estate filled up slowly with elderly people, young single adults and families from ethnic minorities: all the groups least likely to have access to money and jobs. By 1976, 55 per cent of applicants on Haringey's waiting list refused to be housed on the estate when offered a home there. Residents described it as 'monolithic', 'like Windscale' (the nuclear power station now called Sellafield), and strongly predisposed to crime due to its combination of walkways and stilts, which provided dark hiding places. The Department of the Environment told the council that it saw no reason not to demolish Broadwater Farm: there was no housing shortage, and because of its distance from the housing office, the estate had the lowest rate of rent collection in the whole borough. That it had not been pulled down by the end of the 1970s was due largely to the expense and inconvenience of having to rehouse the 2,000 people who still lived there.

According to its tenants, the years between 1979 and 1981 were the worst time to live on the estate. Its very future was in doubt, and the all-white tenants' association was vastly unrepresentative of an estate population that comprised nearly half from ethnic minorities. Many residents could not even move around the estate, both for fear of robbery or burglary and because the walkways were often flooded due to inadequate draining. In desperation, Haringey Council managed to persuade the government to include Broadwater Farm in a pilot scheme designed to arrest the decline of the worst estates in Britain by directly involving tenants in their management. A new youth association, set up and run by a Jamaican mother of six who was liked and trusted by younger tenants, co-existed alongside the tenants' association and a local management team of forty that was brought on to the estate to administer rent collection and repairs. The effect of these measures was swift and positive, and seemed to defy the laws of social gravity. Inter-generational and inter-racial relations began to improve, with members of the mainly black youth association setting up a lunch club for mainly white elderly residents. The presence on-site of maintenance workers and housing management officers made tenants feel as though they had not been left to rot in an inhospitable environment. Everything appeared to be going according to plan: Broadwater Farm seemed to provide proof that estates of its kind could work as long as they were managed properly. Haringey Council began to receive requests from public housing managers all over the world to visit the estate in the hope of replicating its success.

But this was still a fragile community, working against an unemployment rate of 42 per cent, entrenched poverty, persistent racism and the flawed concrete structure in which it was expected to thrive. In the summer of 1985, the youth association took its members on a long-planned exchange trip to Jamaica. The disused shop from which it was run was closed and shuttered for the duration, as crime on the estate had fallen to the extent that it was deemed safe to do so. It was not. As soon as the youth team left, another team, made up of drug dealers, moved into the estate and capitalized on the brief absence of its youth leaders. Within a few weeks, order had broken down: drugs were being sold openly, and joyriders burnt their way through the estate without police intervention. As Anne Power reports in her detailed study of the estate's turbulent life, police involvement was desperately needed, but didn't come forth until riots at Handsworth, in Birmingham, and Brixton, south London, alerted police to the possibility of further civil unrest in inner-city areas.

On 5 October, police raided the Tottenham home of Cynthia Jarrett looking for her twenty-four-year-old son,

Floyd, whom they suspected of driving a car with an expired tax disc. Jarrett died of a heart attack during the raid, lighting a touchpaper that had been smouldering on Broadwater Farm throughout the summer. The police hadn't come when they were needed to deal with the 'bad men' who had taken over the estate in the youth leaders' absence, but had shown up combatively and in large numbers as soon as they suspected that disorder might spread beyond its confines. The estate was consumed by rioting on the night of 6 October, following a demonstration outside Tottenham police station in response to Cynthia Jarrett's death. When a fire broke out on the first floor of one of the estate blocks, firefighters were attacked, leading to the deployment of vast numbers of police. This inflamed the situation further, culminating in the hacking to death of PC Keith Blakelock by rioters.

Something like a miracle followed this descent into murderous chaos. Broadwater Farm wasn't demolished after the riots, but it was transformed for the better. An inquiry into the causes of the riots prodded the government into investing £33 million in the estate – money which had not been spent during its time as part of the Priority Estates Project of the early 1980s. The concrete walkways were knocked down and entrances to each of the twelve blocks were brought down to ground level. Its grey expanses were broken up with colourful mosaics and a grand illustration of a fountain. On-site workshops were opened on the estate, so that tenants could learn skills and run their own businesses, and estate managers were given greater powers to deal with the challenges of living on an estate that, simply, should never have been built in the way it was built.

Broadwater Farm, as the social-policy journalist Christian Wolmar noted in his 2004 BBC radio report *Down on the Farm*, now thrives. Three thousand eight hundred people from fifty different countries live on the estate, 400 of whom participate in the estate football team, Broadwater United, which has produced twenty-five professional players for teams including Arsenal and West Ham. Once again it is seen as a model public-housing project, but this time around, that seems genuinely to be the case. There were no robberies and only one burglary in 2005 – down from 850 in 1985. For the first time in twenty years, there is no permanent police presence on the estate, but there are on-site housing officers whose names and faces are known to every resident. Such difficult, large and multiply deprived estates are only capable of working when there exists a combination of political will, financial resources and intensive management by a resident team of estate managers and maintenance staff, and enough committed tenants to provide a sense of stability and hope. As Anne Power writes, absent or ineffectual local management makes an unpopular estate highly vulnerable to rapid decline. Leave an estate as large as Broadwater Farm to its own devices, and you may be advised to knock it down before it destroys a whole community.

Elsewhere in Britain, estates built at the tail-end of the post-war expansion in mass housing, when virtually everyone who needed a council home had been provided with one, were among the first to suffer decline as a result of poor management. Such decline was reinforced by housing policies that seemed insistent on breaking up poor, yet cohesive, 'slum' communities and dispersing them to faraway overspill estates, or reducing housing density so drastically that areas which once had thronged with people began to feel like ghost towns. Among these estates were the Crescents, built in 1970 in Hulme, an inner-city area of Manchester. It says a lot about the immediate fate of the Crescents that within a decade or so of their completion the upper floors had come instead to be regarded as the epicentre of the city's musical sub-culture. Dewy-eyed ravers still reminisce about how bangin' and sorted it was at The Kitchen, a makeshift nightclub that had been created by knocking in the walls of two empty flats using mallets. One party animal later described it as 'a wonderful lunatic place to live . . . a magnet for every crazy, every loon, every counterculture-inclined freak in the north of England and beyond'.

The Crescents had started life as an ambitious, but typically short-sighted, attempt to reproduce the elegant Georgian terraces of Bath Spa using concrete. The original Bath Crescents house a large number of people in an urban area, but with a similar level of space and comfort to suburban housing. Their Manchester counterparts were intended to do the same. Front doors were to be accessed by means of 'decks', layers of open-air walkways from which tenants could take in the view of large communal spaces and the buildings that surrounded them. The idea was to get some fresh air into Hulme; the reality was an unmitigated disaster. Hulme, once the human engine room of the Industrial Revolution, crammed 90,000 workers into back-to-back housing before most of the area was razed to make room for the new estate. Aerial photos of the Crescents taken shortly after they were completed in 1971 show a scorched, moony landscape, with four uneven C-shapes curling wonkily across the soil like worms that have got stuck. Each house-worm was named after one of four prominent British architects of times past: Charles Barry, William Kent, John Nash and Robert Adam. Only a tenth of the original population was left, the rest having been moved to overspill developments on the edges of the city.

Almost immediately, the estate's infrastructure began to suffer from the same problems that beset Park Hill and Broadwater Farm: leaky roof membranes, infestations of vermin and insects, uncontrollable damp, deserted walkways and an endemic feeling of isolation. The flats were so expensive to warm that many tenants never turned the central

heating on, and communal areas so difficult to maintain that
the council could not cope. When a small child died after
falling off the top-floor 'access deck' of one of the Crescents in
1974, families decamped to the outskirts, belatedly following
the rest of old Hulme. Manchester's city council decided that
it could not justify housing families with children in a building that was unsafe for them to live in, and began letting the
flats to an explosive mixture of young single people, the elderly and, eventually, the homeless. Then, the 24-hour party
people moved in: self-imagined bohemians, squatters, anar-
chists, DJs, musicians, with a raggle-taggle army of drug
dealers and hangers-on bringing up the rear. The Kitchen
never closed: its three knocked-in floors were, in the eyes of
musician and writer John Robb, part of 'a concrete maze perfect for crime and even better for mental parties run under
their own rules'. That must have been great, if you weren't
over forty or on Temazepam for medical, as opposed to recre-
ational, reasons. Long-term residents, disturbed by constant
noise and the behaviour of single, transient tenants whose
mental health problems went untreated, recall having to get
drunk just to sleep at night, becoming addicted to tranquilliz-
ers and maintaining only a tenuous grip on the social threads
that kept them from going mad.

Hulme's old community had been dismantled by this
unwieldy, mystifying series of buildings, whose faults were so
manifold that the council gave up on them almost as soon as
they were constructed. As a result, the overthrow of the usual
rules of civic life could take place without resistance. The
Crescents became a law unto themselves: like Broadwater
Farm, their very structure encouraged anarchy, meaning that
they required constant and intensive management that the
council did not – or could not – provide. Having said that, it
was only the persistent efforts of tenants that enabled the idea
of *re*-regenerating Hulme – which proposed rebuilding the

area and its community over again from scratch, beginning with the destruction of the Crescents – to be taken seriously.

Ten years after the Crescents became the centre of Madchester's lunatic parade, the concrete worms came down one by one, and in their place grew comforting lines of terraced houses and pleasing low-rise apartments with curvy roofs. Some are for rent from the Guinness Trust, and some are for private sale. Even *The Times* has called it 'Manchester's latest hotspot'. Hulme has nevertheless found it hard to shake off its old notoriety, and that has to come from the fact that two generations' worth of social fabric was burnt to a crisp by scorching the earth on which it stands. These days, it's a tense – what developers and talker-uppers call 'vibrant' or 'edgy' – mixture of Manchester's gay villagers, impoverished housing association tenants, and property investors waiting patiently for the day when its bargain-bin house prices begin to rise.

Council tenants didn't start to move off their estates just because many of them had become intolerable places to live in. Most people could either see no other option than to stay where they were, or were broadly contented with a statist status quo that guaranteed them a home, however leaky or unsuitable, and an income in times of hardship. The numbers of people housed by their local authority continued to rise throughout the 1970s purely because councils kept building homes, clearing slums and shortening waiting lists. The gap between the incomes of the richest and those of the poorest in Britain reached its narrowest ever point in 1979 – the same year in which council-house occupation, as a proportion of the population, reached its peak at around 40 per cent. But the unfortunate effect of narrowing inequality in the 1970s was to make everyone feel as though they'd never had it so bad. British people saw no reason to celebrate their egalitarianism, when the apparent cost over the course of the decade had been endless industrial action, government spending cuts, high inflation, rising unemployment, scary punk rockers and National Front rallies. In some small way, a socialist society had been achieved in Britain; it's just that people seemed to find it a dreadful place in which to live. John Lydon rhymed 'anarchy' with 'council tenancy'. No few-chah for you!

There was a point in the late 1970s – probably between the Labour government's embarrassing request for an IMF loan and the strikes of the 1978 'Winter of Discontent' – when the dissatisfaction of many working-class people coalesced into disgust with the very ideology that had been intended to make them fully equal with the rest of society. And yet the light of equality finally seemed to be emerging at the end of the long post-war slog: an end to the old slums, to homelessness, to landlord exploitation and to wage disparities. That's all well and good in theory, they agreed, but in reality, hadn't they been sold a pup? They had been given homes, but not the caretakers to look after them. They had been given front doors, but only on the condition that every one was the same colour. They had bulging pay packets, but at the expense of rampant inflation. There was a sense that what they really wanted – to be individuals, with individual property and individual wealth so that they no longer had to be messed around by governments that provided for them only in a most shoddy and cursory way – could only be achieved by retreating from the state that had given them the space, the health and the freedom to make such decisions. The problem for council housing was that the policy that would give tenants such freedom had a political motivation: to sever the poorest from society and to deny that the role of council housing had ever been to provide the nation with a collective asset that could be shared by all. Privatization would benefit millions of council tenants, but at the time-honoured expense of those who were left behind.

In June 1979, the British electorate (or just over 40 per cent of it) voted into power the Conservative Party, led by Margaret Thatcher – a woman who, only four years earlier, had been nicknamed 'Milk Snatcher' for her stoppage of free milk in primary schools. The previous thirty years had been about giving people freedom from the five giants of Want, Ignorance, Disease, Idleness and Squalor. Most working-class people had benefited from the welfare state, through education, free health provision and mostly, but not always, better housing. Now those same people decided they didn't just want freedom *from*, they wanted freedom *to*. They wanted the freedom to move at will, to paint their doors bright colours, to stone-clad, to pebble-dash, to double-glaze, to extend, to crazy-pave, to Artex. To improve, I guess. To make your house truly a home is a basic human desire, and one that's impossible to argue with. Council tenants, fed up with being answerable to a landlord and exasperated with the way in which many local authorities had seemed to give up maintaining their estates altogether, wanted a ticket to freedom. That ticket was the Right to Buy.

Margaret Thatcher is the person associated most thoroughly with the policy of allowing council tenants to buy their homes at a large discount from their local authority, having proudly announced her aim, upon entering power, to bring about a 'property-owning democracy'. However, both the phrase and the idea were Harold Macmillan's: he dreamed them up in the early 1950s, after which the sale of tens of thousands of council homes took place at the discretion of local authorities. In the 1970s, Edward Heath tried to make the Right to Buy a centrepiece of national Conservative policy, rather than a semi-clandestine practice carried out by mainly Tory councils. Thatcher initially opposed the idea on the grounds that working-class people shouldn't be given the same privileges as those sensible lower-middle-class folk who had saved up to buy private homes built by Barratt or Wates. She changed her mind after realizing that her victory in 1979 depended on the votes of skilled manual workers who had the desire, and the spare income, to buy their homes at a discount of up to 50 per cent, depending on how long they had been paying rent to the council.

There was another, less heavily promoted agenda that was concomitant with the Tories' oft-proclaimed desire to extend democratic participation through mass home ownership: the dismantling of Britain's council housing stock. Local authorities were barred from building new homes to replace those lost to the new owner-occupiers, a policy that forced many councils to raise their rents in order to make up the loss in revenue. Selling off homes to private buyers was the equivalent of floating one of the state-owned utilities on the Stock Exchange. Instead of individuals buying share certificates, they bought their own slice of the national housing asset. This was a massively popular thing to do because, providing you had enough money to pay the mortgage, and enough left over to cover contingencies such as the boiler or the central heating breaking down – no longer the council's job to fix, but yours – the benefits were immediately tangible. You would own bricks and mortar in a society that fetishizes them.

The Right to Buy policy was launched in 1980 by Michael Heseltine, the incoming Secretary of State for the Environment, shortly after the Conservatives won power. Popular newspapers billed it as the 'Sale of the Century', after the television game show of the time. By 1982, the year of the Falklands War (KILL AN ARGIE AND WIN A METRO!, STICK IT UP YOUR JUNTA, etc.), sales of council properties to former tenants reached 200,000 a year, and the *Sunday People* ran a competition offering a foreign holiday to the owners of the most improved ex-council home.

The maximum discount was raised to encourage yet more sales, which generally were to relatively comfortable, middle-aged working couples whose children had left home. As a direct result of the Right to Buy, we could now, for the first time since the introduction of social insurance in 1906, refer to the deserving and the undeserving poor as though they were different species, and not merely the lucky and unlucky sides of the same coin. There were three, now four, now five million unemployed, and it was obviously no one's fault but their own that they were unable to take part in the fun.

On council estates across Britain, individual homeowners began to take over from the local authority as the agents of improvement and maintenance. Better-off households won the right to keep their little corner clean, leaving the homes of the worst-off looking scruffy and ragged. With the advent of the Right to Buy, both poverty and difference became visible: it became a matter of whether you had double glazing or mass-produced council windows; whether your front door was made of strong oak or blue-painted council wood; whether you had brass house numbers or council plastic ones. This was a positive development, in the sense that new homeown-ers took such understandable pride in their acquisitions that estates with a high take-up of Right to Buy began to look far more attractive and less uniform than they had done under council ownership. It broke things up nicely. But looked at from another way, it also broke things up badly.

The Right to Buy was the Trojan horse of privatization: it made the paring-back of the welfare state seem attractive and reasonable, a proposition which, in turn, made those who remained reliant on the state seem weak. I'm reminded here of Thatcher's unruffled comment that her government's pro-gramme of cuts to social-security benefits, to manufacturing subsidies (thereby speeding up the process of deindustrializa-tion, putting even more working council tenants out of a job) and to general public spending would lead to the reopening of soup kitchens. Oh, and there was one more cut: to the rate of tax paid by the highest earners, from 83 pence in the pound to 40 pence.

In the first fifteen years of the Right to Buy policy, 1.6 million homes were bought from councils, leaving their housing stock so depleted – particularly in areas where high sales were matched by high demand for social housing, such as the inner London boroughs – that it became almost impossible for anyone not in extreme housing need to become a council tenant. By 1995, 95 per cent of those housed by local authorities qualified for some form of means-tested state benefits. Despite this, depopulation in areas of high unemployment, seen most sharply in the north, caused the least popular estates to empty out almost completely, except to those who were statutorily homeless: the mentally ill, hard-drug addicts, ex-cons and those who had never worked and could expect never to work.

Between 1981 and 1991, the poorest local authorities in Britain suffered the most from an outwards stampede of economically active households (including those who had made large profits on selling the homes they had bought under the Right to Buy) to more affluent suburban areas, losing yet more revenue from rates and the kind of disposable income that keeps neighbourhoods afloat. Private investors bought up entire streets of ex-council properties in order to collect the housing benefit from the DHSS 'clients' who were housed in them, causing ruin and chaos of the proportions discovered in the late 1990s by the investigative journalist Nick Davies. His book *Dark Heart*, an often distressing exposé of conditions on Leeds' worst estates in the final years of the 1979–97 Conservative administration, portrays gangs of children, sometimes encouraged by their parents, trashing inhabited houses and laying waste to entire streets with frightening displays of nihilistic violence. (Bernard Hare's more recent *Urban Grimshaw and the Shed Crew* discusses the phenomenon of such cut-adrift kids, in the same area of Leeds, but with more humour.) There reached a point on many estates where the very idea of anyone in the area ever getting a job, however lowly, seemed unthinkable. A tenant on one of the twenty most difficult-to-let estates in Britain summed up the situation of millions who were left to suffer the consequences of this monumental act of asset-stripping: 'Joneses to keep up with do help to solve problems, but we haven't got any Joneses.'

The lack of Joneses in areas that could most do with them created a circular effect in which any household with the means to avoid such estates stayed away, causing the remaining tenants to feel even more cut off from society and even less concerned with keeping up appearances. In turn, this gave families who were already beyond the control of the community a sense that they could do what they liked in an area that had been abandoned by the outside world. They could rule nowhere else but their own back yards, and this they could do by attacking firemen called out to attend fires, bullying the isolated and mentally ill, shooting air rifles at passers-by, and keeping the police as far away as possible. As Hare discovers, the same kids who scandalize newspaper columnists with their anti-social behaviour know precisely how to look after their own patch; it's living in the world outside the estate that causes them problems, because the only world they've ever known is the one within it.

Although many people manage to hold themselves together and even thrive in the single-class environment of a council estate, hidden damage is caused by many factors. First, there is the simple knowledge that you are surrounded by poor people – people who have drawn the short straw in life and can see no obvious way of lengthening it. The fact that you are living in a place populated almost exclusively by the poor makes those who are less poor unlikely to enter the area unless they have to, further entrenching its isolation and the stigma of living there. That isolation, in turn, limits the aspirations of those poor people by presenting few clear alternatives to the lives they see being lived around them. If those lives seem mad and chaotic, that madness and chaos will spread to those who are most susceptible. So it spirals down. The sense that you are fettered by circumstances beyond your control – lack of money, a house that you have not chosen to live in, noisy or anti-social neighbours – will, if left unchecked, inevitably lead to depression and general poor health. Residents on eight Gateshead council estates of varying quality and reputation report worse mental and physical health the worse their estate is perceived to be. In American housing projects, the 'ghetto miasma' that is said to cast a pall over the lives of the (overwhelmingly black) poor lifts miraculously from anyone who is moved out of them into single-family homes on the edge of the countryside. It's clear that the subjective experience of poverty is far worse when accompanied by a belief that your living conditions are as bad as they could possibly be.

In her research into living conditions and common experiences of entrenched poverty and decline on five European housing estates, Anne Power found that social housing not only tended to be clumped together away from the main body of cities and towns, but stood out like a sore thumb on account of its design, density and height. This was intentional, she says, for the architects and planners whose brainstorms resulted in such estates were convinced that their projects' distinctiveness was in itself prestigious. Power writes of her case-study estates, in Denmark, Ireland, France and western Germany, that Corbusier-influenced 'streets in the sky' are 'anti-social in character'. Yet it's not the concrete that corrupts, so long as it's watertight and well-heated, but the mould into which it is poured, and the way in which that mould is repeated on its plot of land. If the pattern is faulty – if the buildings are stacked and grouped in such a way that dead-ends are created, inviting drug-dealing, loitering and the whirlpools of wind that trapped us on our way to school – an estate will become undesirable no matter what material it was built with. In the phrase of the architectural theorist Bill Hillier, 'space is the machine' which traps social-housing residents in a perpetual night-time where the sun never shines and where every inch of public space seems more threatening than inviting.

Buildings and communities grow and adapt as the people who live in them do, but that growth can be stunted by a lack of care and attention to that very process of adaptation and change. Britain was first transformed by mass social housing at a time of full employment among the people who used it, and in a time when it was believed that modern planning and building techniques would somehow mean that maintenance and investment could be forgotten about. Now there is no such thing as mass social housing. The term 'full employment' has been appropriated to mean a lifetime of short-term contracts, early redundancies and successive retraining. Estates that once won awards are now reviled because nobody has seen fit to keep them in the condition they were in at the time of building.

Many of the post-war New Towns are suffering palpably, both from the invasion of concrete in the 1960s and the failure of later governments to maintain investment in the large council estates that formed their backbone. Millions of new homes were built in a spirit of optimism, as a once-and-for-all solution to the depredations of slum life, but were then expected – like the people who lived in them – to look after themselves. As the journalist Jason Cowley writes of his native Harlow in Essex: 'The town, built to a master plan by Frederick Gibberd to provide cheap, efficient housing and a pleasant semi-rural environment for the urban poor of north-east London, today feels like the kind of place you want to pass quickly through on the way to somewhere else: a place that has been forgotten.' Harlow's Labour MP, Bill Rammell, adds: 'If you build everything at the same time, particularly using experimental techniques, then everything is going to go wrong at the same time.'

It's not that the experimental techniques were inherently a bad idea, merely that if large numbers of homes – particularly in the social rented sector, which does not reap the benefits of owner-occupiers looking to increase the value of their home through regular home improvements – are to be built at the same time, their maintenance and improvement over a long period is integral to their long-term success as communities. When planners and architects dream of creating new ways of living through new ways of building, it is often in terms of trying to make sure that people stay in a new area for long enough to establish roots; but those roots will only take hold if living conditions are seen to be improved, or at the very least maintained. Homes, inevitably, suffer wear and tear after heavy use over a number of years. The block of flats in which I live hasn't seen a lick of paint since it was built in 1981: every wooden surface is peeling and exposed, like a sunburnt face that's had no cream applied. If the longevity of a home and a community is to be preserved, the fabric of the present has to be refreshed all the time, and not allowed to become foetid and rotten. Homes are built from materials that do not exist in perpetual deep-frozen perfection; but from the lack of attention given to them – by overstretched local authorities and by short-sighted central government – you might think that they were.

In taking so enthusiastically to the idea of buying their homes from the council, over a million British households participated in the dismantling of mass public housing in Britain. In so doing, most of those households would have acquired the first assets they or their families had ever owned. For the first time, they had wealth that could be passed on to their children. At first, it's hard to think of this as being a bad thing. In emphasizing the right to realize individual wealth over preserving the collective wealth of the country, successive governments – both Conservative and Labour – have cleverly made the Right to Buy seem a progressive, even redistributive, policy. Look at us, they said: we're giving hard-working people the chance to own a stake in their lives. We're giving them the chance of passing an inheritance on to their kids. We're giving them the kind of expectations and healthy responsibilities that the middle classes take for granted. We're dividing the poor up into deserving and undeserving, so you can tell the difference, just like you could in the days before the welfare state was formed. But they never said, Look at us: we made a balls-up of building council homes after the mid-1950s. We made children live on top-floor flats so their parents couldn't let them play outside. We've made the class divide worse by allowing the better-off to run off with the profits of their homes, and preventing the worse-off from having new council homes in their place. We've made sure that the poorest people in society are back in the same relative position they were before the first council estates were built.

The 1980s ended with a mission largely accomplished: to privatize as much public housing as possible, thereby reducing a once monolithic pillar of the state to a manageable rump. Once council housing had been carved up, and its inhabitants divided up into deserving haves and undeserving have-nots, the government could begin to work out how to replace once-powerful local-authority housing departments with housing associations, which didn't come with all the leftist political baggage of urban councils. Housing associations were officially adopted as the favoured providers of new social housing from 1988, and a year later began to be funded through private finance initiatives. The results could be seen from the sudden popping-up of *Brookside*-style culs-de-sac on the edges of council estates where once a tower block might have been squeezed in. The change in design ethic was not only in response to overwhelming evidence that high-rise flats were the hardest of all council homes to let, but because the appointment of housing associations came with an important caveat – the Tenant's Guarantee – which required the new providers to consult with residents before they built. Meanwhile, the Housing Action Trust's sustained efforts at consultation with residents transformed the likes of Old Ford in the East End of London, and Castle Vale in Birmingham, from streets in the sky into streets on the ground. Councils were encouraged to become enablers, rather than providers, in the housing chain: in practice, this anticipated tenants buying their own homes wherever possible or, more charitably, ensuring that the most difficult estates were managed consistently and, in places where they could no longer be managed at all, assessed for demolition.

Housing associations came into their own in the first decade of the twenty-first century as part of the latest – and, to all intents and purposes, the last – stage in the breaking up of mass council housing in Britain. Conservative-controlled local authorities were the first to wash their hands of their problem homes by transferring them to housing associations, as Labour authorities were repulsed by the idea of losing huge amounts of stock, revenue and votes. By 1997 only two Labour councils, Wyre and Lichfield, had handed over their stock to outside managers, but any local authorities that had expected the incoming Labour government to reintroduce state support for council housing would have been disappointed.

During the 1980s and 1990s, a backlog of overdue repairs and renovations to council houses grew so huge that, by the time Labour entered government in May 1997, £20 billion worth of investment was needed to bring every council home up to a reasonable standard. Tenants, for once empowered (to the extent that their decision could decide whether their estates were taken over by housing associations or left to rot), were told to vote for change and like it, otherwise they would never see double glazing or a new bathroom in their lifetimes. As a result, 120 councils had transferred their stocks to registered social landlords (RSLs) by 2001 on the understanding that, if they failed to do so, no money would materialize from the government for repairs. The stock would fall further into ruin, its residents further into despair and, ultimately, entire estates into chaos or dereliction.

The significance of removing from local authorities the power to house the people who vote for them is double-edged. It punishes councils for behaving, over many years, as though they were not accountable to their voters – Labour councils in the belief that their council tenants would probably continue to vote Labour whatever the quality of their housing, Tory councils in the knowledge that their tenants formed a tiny minority of their electorate. Housing associations are generally smaller organizations than local authorities and are therefore, in theory at least, more accountable than the unbudging blank face of town-hall bureaucracy. But there is also the fact that, especially once the Right to Buy policy took hold, local authorities were as much the victims of governments' desire to play politics with housing as were the tenants. They were prevented from building and maintaining their stock using Right to Buy profits, which made them look lazy and incompetent. (Perhaps that was the idea.)

Then there is the 'enabling' factor. Since 1980, governments have been keen to disabuse voters of the notion that they will provide from cradle to grave. So keen, in fact, that most forms of state provision now come with the warning that they are intended only to enable you to reach, as quickly as possible, a point of self-sufficiency. The enabling state – as opposed to the providing state, which promised to raise us up universally on a sort of giant cushion from which it was impossible to fall – offers help temporarily and conditionally, to sort you out while you're down on your luck. Housing associations are also seen as enablers, whereas local authorities will forever be seen as dependency-encouraging providers. There may be no more than a cigarette paper of semantics dividing the two, but the suggestion is that local authorities, which once housed half of us, will one day house none of us, and that we had better be prepared.

The country that created my religion, the NHS, is the same one in which the secure jobs once enjoyed by council tenants have slipped away, to be replaced by flimsy contract work that makes a life seem as solid as fluff. Since the contracting-out of public-service jobs began in the early 1980s, in tandem with the partly inevitable, partly politically moti-vated decline in well-paid manufacturing work, 62 per cent of workers in the public sector earn less, 44 per cent have lost their job security and 53 per cent have seen their sick pay decrease or disappear altogether. The prosperity of estates, populated by a single class of people doing a similar and rarely well-paid range of jobs, declines on the back of the quality and quantity of work offered to their populations. In the late 1970s, fathers began to be squeezed out of 'jobs for life', which had given rods to their backs and made them proud. They rowed with their wives over money and left their children wondering for the first time whether there was a connection between how much they were loved and how much they could expect to receive for their dinner. The pres-sures on already difficult lives increased just as their houses, all built at the same time, began to look flaky and shame-inducing. It all happened at once.

This is what remains; it's all that remains. Estates have come to mean more as ciphers for a malingering society than as places where people actually live. In the eyes of many people, council estates are little more than holding cages for the feral and the lazy. Sure, if no one in your family has worked for twenty years, or you stopped going to school when you were twelve, you're not going to have much basis for a regular and disciplined life, but then neither are you particularly well placed to create one, because you're likely to be surrounded by people in the same situation. On the most marginalized estates, 60 per cent of adults are out of work, and yet those same adults find themselves blamed for the poor conditions in which they live. This is no longer a society in which you can be proud, still less be seen to be proud, that your home has been provided by the state: it doesn't work like that any more, not when you, the council tenant, exist in a minority of 12 per cent.

Council housing, once the cherished centrepiece of Bevanite socialism, took just twenty years for successive governments to pick apart. Design fads, unimaginative builders and concrete helped them to do the job, whether intentionally or otherwise: but then, cracks began to show in policy long before they became visible in tower blocks. Once the dream of a large cottage for every worker was demoted to a high-rise flat for every worker who couldn't afford to buy a house, its decline was inevitable. It wasn't so much that many council-built homes turned out to be unsuitable, ill-thought-out or plain cynical; more that, from the mid-1950s onwards, council housing was prioritized by governments only as part of a wider house-building policy, not as a means of bringing about equality. Once Bevan left office, more private houses were built than council houses in any given year, making council tenants an instant minority and meaning that, in order to have a wider choice of housing in a less class-segregated area, you would always be forced to 'go private'.

Widening inequalities, caused partly by the mass windfall enjoyed by the better-off working classes after buying their houses in the early 1980s and selling them in the late 1990s, are turning the poorest nasty: those who have least plainly have little to lose. In towns and city centres, you can tell which buses are going out to the estates because the people at the bus stop look angry and exhausted. So, often, do their children if they're not pacified by sweets or pop. As Andrew Adonis and Stephen Pollard write in their 1998 book *A Class Act*, 'Twenty years ago, if you wanted to find a poor family, you had to ring a number of door bells of typical council flats before you found one. Today, arrive at a council estate, ring any bell, and you have probably found one ... no one chooses to live in a council house – especially if they want to get on.' The council tenants of today, in comparison with those of thirty, forty or fifty years ago, don't see their home as a reward or a privilege, because it is precisely the opposite.

4

The Wall in the Head

Since the fall of the Berlin Wall, a phrase has been used to describe the outlook of former residents of the communist GDR who can't quite get over the fact that their country has been subsumed into its larger, richer, democratic neighbour. They call it *die Mauer im Kopf*, or 'the wall in the head'. This reluctance to accept the end of history may present itself in a preference for Spreewald gherkins over *cornichons*, or an insistence on wearing a mullet and stone-washed jeans when more up-to-date fashions can be purchased at a reasonable price from H&M. They cannot stand the 'elbow culture', the former Easterners, by which they mean the every-man-for-himself nature of capitalism. They are convinced that the 'Besser-Wessies' – smug former West Germans – have something against them, in which case they'd be right. Many Wessies consider Ossies – the Easterners – to be lazy, and undeserving of the billions of euros they receive in subsidies through a 'solidarity tax' levied on Wessies' wages in an effort to make the two Germanys more equal. Most Ossies, for their part, feel eternally working-class, proud of their simple tastes and at once envious and dismissive of the West's showy confidence.

To be working-class in Britain is also to have a wall in the head, and, since council housing has come to mean housing for the working class (and the non-working class), that wall exists unbroken throughout every estate in the land. The wall may be invisible, in that no one has built a fortress of bricks around every area of municipal housing, like ten thousand Cutteslowe Walls, but it's there, heavy and strong, and as thickly invisible as Pyrex. The trick is to find a crack in it and whittle out a little escape route, but that takes strength from your side and help from the other, which you're not going to get if you snap at the hand that's reaching out to you. It requires a degree of self-awareness, good health, a better than average knowledge of where you intend to go once you've made a run for it, and a sort of cheek. You're going where you're not supposed to go; you might be leaving behind people who do not want you to go. The people on the other side might not want you to stay.

The wall in the head is built up slowly, brick by see-through brick, over the course of a lifetime. Your knowledge of what's out there, beyond the thick glass walls, is entirely reliant on what you can glean from the lives of the people you know, which usually means your own family members. If your family and friends all live on the same estate, that's a little wall built for you right there. If you have links outside it – friends who live in a different area or type of housing, activities that regularly and repeatedly expose you to new experiences – then you've one less wall to knock down. This is what is known in think-tank speak as 'social capital'. If you have friends and close family who have had a wide range of experiences either through the type of jobs they do, the level of education they have had, or the places in which they've lived, you are likely to have more of it.

Social capital is more important for people who live on class-segregated estates than it is for anyone else: not only are your prospects of social mobility dependent on it, but so are your chances of having a life that is fully connected to the wider society. Otherwise, you can add three more walls and a lid and call it a box. If a map were to be drawn showing how the traffic of people and cars flow through London, its legion council estates would show up as large areas of blankness. The world seems to stop on the edge of every estate. You park your car – if you dare to – on the edges and enter the concrete labyrinth as though entering a foreign country. It's a wonder no one asks for your passport. To quote Tina, the protagonist of Channel 4's council estate-set drama *Tina Goes Shopping*, 'No one ever comes here, and no one ever leaves.'

'He loves me to bits. I really wanna have a baby with him now. I've told me mom, she says it's fine if I can look after it.'

I remember these words, spoken by a classmate in a Home Economics lesson in our fifth year of secondary school. Eight of us, for no obvious reason other than we were all girls and the other three pupils in the class were boys, were shoehorned around a table made for four, creaking on ancient steel-and-Formica stools next to the scratched Perspex windows. Between us and the outside world lay a grid of steel mesh to prevent the windows being removed for ease of burglary. She wasn't speaking to me directly, but to the girls on either side of her, as they absently plaited their long dye-streaked hair without looking at it and fiddled with giant cans of Superdrug mousse under the desk. They teased their permed fringes upwards and across, four inches high and hard as ironing boards. She had moved in with her boyfriend, after a row with her mum meant, evidently, that they could no longer live in the same house together. Another girl interjected, who I remember would eat toothpaste on the way through the school gates so she wouldn't smell of smoke.

'My cousin came round last night and she had her baby in these little Fila boots. Aaah, they were so cute.' A chorus of 'Aaah's rose as they would in an episode of *The Royle Family*, while the gingerest boy in school swung his legs on the worktop and pretended he was Jamaican to be more like his mate sitting next to him, who wasn't Jamaican either, but had parents who were. He had the same birthday as me and wore a gun holster strapped around his shoulder. 'Raaas claaat,' they muttered at us, half proud, half embarrassed, falling somewhat short of the requisite louche scorn that would have given the term its full potency.

The teacher was absent, and there was no replacement that I can remember. Not a lot of cooking tended to get done in Home Economics, although careers in catering were promised to many of us; usually at the nearby airport, whose historic commitment to the minimum wage – that is, the minimum wage and not a penny more – slurped up the local labour slack like milkshake through a straw. To me, cookery lessons seemed like a gift: cooking was a hobby and a treat. The point for most of us was that it was a doss, mainly because teachers of 'euthenics' – the suspicious-sounding collective name for the HE, textiles and childcare department – tended to be hopelessly ineffectual at dealing with children and young adults whose worlds were so small that they didn't extend as far as the kitchen, and so big that they encompassed motherhood.

Think of the pity of what she said: 'I've told me mom'. There is pity in the idea that no one found the statement particularly strange, or that you might find the child's trainers more interesting than the child. There is a lot of pity in the thought that a girl's life had come to this at fifteen, and that she had little idea of what this could mean for the rest of it.

I hardly knew her, except that it seemed extraordinary at the time that she was living on her own with her boyfriend: it seemed to me not grown-up, but catastrophic. Maybe it was she who, twelve years later, would refuse to fill up her estranged husband's Pot Noodle and, in so doing, be rewarded with an attempt at strangulation. But I know it wasn't, because she died aged twenty-five in a car crash, leaving behind five children.

If you attend a school on a council estate, having come from a council estate, you get a council-estate education. It's not so much that you get told that kids like you can't ever hope to achieve their full potential; it's just that the very idea of having lots of potential to fulfil isn't presented. You don't know what your potential is, because no one has told you about it. Nobody tells you that there are universities, where you can learn about more things than you ever knew existed, because it's simply assumed that you'll never get that far. If you do what is hoped, but not expected, of you and find these things out for yourself, you have to *tell* your teachers precisely how far you are going to go in life, and even then they're not always going to believe you. Inculcated into every child at a council-estate school is the idea that you shouldn't hope for too much. If you want a lot out of life, go be a pop star. Don't expect us to school you in the ways of excellence. Your best bet is get a place on a vocational course at the local technical college, where you'll get to hang out with lots of other kids whose educational attainment is scandalous in an affluent, highly technocratic society. If you're lucky, there will be a special branch of the college on your own estate, offering training in lots of different skills, from customer service to hospitality and catering, meaning you never even have to leave. I guess that is what is known as being realistic.

Unless you show extraordinary levels of ability, initiative and maturity – in a school context where 'extraordinary' can mean anything from merely turning up, to showing an interest and then applying yourself – you are unlikely to be let in on the little secret that is the World Beyond the Wall. I am a child of the little secret, which is not to say I showed extraordinary levels of ability, initiative and maturity. Indeed, I showed the sort of qualities that most middle-class parents would regard in their children as deeply average, which is to say that I was quiet, conscientious, anxious to please, anxious full stop. My teachers – the only middle-class people I knew – let me in on the whole thing purely because I stuck out. I showed signs of knowing, or suspecting, what was possible if I put my mind to it: signs that the wall in my head was lower than could usually be expected in a place like ours.

The wall is about *not* knowing what is out there, or believing that what is out there is either entirely irrelevant to your life, or so complicated that it would go right over your head if you made an attempt to understand it. It's hard to articulate: it's sort of like living in a black and white television and colour TV hasn't been invented yet, and even if it had, it wouldn't be any better because it's just the same pictures, only in colour. Here's an example that might better illustrate what I mean. The first time I saw a broadsheet newspaper, when I was about seventeen, sitting in the upstairs library of my sixth-form college, I thought it was an obscure subscription service for professors. It was the *Guardian*. I never for a moment imagined that I – armed with seven grade-A GCSEs and a shelf full of books at home – would ever be able to read it and understand it. *It wasn't for me*. It was completely unlike anything I'd ever seen. That's not to say I didn't know lots about the world; I learnt to read early by reading the *Daily Mirror*, which gave me my world-view, and which is why to this day I defend it and other allegedly 'down-market' newspapers against snobs who somehow think that petit-bourgeois bile is better. But I'm glad I got exposed to newspapers other than the *Mirror*, because they gave my knowledge breadth and depth, and they helped me to understand the value of analysing things, and of scepticism, as opposed to mere cynicsm.

Richard Hoggart's *The Uses of Literacy* describes the unexpected intricacies of a life drawn with a limited palette. His version of working-class life, which I recognize and identify with, is lurid and comforting, but it's also stifling and repetitive, emphasizing conformity above all else and too readily falling for plasticky, monochrome versions of the real thing: relationships, art, books, life. Hoggart acknowledges the role of popular culture, when it's done well as it can be, in enriching life. It needn't be a mere palliative: it can teach you more than any mediocre example of high culture ever could. Back on the Wood, I had conspirators called the Pet Shop Boys. They didn't know they were conspiring with me, obviously, so here is a belated thanks to them. They gave me a life-changing glimpse over the wall. The Pet Shop Boys were my favourite pop group from the age of nine, when they sang a song about the West End of London and made it sound like the most exciting place in the world. They had other songs, about the kinds of lives in which you had the choice of becoming a pop star, a writer, a composer or a revolutionary. Their lyrics were as valuable to me as books, to the extent that I actually stopped reading books and just read their songs instead. That I was an obsessive sort of person anyway – I had a comfort-blanket attachment to daydreaming and collecting things – helped, because I latched on to their world as a way of confirming that there was something outside the Wood that was worth directing myself towards. I only had the vaguest, most nebulous idea of what it was – the fact that the Pet Shop Boys were middle-class and I wasn't kind of passed me by at that stage – but I knew that it was somewhere I would have a better chance of making friends, of finding people with whom I had things in common, who were able to celebrate the way they were and what they liked, rather than hide them for fear of being picked on.

That wall in the head springs up just when you most need a hammer to knock it down. It manifests itself in ways of speaking, ways of dressing, the ways in which opinions are exchanged and how entitled you feel to express an opinion at all. When I arrived at a sixth-form college in the southern part of Solihull, I was the only girl, along with a small handful of boys, from my school year to go there. I was armed with my good GCSEs and a profound conviction that I had endured the worst and that life could only get better. Survive a childhood and you can survive anything; survive five years in a school on a council estate and you get a medal from the Nietszche Society. The sixth-form college was a place full of nice people who didn't have a problem with the fact that I sometimes wore glasses and didn't like New Kids on the Block; therefore, I was all set, for the first time in my life, to fit in like that last satisfying counter in a game of Connect 4. But really, I had no idea. I mean, I had *no idea*.

You should have seen me and my mate Richard when we first met. We were the much-talked-about, little-practised coming together of north Solihull and south Solihull, a clash of the provincial titans to match Adrian Mole and Pandora – except, I hasten to add, neither of us harboured romantic feelings for the other. At least I don't think we did. We must have looked hilarious. I was five feet tall and five and a half stone, he was six foot five and three times as heavy. I got a crick in my neck just trying to keep up eye contact, a skill I was still in the early stages of acquiring. Richard spoke as though he had learnt his communication skills exclusively from watching Roger Moore films, wore kayak-like tennis shoes and was obsessed with the 1960s, from the assassination of JFK to Scott Walker and Simon Dee. He was in my A-level Politics and History classes, and to start with I knew nothing about him other than that he seemed immediately to rub everyone else up the wrong way. He knew lots: he knew too much. He was too quick to speak up. He seemed to have an innate grasp of affairs current and past, and a phone-book memory for the people involved. Entitlement, that's what it was. He felt *entitled* to articulate his opinions. This was completely new to me. I've no idea why, but we ended up sitting at right-angles to each other in both classes, never quite acknowledging each other at the start of each day but somehow ending it in conversation.

The daily exchange, let's call it, would go something like this. We would be walking between the college campus and the High Street, a good fifteen-minute dawdle through salubrious parkland, with Richard in his bright red baseball jacket and me in spray-on leggings and a smoking jacket. It was perpetually raining, so he would have to hold the umbrella for obvious reasons, but he was so tall that it would get caught in the lower branches of the trees along the pathway. Dodging the weeping willows and umbrella spokes, Richard would say something about the importance of John Smith not making the Labour Party too left-wing, and I would reply, 'Oh, Richard!', implying that the whole point of the Labour Party was to be left-wing. Or he would say something about Kate Bush's bush, or Tori Amos's baps, or how marvellous the latest issue of Q was for its full-length nudie pic of Sophie B. Hawkins. And I would reply, 'Oh, Richard!', implying that he was really very rude and should shut up immediately.

'Lyns!'

'Er, what?'

'Have you ever heard *Young Americans*?'

'Er, no.'

'Apparently Bowie can't even remember making it, you know. It says in Q this month. He can't remember the whole of 1975 or 1976 either. And have you read the Tony Parsons interview with him in *Arena*?'

'Er, no.'

'He says he was living in the spirit of Dionysus and that when he had his CAT scan it showed up ninety-six holes in his brain. And have you seen about the Harold Wilson MI5 papers?'

'Er, no.'

'They've just released them under the Thirty Year Rule, it was in the *Staggers* today. Did you get the *Staggers* today?'

I thought, what's the Staggers? (I kept that to myself.) What's Dionysus? What's a CAT scan? What, in David Bowie's name, is the thirty-year rule? It was all too much. It was more than I knew about. You just didn't get this stuff on the Wood. I wanted to know about everything, but I felt a barrier stronger than I was capable of breaking down alone, a barrier that seemed to exist only in my mind but was no less solid for it. I had left school in the belief that, once I had been told the little secret about, you know, life and stuff, there was nothing else to know. But I had so much to learn. I had to learn about things like indie rock, and buying army-surplus jackets from the flea market, and how to have a conversation with people. If I was to fit in and make the friends I longed for, I had to learn how to become middle-class.

It was horrible. It felt like exchanging one wall for another. I didn't *want* to join the Socialist Workers Party, thank you – I already was a socialist worker, sort of. I didn't *want* to smoke bloody doobies – haven't you seen what drugs do to people? The thing I least wanted to do in the whole world was go to Glastonbury, which was revealed to me through the breathless exhortations of festival regulars as some sort of mud-encrusted bourgeois Scout camp. I did want to know more about this David Bowie dude, though. He looked like he had the right idea. He was glamorous and existential (my

favourite new word of this period, which got me into terrible
trouble with my mum for confusing my grandparents with it,
who had told her I'd been bandying such words about and
unwittingly making them feel uneducated) and kind of bendy;
he didn't have any walls around him. I listened to Richard
because I trusted him; he was only a few months older but, in
the nicest possible way, I think he saw me in those days as an
experiment. At the very least, he saw that I was floundering –
that I had leapt over one wall but was shocked by the height
of the next – and gave me hope that, once I had got over this
one, that would be it. No more walls, just freedom.

This one-sided barrage went on for months. I never knew
what to say to Richard, but still, he kept talking, about things
I didn't know but wanted to know. The rain never stopped;
Richard's golfing umbrella got caught in the trees as regularly
as I was stumped for a response to his filthy jokes. He
insinuated his way into my Platonic affections simply by
continuing to talk to me until, eventually, brow-beaten and
weary, I talked to him back. It helped that we'd both signed
up to write for the college magazine on Wednesday afternoons, when we were encouraged to pick an extra-curricular
activity that would look good on our UCAS forms (a sign of
the college's high expectations, this. In our last year at secondary school, by contrast, we did compulsory vocational
courses once a week at the further-education centre on the
estate. Girls had the 'choice' of doing hair and beauty, boys
the 'choice' of doing car mechanics. It's probably fair to say
that I'd not really thought of hair and beauty as my vocation.
I endured a brief nuclear winter of the soul the day the other
girls 'volunteered' me for a perm).

Every Wednesday at two, after I'd locked myself in the
cloakrooms and eaten my box of raw vegetables, Richard
and I would wait expectantly outside the door of the English
seminar room for our course tutor to arrive. We never admitted

it to each other, but for both of us it was the most exciting hour of the week. Moderated in the loosest terms by the tutor, Richard got to argue the toss with another snappy youth called Ian, who wore a tartan waistcoat and seemed entirely self-possessed. One week, they nearly had a fist fight over whether the government should pull the troops out of Northern Ireland; the next, they tore up the cover of our mildly anticipated weekly dispatch because each of them wanted to have a different *Private Eye* joke on the front. They used to make observations – not unkind, but curious, envious ones – about the intellectual lives of famous people, but I didn't recognize the names of any of the people they mentioned. For a year I stayed silent, absorbing as much as I could, scared of opening my mouth lest I got it wrong. Then, slowly, it began to make sense. I began to knit together the strands of this other world to make a rope that would carry me over the final wall.

In the second year, things were different. I'd saturated my brain with information and gradually found the confidence to say out loud what I'd learnt and what I thought of it. Richard ripped into my sudden love of David Bowie, but for the first time I realized that it was affectionate and that I reserved the right to tell him, equally affectionately, to get stuffed. I knew I could do this because I'd gone into the second-hand record shop and bought myself primers in the Velvet Underground, Brian Eno and Roxy Music. Hey, boys! I can do this 'knowing stuff' stuff, too! I found myself suddenly able to add my tuppence worth to Richard and Ian's flailing arguments about what the Labour Party should do to get into power.

'Redistribute the nation's wealth!' I'd say, barely able to suppress my pride at now knowing the meanings of the words I was saying. I had got into a sticky situation earlier that term in our Politics class when I was the only one who put my hand up to say that nuclear power stations shouldn't be decommissioned, as I'd thought that the meaning of the word 'decommission' was 'to keep open', not 'to close down'.

'Don't be such a leftie!' Rich would say. 'What's wrong with meritocracy? Then people like you would be able to do as well as you deserve to.'

After another sodden walk into town, we'd split at the top of the High Street for our respective buses, he to the Birmingham suburbs with hordes of other sixth-formers, I to the Wood with familiar kids, now at technical college, whose rowdiness had barely subsided from school. So different were the lives lived at either end of my half-hour bus route to college that I could almost feel a physical change taking place on the way from one to the other. Every day Richard prodded me a little further out of my shell, only for me to retreat back into it as soon as I returned, because there was nobody there of my age with whom I could share it. The most ridiculous thing about this is that Richard, and college, and my other life, was only four miles away. Four miles and a world, that's all.

A new and different gap was emerging between my life and that of the other kids on the bus. At school, I'd been seen as nothing more than an oddball, a boff, someone from the same area but who inhabited a different internal world. I began slowly to realize that my external world was now changing to go with it. For the first time, I was moving in completely different circles, ones in which I seemed to be accepted, even liked. Not just by Richard – perhaps we were as awkward as each other in our own way – but by people who, I now see, had the self-confidence, the lack of insecurity, not to judge others on their appearance. It appeared to me that the kind, sensible, thoughtful people I'd met at the sixth-form college – and who represented the vast majority of students there – were all middle-class. I seemed to be more on their wavelength than anyone's at school; therefore, I thought, I must be middle-class.

Of course, I wasn't – my family existed in a painful limbo region somewhere between the upper end of the working class and the lower middle class: neither at all rough nor at all posh, poorer than a skilled manual worker's household and yet able to afford day trips – but I was comfortable with this assertion for a few months. I shed my snow-washed jeans and pointy boots for tie-dyed maxi-skirts and vast woolly jumpers – which, back in 1993, was an appropriate look for my new identity. One weekend, I dared to wear my new Doc Martens to the KwikSave on the Wood and, with crushing inevitability, was called a 'lesbian moose' by someone who, with crushing inevitability, was called Darren. He was still in Year 10. But it was too late for him to get to me: the council-estate clam had opened up in the steamy hothouse of intellectual awakening. I wore Ziggy Stardust T-shirts and fur coats, because now I could and it didn't matter if I did. Nobody, whether they were called Dean, Sherry, Wimple or Bumtish, was ever going to stop me. I started getting the *Guardian* on weekdays and the *Observer* on Sundays; our politics teacher advised that it would help me with my A levels; the newsagent had to get them in especially. It felt as though everything was opening up to me: the richness of culture, the power of language, the usefulness of politics and, most importantly, the possibility of deep and lasting friendships rather than bully-acquaintances.

The first wall had fallen, but that didn't mean I was happy. The shock of realizing how much, and how rapidly, I was changing was almost too much to stand. There were many ways in which I was frail. The certainties that had bound together our small, isolated family-island began to come apart, as though the centre could only hold if we all remained exactly the same for ever. I stopped eating and got a part-time job in a cake shop so I could look at food all day without tasting it. My head felt like it was being crushed slowly in a vice (it really, physically felt like that: as though the walls were closing in and I would die if I didn't get out).

My parents waged civil war in the house, outbreaks of which I tried to duck but they wouldn't let me: they were scared. I told my dad I was depressed. 'But people like us don't get depressed!' he raged, depressed. For the first time in my life, I felt entitled to be treated for feelings that I knew were treatable, rather than an inescapable by-product of living a life in which you don't really feel entitled to anything. The GP in the flat brick clinic told me not to be silly, but – to his eternal credit – he didn't put me on My First Prozac as preparation for a lifelong trek along the vale of tears. Instead, he signed me up to a course of therapy in which, once a week, I'd reel off every one of my bizarre new discoveries about the world and its workings to a sympathetic psychologist. It worked amazingly well: a year later, I left home for London, never stronger, never to return to live. I knew then that everything was going to be all right. I had reached the other side of the wall.

Those are the facts of the wall in my head. Eighteen years of dedicated building could not prepare me for the suddenness of its fall; in some small way I was like the Ossies, holding on to their bad hairdos and food in jars. The wall in the head is just that – a state of mind – but it would not be so strong, or so seemingly insurmountable, were it not for the real walls that serve to strengthen it. Coexisting with the state of mind is a state of economics, a state of health and a state of education, a state of government policy and a state of segregation by class. You build the internal wall in order to deal with the one that exists outside. Knowing there are forces that exist actively to hold you back and smother your potential, you need to develop a rationale, a way of coping with it, in order to avoid going mad. Living in Britain's poorest areas, which almost invariably are inner-city or peripheral council estates, will shorten your life by up to ten years, and will ensure that your children are one-seventh as likely to go to university as those who grew up in areas of affluence. Not only that, but going to school on a council estate, or in an area whose catchment area includes a high proportion of council housing, means that you have a 10 to 15 per cent chance of leaving school without any qualifications whatsoever, and, at best, only a 25 to 30 per cent chance of getting the five A*- to C-grade GCSEs you need to do just about any skilled job. Estates are like ghettoes, in the sense that the worst-planned and poorest-served of them are so cut off from their surroundings that they may as well have walls built around them. They can't easily be compared to ghettoes in the conventional, racial sense. Rather, estates are class ghettoes, places where few middle-class people aside from those who are paid to do so ever venture.

How can this state of affairs have come to be? Britain is a country that has universal free healthcare, a free education system up to the age of eighteen, and – even today, after twenty-five years of tax cuts and reverse redistribution that have most benefited the richest – a system of state benefits that ought to act as a safety net below which no person living in Britain should fall. But it doesn't. Something goes wrong along the way, punching holes in the net and causing the very worst-off to fall through to a place so low that teams of social workers, teachers, counsellors and mentors have immense difficulty in pulling them back up. An important part of that safety net ought to be housing, but, increasingly, housing is the very hole through which people in need fall through. That is because of the way in which so many estates have been built: isolated, cut off from passers-by, car routes, local shops and every class of people except the people who live on them. They have hived off poorer working-class people from affluent society when, all the while, governments have claimed that we are progressing inexorably towards a state of classlessness.

In the ghettoes of America, it is said, there exists a miasma, a cloud of poor health and very early mortality, which hangs over the people who live there. It may seem obvious that, if such a thing exists, the cruelty of unfettered market capitalism must be the reason why the poor die early; not from shootings or overdoses, but from cancer, asthma, diabetes and heart attacks. A 2003 report in the *New York Times* listed a horrifying litany of diseases that have befallen young men and women in the largely African-American housing projects of south-west Yonkers, which form part of an otherwise fairly affluent conurbation just north of New York City. A thirty-six-year-old woman, who had recently moved from School Street, a Yonkers project, to another in Brooklyn, was suffering from diabetes, arthritis and asthma. She was grieving the recent deaths of six friends, all of them younger than her, from similar diseases and from various forms of cancer. Another woman, aged forty-eight, had her first heart attack in her twenties, watched her brothers die at forty-five and fifty, lost a sister at thirty-five, and has witnessed eleven young people in her neighbourhood perish not from guns or drugs, but from the kind of illnesses we associate with people in their seventies.

'It makes you wonder whether there is something deadly in the American experience of urban poverty itself,' states the author of the report, taking heed of Orwell's dictum that the first duty of any writer is to state the obvious. The project dwellers she speaks to are hunched with the stress of everyday existence in an area so crushed by disadvantage that the bodies of teenagers grow rapidly old in preference to drawing out a luckless life. Neighbourhoods characterized by rubble, abandoned buildings, burnt-out cars and the dead-end hustling of men who will never work a legitimate job seem literally to sap the life out of those who have to live in them. Similarly impoverished people, whether black or white, live longer in projects that have managed to avert total ruin. That's because each little piece of evidence that the world around you has broken down is another source of stress, which infects your body in the form of the hormone cortisol. Small doses of cortisol do you good when you have an exam, or when you walk dozily into the path of an oncoming car and must run for your life to avoid it; it's when cortisol streams through your body like blood, all day every day, that it begins to cause terrible damage. It weakens your immune system and damages your essential organs. Constant stress kills.

As the American sociologist William Julius Wilson trenchantly recounts in his book *The Truly Disadvantaged*, the post-war deindustrialization that took place in the large cities of the US affected the black working class disproportionately badly. Until the mid-1960s, the nation's manufacturing base was strong enough to support a good proportion of migrating African-Americans who had moved to the industrial north from the south in search of work, and who had found subsidized housing in new mass housing projects such as those in south-west Yonkers. Industrial decline took work away from the low-skilled at precisely the same time that well-qualified black middle-class families were enabled by the socially mobilizing effects of the civil rights movement to move out of the ghetto. Those who were left in the projects, quite suddenly, had nothing: no work and no prospect of work, no support from the better-off and better-connected, no voice except that which they could raise themselves. Not only were the projects single-race, they were now also single-class. Not even working-class, says Wilson – perhaps we should be unafraid and call those who were left, cut adrift from the dignifying life patterns of work and family, America's underclass.

In *Respect: The Formation of Character in an Age of Inequality*, another US sociologist, Richard Sennett, describes his experience of growing up on Cabrini-Green, an estate of terrace houses and low- to high-rise breezeblock apartments built by the Chicago Housing Authority in the early 1950s as part of the city's slum-clearance programme. (There was, and remains, little precedent for public housing in the United States: local authorities own and manage less than 5 per cent of the national housing stock.) As a child, Sennett holed up in a book-lined apartment listening to classical music and learning to play the cello while his social-worker mother observed, from a respectful distance, the curiously noisy daily life of their working-class neighbours. He was fully aware, he writes, of the fact that he and his mother stood out, despite the evident lack of money that had drawn them to this heavily subsidized inner-city project. And yet, this brand-new housing block had started out with a veneer of social glue. People had steady jobs in local industries, which enabled them to keep their families together and their rent paid. It was only when the municipal authorities began to withdraw from the neighbourhood, leaving families to maintain their own housing as best they could on varying resources, that divisions began to arise between those who had more success in keeping their homes and gardens tidy than others. Once-plentiful manual jobs, in heavy industry, shipbuilding and mining, became scarce as deindustrialization took hold in the major cities, with the poorest, mostly living in public housing, becoming the worst affected by long-term structural unemployment. When Sennett left the estate, aged seven, Cabrini-Green had already begun to be afflicted by racial segregation, vandalism and the flight of those – he and his mother included – who had the means to leave.

Wilson's analysis of the factors that caused the poor, segregated but cohesive and class-integrated ghettoes of the 1960s turn into the chaotic race-and-class ghettoes of the 1980s onwards shows how Americans living in the inner cities had their life chances stripped away to the extent that many of them could no longer function properly, either physically or psychologically. Often, their bodies gave up before their minds did. Their ability to live the kind of lives with which the rest of America could identify was taken from them. That, if anything, is the definition of the ghetto: a place that doesn't just punish you, but kills you, for living there.

Does the same rule apply on Britain's council estates? Do stressful, polarizing, isolating factors build up here to the extent that council tenants live under a 'ghetto miasma' of poverty, even though they can still rely on much of the post-war safety net to soften the constant blows of inequality? To an extent, yes. Extreme health inequalities do exist between areas of council housing and their private counterparts. If you belong to the 'Hard Pressed' social group, using the ACORN method of mapping social and economic discrepancies across Britain – that is, if you live in council housing whose associated qualities vary from 'poorly off' to 'high unemployment' to 'inner-city adversity' – you are more than twice as likely to smoke than if you belong to the 'Wealthy Achievers' group (those who live in executive, affluent, owned homes). Again in the 'Hard Pressed' group, you have a 34 per cent likelihood of reporting bad health, as opposed to a 16 to 18 per cent likelihood among 'Wealthy Achievers'. On the poorest estates, there are high rates of chronic joblessness. The supply and abuse of drugs can overwhelm a community, as they did in the 1980s on the Ford Estate in Birkenhead – not far from the gingerbread-style cottages of Woodchurch – to the extent that it was later renamed Beechwood in an attempt to vanquish the stigma of its old name.

The most thorough exploration of whether council estates have become social ghettoes comes from *Swimming Against the Tide*, the investigation carried out by Anne Power and Rebecca Tunstall for the Joseph Rowntree Foundation which documents fifteen years' worth of regular visits to twenty of the most troubled estates in England. They found that, as a direct result of post-1979 economic and social policies, which were designed to cleave the poorest and worst-educated part of the working class away from the better-off – effectively, to create an underclass – the most vulnerable people were cut adrift on islands of grotesque disadvantage compared with the rest of society. Over the course of the 1980s, the rate of family break-up on the estates studied increased far more rapidly than the national average, and the proportion of tenants from minority ethnic groups on the estates in London increased, as unemployment among black people increased disproportion-ately to the rest of the population (most council estates outside London remained largely 'white', even those in otherwise multi-cultural areas; the wood being a prime example). The fear of complete social breakdown on some of the estates grew to such an extent that, as on Broadwater Farm, intensive local management was required in order to maintain basic order. The 1980s were disastrous for the people marooned on estates such as the ones surveyed by Power and Tunstall, but whether the damage was enough to turn them into permanent features of a parallel, ghetto-like landscape is another question. The threat of social disintegration *can* be fought off by well-organized tenants whose efforts work and are recognized, not patronized, by outside parties.

The wall in the head can be approached another way. I want to know whether the very existence of areas of concentrated poverty and disadvantage suggests that we live in a society that is too tolerant of hierarchies, of invisible walls. Does housing the poor on council estates enable us to forget about them, except when they have stolen something of ours? Does allowing the rich to put electronic gates between themselves and the world allow the rest of us to get on with our lives without having to be envious of them? Does the fact that middle-class parents will do anything to avoid sending their children to largely working-class schools amount to an admission that they would never accept a comprehensive system for the greater good? If we were to attempt to destroy Britain's pernicious class system by tearing away not its physical structure, but the way in which we inhabited it – if, perhaps, we all woke up tomorrow and were given a piece of paper that randomly assigned us a new place to live on which our current salary, occupation or ethnicity had no bearing – we might not survive the shock of having the visible evidence of our social position removed so suddenly. Our place in the environment is, by extension, our place in life. We gravitate to where we feel most comfortable, and, if we can, stay away from places that make us feel uncomfortable. By building environments that can be so closely related with class – high-rises for the poor, semis for the muddling-along, mini-mansions for the rich – we have endorsed the idea that the class system is so immutable as to be a caste system.

Perhaps you could call the entire working class one great big ghetto, partly as a result of that peculiarly British attachment to caste-like class roles, and partly because the working and middle classes exist in a permanent state of mutual incomprehension and prefer to maintain this state by keeping to their own areas, schools and eating habits. I wonder whether the man who lives on a council estate is more likely to die early because he has eaten more pies than his owner-occupying compatriot, or because the cumulative stress of knowing that he is at the bottom of life's laundry pile has caused fatal damage to his immune system. Then again, he might have eaten all those pies in order to comfort himself about his relatively low position in the social hierarchy. Inequalities in health, wealth and education are the logical consequences of an economic system which over-rewards those who least need rewarding, but in Britain, they are also the result of a social system which dictates that good health, fulfilling work and a decent education are the preserve of the middle and upper echelons.

That doesn't necessarily mean, of course, that every working-class person is equally poor, or equally ill, or equally ignorant: you only have to read Tony Parker's wonderful work of oral history *The People of Providence*, about the residents of a south London council estate, to know that the reverse is true. In the book, real-life Alf Garnetts spit out bigoted clichés about 'the blacks' who live among them, while young white couples without an O level between them tell Parker, a gifted listener, that 'you couldn't want for nicer people than we've got for neighbours anywhere in the world'.

But there are certain standard assumptions – in my experience and that of many others – that persist within the working class that serve to thwart any attempts they may make to improve their lot. The worst of these assumptions tend to reinforce a pervasive stereotype which suggests all council-estate dwellers are ignorant, and that all ignorant people dwell on council estates. The first is that participating in education beyond the age of sixteen is a waste of time when you could be out there earning money, or even, in a teeny-tiny minority of cases, that it's not worth going to school at all because there's no job worth doing at the other end that pays more than selling dope outside the shop. It's important to state here that this observation is by no means intended to generalize about working-class schoolchildren and their parents; more that, in single-class areas such as council estates, a take-it-or-leave-it approach to learning for learning's sake is prevalent enough to invade one's inner pathology, resulting in low expectations of the education system, the effect of which is aggravated by the collusion of some teachers in believing this damaging stereotype.

I like to think that I know what I'm talking about. I went to a school in the lowest 5 per cent of all schools in England in terms of academic achievement, measured by the rate at which sixteen-year-olds pass five GCSEs at grades A* to C. The year I left school, twelve of us out of 120 school leavers got the coveted five A-to-C grades. My B in Maths tells me that 12 out of 120 equates to a GCSE success rate of 10 per cent. My school was an estate school, built on an estate to serve the children of the estate. But because the estate was built new from scratch, its schools were free to break the mould. This one opened in 1970 as a co-educational comprehensive school, whose lofty aims included breaking down the traditionally rigidly authoritarian teacher–pupil relationship by banning school uniforms, and encouraging lateral thinking in preference to rote learning. At a reunion held for the school's first intake, some of its original pupils, now in their forties, told me how exciting it felt to be able to call their teacher by their first name, to turn up to class in jeans and a top, and to have their minds stretched in directions they never knew existed. Others thought it was, and I quote, 'a load of crap'.

This method of teaching and learning might not have harmed the prospects of those pupils whose imaginations were fired by this approach – those pupils who, before the advent of comprehensive education, might have been creamed off by the 11-plus exam and sent to grammar schools – but some slackness, a certain lack of conviction in the aims and methods of the education system, must have begun to set in. It soon became exactly the kind of school that people expect schools on council estates to be like, allowing many of its graduates out into the world without a single qualification, and the vast majority of them without the GCSE passes they would need to apply for most decent jobs. The school I began attending in 1987 wasn't *terrible*, but neither did it do much good, at least academically, for an awful lot of its pupils. No official policy on bullying seemed yet to have been instituted. There existed an air of mutual incomprehension between the least effective teachers, some of whom told us that we didn't know we were born – they grew up in the slums without two saucepans to bang together, here we were in a nice warm classroom and we couldn't even be bothered to listen – and pupils who didn't know any different, but who still deserved to have their horizons widened through education.

When I passed my GCSEs and left to attend college, I was told by some that, 'Oh, but you were the sort of kid who would have done well anyway.' The implication seemed to be that I'd survived a sub-standard education unscathed. While I had several excellent teachers, even the most encouraging of them weren't wholly immune to damaging preconceptions about the prospects of their students. It was assumed that certain work-experience placements were beyond our reach – namely, professional ones – and, by extension, so were certain careers. There was also the suspicion among some, on the quiet, that our parents weren't that bothered either way because the boys would go and work at the Rover factory and the girls would have children (a germ of truth here, though thankfully not in the case of my own parents). Also, because of the policies of the government under which we were living at the time, it was presumed that we were unlikely to benefit from any social mobility that might have been hoped for for us in previous generations. On the last count, they may have been right: those of us born in the 1970s have since been shown to be far more likely to remain in the same social class as our parents than those who were born a generation earlier, in the late 1950s.

I asked a consultant for Solihull's local education authority which he believed came first when assessing how schools on council estates serve to reinforce the walls that exist between the classes: low aspirations on the part of pupils and their parents, or low expectations on the part of teachers? The consultant works with some of the most socially and economically polarized school catchment areas in England, meaning that he has a clear view of how differently pupils in the affluent south of the borough, attending largely middle-class schools, fare in comparison with those who attend exclusively working-class schools on the council estates of the north. Just as the gap in life expectancy between the north and south of the borough is vast, so is the gap between levels of educational attainment, with schools in the south achieving an A* to C pass rate of between 70 and 100 per cent, and those in the north (excepting the borough's City Technology College, which selects its pupils according to ability) averaging 30 per cent or less. He believes that the more closely linked a school is with a council estate, the lower the results: 'I do believe that most of the schools in the north of the borough are under-achieving, and the potential of the kids is just not reached. Although there's much excellent teaching in these schools, the impact of bad teaching is far greater in a challenging school. I've had colleagues in the north say to me, "Kids like this can't do this, can't do that" . . . I'm sick of hearing, "What you've got to understand about kids like ours is that . . ." They're building in excuses for underachievement all the time.'

Pupils, parents and teachers have long colluded to perpetuate the myth that working-class children are destined for ever to remain stuck in the working class, and that if you come from a council estate your only hope of health, wealth and happiness is to get out of it. To a certain extent, the assumption is true: the limitations of estate life only become obvious once you see what lies outside of it. *Die Mauer im Kopf* again. One of my former English teachers argues that one set of assumptions feeds the other: 'I would say that if there are low expectations, its not just in the classroom, but generally in the experience of the council estate, which is really very insular. I wouldn't agree that it's just teachers' poor expectations, it's more that the school is part of a community which has poor expectations generally.' If estates are to become something other than disregarded blots on the affluent home-owning landscape, then perhaps the only way of doing this is to bus children out of their estates into schools where they'll meet people whose range of experience is wider, and where they might begin to form a view of a world that's not only bigger, but more accessible, than they ever believed. I wonder whether bussing, which has been suggested as a way of narrowing the discrepancy in achievement between working- and middle-class children, is really such an outlandish suggestion. If single-class estates are to continue to exist, and they will for as long as council housing is viewed with disgust and suspicion, then surely the most obvious way of ameliorating the disadvantages associated with growing up on them is to give children the opportunity to become familiar with a world outside the estate, if only for part of each day. Otherwise, how will you ever get to know what is out there to aspire to?

Health and education inequalities are not the only ways in which class barriers are enforced on many council estates. What you eat, and where and how you are able to buy your food, is influenced by the area you live in, to the extent that those who live on both inner-city and peripheral estates are virtually prevented from having a good diet, whether or not they have the money to afford one. Big branches of the mainstream supermarkets – the Sainsbury's, Tescos, Morrisons and Waitroses – stay away from poorer areas, leaving estate dwellers with the narrower choices provided by KwikSave, Somerfield and discount chains such as Lidl, Netto and Aldi.

Even then, such supermarkets are poorly served by infrequent and ineffective public transport and are often inaccessible on foot, leaving the most isolated to rely on corner shops (now, ironically, increasingly supplanted by Sainsbury's Local and Tesco Express, which are often more expensive than the larger branches of these brands) and unhealthy takeaways. A 1999 report by the social-policy think-tank Demos showed how residents of four council estates found it difficult to travel to markets and supermarkets which offered the variety of good-quality, affordable food that the 'mass affluent' – the 70 per cent of people who are starved for time, rather than money – take for granted. One estate in inner London had no main-stream supermarket within reasonable food-carrying distance, yet its shopping parade could boast fourteen takeaways offering greasy, salty, nutritionally deficient ready-prepared food. The choice for residents without a car was between paying for a mini-cab to take them home with their shopping, or making use of the scarce outlets available locally. Another estate had no large supermarket within half an hour's bus ride. Another, in a rural area, was six miles from the nearest town and served by five buses a day, which ran only on weekdays. They could not utilize supermarket delivery services because these were most often subject to a minimum purchase level set too high for their budget, or charged £5 for delivery, which they couldn't afford. Sheer canniness was often the only way to ensure a food intake of any kind, let alone a good one.

Again and again, a life spent on a council estate is proved to be an endurance test. To live in council housing in Britain is to be bound and trapped in all manner of ways. There is not only a wall in the head to contend with, but barriers to full partici-pation in almost every area of mainstream society. We seem reconciled to the existence of poor and marginalized people, while failing to integrate them in ways which might not only relieve their poverty, but could transform their status from unequal – humiliated, vilified – second-class citizens into equal, first-class ones. Instead, we reinforce all the things that serve to make people poor: we house them on large, blank-faced, inaccessible estates, we make them ill, and we are content to offer them a peasant's education and a pauper's diet. And still people say that poverty and low status are exclusively in the mind.

The problem with having a wall in the head is that it makes you look thick to people who don't have one, or whose walls were only knee-high and could be jumped over without much effort. Invisible barriers to knowledge, self-awareness and social mobility seem to irritate those who think that they don't exist, to the extent that they will happily describe walled-in people as 'scum' or, in the current argot, 'chav scum'.

Chavscum.co.uk, a website hosting reams of virulent abuse against the 'undeserving' poor, would be shut down immediately if the same dehumanizing language were to be directed at people of another colour or a different religion. But because its targets are merely of another class, we can log on and have a good laugh. 'Chavs', its members write, are most often to be found on council estates, wherefrom they 'swamp' and 'take over' more affluent areas by dint of their rampant and regrettable fertility. According to one foamy-mouthed contributor, 'these people are not human!' Classism has begun to supplant racism as the nation's favourite conversational kickabout.

Darren, the boy who called me a 'lesbian moose', was a member of the social group that is now known as 'chav scum'. He wore Adidas tracksuit bottoms with a Reebok tracksuit top and grubby trainers, and was violently ignorant. In those long-gone days, when credit was still reasonably difficult to obtain, there was less shame inherent in wearing trainers that were more than a day old, although the mothers with whom I worked at Braggs the Bakers did their jobs purely so that they could afford new ones for their children every few months.

'I can't believe my Jordan,' said Lynne, a gently permed, size-8-uniformed smoker of Lambert & Butlers, of her eleven-year-old. 'He wears 'em out playing football and then I have to gerrim a new pair. That's another seventy pound. Then 'e wants a Nike tracksuit, that's another 'undred pound, then 'e wants football boots, they're another eighty pound. And a Blues kit, Christ alone knows 'ow much tharris. So he'll have to wait for Christmas for that.'

The word 'chav' is derived from the word 'charva' – itself, like the similarly pejorative term 'pikey', an abusive name for gypsies. It's what we're allowed to call working-class people who wear the wrong kind of gear. Don't get me wrong: it's a terrible look, from the cavernous tucked-in trackie bottoms to the garlands of drecky gold jewellery. It invites looks of disgust among people who know how to wear Burberry and Hackett properly – there is a proper way, apparently, although I've yet to discover what it is – and whose label-adorned gym kit costs almost as much as a Lacoste shellsuit. Taleb, my brother-in-law's lodger, will tell you, with a shake of his head, how much one of those will set you back. 'A hundred and forty pounds. A hundred and forty!' He's an Iraqi Kurd who exchanged guerrilla warfare in the mountains for a job working seven days a week at the covered market in Liverpool, and he knows that as long as the people of Norris Green and Speke want to wear hummus-coloured rustling sweet wrappers that hug their legs like clingfilm at the slightest breeze, he won't be wholly unwelcome to stay.

The Lacoste sportswear brand grosses 8 per cent of its British sales in Liverpool, a city that contains less than 1 per cent of the British population. You only have to step off the train at Lime Street to see enough evidence to support this statistic, but the ubiquity of the Lacoste tracksuit – available in a range of mood-lightening colours including taupe, maroon and navy – in Liverpool is such that it serves to remind the visitor that the city

is a law unto itself. You hardly ever see anyone outside
Liverpool wear the Lacoste brand, and when you do, the chance
of them wearing a maroon shellsuit is negligible. Arriving in the
city one afternoon, I bumped into half a dozen Lacoste-suited
twelve-year-olds making mischief, in an inimitably Liverpudlian,
giddy, nose-thumbing way, by running back and forth through
the revolving doors of the Walker Art Gallery. When I asked
them – more curious about their tracksuits than their choice of
entertainment – what they were up to, their faces lit up.

'We're just arsin' about!' giggled Paul, a red-haired, yummy-
cheeked boy in a bottle-green trackie.

'Yeah, its 'alf-term, we've got nott'n else to do!' said David,
whose Lacoste was dark blue. They all had solid, age-old,
classless names, not curious new ones that date and class their
owners instantly. They answered in unison when I asked them
how come they were all wearing Lacoste tracksuits.

''Cos everybody wears 'em!'

Why everybody?

'They just do, don't thee? It's the fashion, it's the trend.'

Aren't they expensive, though?

'Yeah, but nobody's bothered. Everyone's got about six of
'em each.'

How much are they, then?

'They're a hundred and twenty-five from St John's, or a
hundred and fifty in Wade Smith's.'

Six at £125 each?

'Yeah, I know, yeah! The thing is though, you can't get the
fake ones 'cos they look crap and the crocodile hasn't gorr'
any teeth.'

'Naw, you don't wanna be seen wearin' one o' them.'

The children quickly got bored of my asking why they
wore things they wore – things they just had to wear and had
to have – and ran off towards the market. Perhaps they were
going in search of Taleb's stall. Later they'd be getting the 82

bus back to Dingle, or the sprawling satellite estate of Speke. They hadn't said a lot, but it was what they'd implied that mattered more: tracksuits are uniforms like any other. Only the real ones, and the people wearing them, count.

It takes reserves of strength – reserves that many people don't know they have until they are forced into life-or-death circumstances – to stand out, to climb over the wall in the head, which is precisely why huge groups of people wear the same things without really knowing why. Despite its cheap-looking expense, sportswear is worn by those people – mainly the young, many of them living on estates, whose single-class nature invites a culture of extreme conformity – who want to show to the people around them that they're not tramps. Money doesn't come into it: if something's in fashion, you have to have it, otherwise you're a 'tramp' or a 'scruff'. 'Scruffs' and 'tramps', by the way, are what those people we call 'chavs' call each other when they lack the money or the desire to conform as precisely as they require.

I can measure just how far I've moved up the social scale in the last twenty years by how much I now loathe sportswear – what it looks like, what it represents – compared to how much I once coveted it. Taking my cue from Dean and Steven, the pec-puffing, peacock-strutting ten-year-old overlords of my primary-school class, who could recite the names of their embroidered insignia collection as others could the Lord's Prayer, I tried to amass as many items of labelled clothing as I could. I sat next to Dean every day in Class 4 and would lean over his shoulder, not to copy his sums (put it this way, only one of us got them right, and it wasn't him) but to mem-orize and trace the cover of his workbook, which was webbed in blue Biro motifs like a heavily sponsored Delft plate. Sergio Tacchini, Adidas, Puma, Diadora, Reebok: names that sounded as exotic as fine perfumes, and available from all good sports retailers.

Every trip to the shops with my mum became a treasure hunt for quality labels at knock-off prices. I would sooner have gone to school naked than be seen without my orange and black Nike windcheater, after a glut appeared in BeWise one half-term at £9.99 each. I revelled in the fact that there were no girls, only boys, who had the same Adidas Kick trainers as me, which I'd also acquired for a snip at a cash-and-carry in the city centre. Hi-Tec trainers were only worn by kids whose mothers were really *really* poor, or who were sensible and unimpressionable enough to know that £79.99 trainers are no less likely to suffer from fatal grass staining than £7.99 ones. In my windcheater and Kicks I was a vision in day-glo orange: the long-lived era of sportswear had arrived, and I was one of its miniature standard-bearers. I was conscious that, for the first time, I looked exactly how young people on the Wood were expected to look, both to those who lived there and to those who lived outside. (Coming back from work at the bakers one day, a middle-aged woman told me, with the certainty of a preacher, that she would not be boarding the bus to the Wood because 'That place is a den of iniquity!') Now I could stand without shame on the edge of the linoleum that truanting older boys hauled over the primary-school gates and carried to the playing field so they could practise their breakdancing in peace.

Walls in the head are insurmountable because they are invisible to the naked eye. It makes it easier for those who don't possess them to pretend that they don't exist at all. Brick walls are easy to climb, if you're agile; mental ones less so, when your mind is bruised by 'the hidden injuries of class'. That's the nature of housing people according to their social group, in places where other people don't have to live or work. Those other people are far luckier because, according to the jolly-looking man who sat next to me on the bus one day, 'they'd sell your granny for a fiver down the Wood'.

You can only begin to laugh at slights like that when you know your life is going well. If it isn't, well, you can always join them if you can't beat them, and act up to a stereotype that many people on the outside seem to want so desperately to believe. One of the problems with breaking down social barriers is that it's easy for the person who has surmounted them to tell the person who hasn't that it's their own fault for being too weak to do the same. Whether it's the whole of society telling you, or your parents, or your inner demon, this corrosive whispering campaign only increases the feeling that you are simply not entitled to the best things that life has to offer. Wear tracksuits, beat up the elderly, live off the proverbial Pot Noodle – do anything as long as it means that you can more easily be blamed for your own plight. Anne Power's book *Estates on the Edge* describes how stigmatized estates, not only those in Britain but also ones in continental Europe, seem to suffer disproportionately according to non-dwellers' perceptions of them. The worse an estate is perceived by outsiders, the worse the estate seems to become, largely because it is only the absolutely desperate who then agree to be housed there: a place where the fear of other people is such that you will only go there when all other options have run out. Accordingly, throughout Europe, further research shows that estate dwellers' incidence of long-term illness decreases when they are moved from areas perceived as 'rough' to newly built estates that have yet to acquire a bad reputation. They visit their GP less, are less likely to be prescribed anti-depressants, and are more likely to feel that they have energy and vitality when they get up in the morning.

Estates in Europe look intimidating in a way that heightens their allure: they often seem transformed from giant filing cabinets into proud monuments celebrating man's pyrrhic victory against nature. But that's tourism for you: nothing ever looks the same when you're on holiday. If you watch *La*

Haine, Matthieu Kassovitz's 1995 film about three youths trying to keep their lives together under malevolent police surveillance in the nightmarish *banlieues* of outer Paris, you will see that it is filmed in black and white, a device that serves to distance reality. The starkness of the photography becomes the estate: it sharpens its angles and lines and gives them an elegance that Le Corbusier would have delighted in. The sun shines off the flat roofs as though it were a car commercial, and not a film intended to wake up the *haute bourgeoisie* to the rotting lives of its estate-banished underclass. And yet the bleak vision offered a decade ago by *La Haine* seems recently to have come true. Kassovitz made the film partly in response to the death of Malik Oussekine, a French student of Arab descent, at the hands of the police in 1986. And in the autumn of 2005, weeks of riots inflamed the peripheral estates of dozens of French cities after anger spread at the accidental electrocution on the Parisian outskirts of two teenagers, one of Malian and one of Tunisian parentage, who were said to be running away from police. Physically excluded from the wealth and opportunities of the cities they live in, the children of the *banlieues* find themselves the persistent target of random ID checks and, argued Kassovitz in a letter to the French Interior Minister Nicolas Sarkozy following the outbreak of rioting, brutal racism from much of the French police force. The director and the cabinet minister have since exchanged a series of angry letters over who is most to blame for the parlous state of the French estates. Sarkozy, who during the riots called the car burners and bottle throwers 'scum' who need to be washed from the streets, refuses to accept Kassovitz's claims of economic and racial discrimination and police brutality against *les exclus* – the excluded French of the estates. Kassovitz reviles Sarkozy for his and successive governments' refusal to accept responsibility for the deep divisions in French society caused by a policy of physically keeping the poor away from the rich. The dire warning given by *La Haine* to the majority who live on the right side of the divide has yet, it seems, to be heeded at the highest level.

In British films, as in newspapers and on television, council estates are used as ciphers, as shorthand to make a point about the society we live in. When estates feature in art and advertising, as they do with increasing regularity as a way of symbolizing all that's wrong, unequal or grimily 'real' in British society, they're often chosen precisely for their horridness, for their brutal dissimilarity to 'normal', characterful, private housing. Depending on who is wielding the pen or the camera, they can either represent the shame of a society that allows its people to be segregated according to their class, or the shame of people who, despite being given homes, food and clothes by the state, seem unable to look after themselves.

Inequality exists in Britain both in spite, and because, of the welfare state. Just because a lot of good-quality housing was built in the 1940s does not mean that the insular nature of the working class has been ironed out and made more palatable for the aspirational majority, and similarly, just because a lot of poor-quality housing was built in the 1960s does not mean that all working-class people suddenly became slovenly and work-shy. As William Julius Wilson argues about America's ghettoes, Britain in the 1980s and 1990s made its poorest council tenants suffer the consequences of deindustrialization and cuts in public investment disproportionately to the rest of society. It was decided for them by the state that they should sink or swim, and that those who could not keep up would have the safety nets of benefits and education cut back, allowing the worst-off to fall through. Even now, it takes a millionaire car salesman with the mindset of a Victorian missionary to promise better exam results for children on council estates through the funding of 'city academies' that replace schools deemed by the government to have failed. Pessimists would argue that council housing has made class segregation worse, by bunching together people of similar social status in places where they can't leave without a combination of good luck and Herculean effort. Optimists would have trouble trying to find something positive to say about a situation in which class mobility has decreased as social-housing provision has increased; about the fact that a policy designed to improve the lot of the worst-off has done little to close the gap in expectations and outcome that exists between the poorest and the richest. That is because the walls in the head are often the hardest to break down.

5

Begin Afresh

I can hear noises outside. *Ouf! Wooooargh! Oooooy! Caaaant! Unnnngh! Boof.* A thud; the sound of a car boot getting jumped on; a prang as the garage door goes *boing.* An engine starting up like a smoker's cough, then back wheels burning black marks into the ground and rumbling the photos off my shelf. I can't tell if the car ever goes anywhere after being revved up for escape. Probably not: the kids are going nowhere fast, and they know it, which is why they come back here every day, growling and prowling, grooming their get-aways in a ritual of wishful thinking. This is all in an afternoon's fun. It starts at about three as the boys' school across the road, the one with the GCSE results even worse than the one I went to (9 per cent, I think), sends its charges towards the dark recesses beneath us. Our flat-block is built on stilts, a long concrete snake clad with brown bricks, under which a series of disused garages clatter day and night, where young boys – and the odd girl – throw stuff, set stuff on fire and shout stuff at each other without making any sense, either to themselves or to the rest of the world. A chip shop abuts the empty lot, dispensing claggy fat aromas through our open windows and those of the world's most depressing post office, whose carpet is made of crushed crisps and where every day the same man queues up to buy precisely £7 worth of lottery scratchcards, all of which disappoint him before he gets as far as the door.

In this part of east London – Tower Hamlets, a thickly populated inner-city borough that's one of the five poorest in England – the flats squash up against each other like a bunch of toes trying to fit into winklepickers. Tower Hamlets has been rated the area with the least 'physical capital' in the country: its cramped, shabby unattractiveness, as much as its poverty, makes many of the people who live there feel miserable. It's not like the Wood, where you can see the sky, even if it is always grey. The tower blocks rise up out of every spare space: in triplets, like the 'Three Flats' estate visible from our living room, or in pairs, like the British Estate, which squats on the far horizon of the view from my study. Sitting here on the settee I can see the twenty-five-storey stack of poo-coloured industrial slabs out of the corner of my eye: a pound-shop Barbican waiting its turn to be redeveloped into private flats.

Our block, which contains twenty flats, is small and self-contained as long as someone gives the security door a good slam when they go in or out. We are shoehorned behind a listed building – a pub outside which some of the key meetings of the suffragist movement took place. It's an orphan of the old road that, until 1981, extended from Bow into the deep east of Poplar. The pub looks incongruous in the dark twee shell that surrounds it: at once stately and utterly dishevelled, like an old war veteran left to grow infirm alone. Some der-brain has painted its follyish Victorian façade black and magenta, suggesting it may have experienced a short-lived incarnation as a goth rockers' hang-out. Now it's piss-head central: handy for the legion rotting council flats it serves and even handier for the betting shop next door.

Although our flat isn't rotting, it's surrounded by ones that are. The road that was paved over – to create, said the planners of the Greater London Council, a pedestrianized market thoroughfare – is overlooked by a system-built block of such poor quality and irregular maintenance that small children have been known to pull off the main entrance door and use it as a bike ramp. The pedestrianized market thoroughfare is now brown-asphalted wasteground, populated by two desultory stalls that pack up just after lunch, leaving behind an empty trestle on wheels that the schoolkids use as an insult-trading centre till long after dark. (It strikes me that the pedestrianization of former roads is less a concession to people on foot than an admission that, everywhere else, cars have won the argument over who – pedestrian or driver – is more deserving of our public space.)

If I leave from the front door of the block – there's also a more commonly used side door which leads on to a quieter street – the landscape is so crushing, both aesthetically and physically, that I trip over myself to leave. It feels as though I'm locked in an airless room and I'm running out of oxygen. The betting shop's concrete awning, directly to the right of the door, shelters a six-strong array of harmless drunks day and night, but also young men in pastel tracksuits who circle the dead space outside, following the same pattern as the swooping seagulls who have followed the smell of cod and chips up the Thames. They talk in code; they shift off every so often to a corner of the knackered tower block, where a tall boy crouched crookedly on a child's bike is making the same circling moves on his miniature wheels. They're up to something, and it so happens that they do their something between my front door and the Londis grocery twenty paces away, where I need to get my milk.

Everyone around me is making a noise, all at the same time – an aggressive cacophony that bears no resemblance to happy, functional bustle. The drunks are doing that grunty thing; the kids are screaming at each other with violent urgency. At night, I have heard men break beer bottles on the side of the pub wall and prepare to slice chunks off each other's faces. I'm sure – and this is where my stomach turns at its proximity to the kind of lives that are only noticed when they end – I've heard one man being killed, or at best grievously injured, by another. Of course we called the police, but the sound of sirens is so constant that I wouldn't have been able to tell you if the wail we heard five minutes later was a car arriving in response to our call, or just another fire engine tending to an exploding bottle bank or combusting mattress. The noise is constant, and never soothing or life-affirming: it's never children giggling or postmen whistling. It's always people having rows with each other because they don't know how else they can tell someone that they hate a life that takes them nowhere further than this grim patch. Or it's jobless boys parping round and round the walkways on *put-put-putty* little motorbikes, like wasps trapped between the curtain and the window.

If I get to the Londis and back without my shoulders curling rigid with anxiety, I treat it as a bonus. And I'm the one who has an attractive, orderly home to go back to. My shoulders were often curled rigid with stress back on the Wood, but this feels different. It's inner-city stress. Do you not find it strange how someone with a secure life and a steady job can claim to experience inner-city stress when they don't have to rely on a fortnightly cheque to survive, or when they've never had a gun pointed at them? My adult neighbourhood is more hostile an environment than any in which I've ever lived, despite the happy life I have now. While many of the social problems I associate with the Wood are present here, they are compounded by an inability to keep up with the transience of the area's population, meaning that many people don't know who their neighbours are from one month to the next. There's also the thought that smug-looking, together-looking people like me rub up in the post-office queue against those who need the clerk to fill in their forms for them, or who try to smash the window if their money hasn't come through. Everywhere I look there are examples of how wrong this place feels, how wrong it is that people should have to live like this. You have the main trunk road from central London to Stansted Airport running parallel to the estate, squared off by a flyover. You've got the church and the chip shop competing for custom as cars flood past them twenty-four hours a day. There's the slump of dead space in front of the pub: a good fifty yards square of emptiness, which seems to prove how you can design desolation into an environment.

This part of the East End is changing. It's presently a sea of cranes from the Regent's Canal to the River Lea. On loose-end bank holidays I've walked around most of the estates here, partly because a Travelcard is so expensive these days, and partly because every block is different, and changing before my eyes. I've needed to fathom how so many people could live in such a small area, next to a motorway, where silence is impossible to achieve without plugging your ears. Since I moved here in 1999, out-priced incrementally eastwards, the landscape has changed more radically than I ever saw the Wood change in eighteen years. But this is London, giddy London, home of the £300,000 postage-stamp plot and some of the poorest people in the country. There are council flats everywhere you look, piled pell-mell on to expensive land, mocking the rich with their sheer visibility. In London, as on the Wood, you can't get away from them, but here there are even more. The city is a hive.

We loved our little flat when we first moved in. I slept in the living room and my flatmate had the bedroom, hiding the exposed pipework with creatively placed furniture and giving the walls a weekly rub-down with mildew spray to prevent a black mushroomy bloom from creeping towards us. Our immediate neighbours were so quiet that we wondered whether they existed: in fact, as we discovered when we burnt up a Black & Decker drill trying to install a shelf, the dividing walls were made of solid concrete a foot thick. It was the only council flat I'd ever been in where the walls had been anything other than hollow and paper-thin. The same, however, couldn't be said for the windows – they are single-glazed – and the front door, which even a weakling like me could knock off its hinges in the right, or wrong, mood. Through them, all you could ever hear was the gnawing sound of people having rows outside, as though an unending episode of *EastEnders* were being filmed. The diurnal cacophony of the inner-city council estate is something I've failed to get used to in the six years since we moved here; it has made me realize the importance of quiet if your nerves aren't to be frazzled permanently. It's the complete opposite of the experience of living far away from the centre of town, on the periphery, where the endless eerie silence can drive you mad in a quite different way. Too much noise grinds you down; too much quiet alerts you to your own isolation. Both are capable of making you feel lonely.

We weren't lonely, though, when we moved into the block. We learned that eighteen of the twenty flats had been bought from the council by their tenants, suggesting that they had been satisfied enough with these solid dwellings, and with the area, to stay for good (or at least for long enough to cash in their equity). It also suggested that they were, in the main, less poor than the people in neighbouring blocks, where few or no flats had been bought under the Right to Buy. Whether this is further evidence of a selective housing policy I cannot verify, as most of our neighbours had been living there since it was built in 1981. What is more likely is that tenants here stayed and bought because of those thick concrete walls and spacious rooms, whereas other tenants on the estate – those who were stuffed into tower blocks or squirrelled away behind the garages with little natural light – sought transfers from the council. It was another reason to feel lucky: our neighbours all knew each other and had gone out of their way to create what the woman next door described as 'a little Shangri-La', erecting honeysuckle-covered trellises to block out the sight of the pub and filling the concrete planters with flowers when the council stopped bothering. We all said 'good morning' when we bumped into each other in the stairwell, and we helped each other to squeeze our bags of rubbish down the undersized chutes using broom handles and wooden spoons. These small acts of neighbourliness far outweighed the nightly annoyances of hearing drunken karaoke drizzle out of the pub, or smelling the acrid smoke of frying bins.

After two years of saving up by working overtime, I managed to put down a deposit to buy the flat next door from our neighbours, a cat-loving, vaguely bohemian retired couple who had exercised their Right to Buy it from the council in 1997 and received the maximum discount of 48 per cent on the purchase price. There are those who think that buying homes that were once intended to house the poor is a heinous crime against those in housing need. My view is that, once the deed has been done, there's no going back, and you're not contributing to the suffering of people on the waiting list if you're buying from people who have already relieved the council of a house. Buying an ex-local-authority home, in any case, is increasingly the only way for people on low-to-middling incomes to avoid feeding their wages to people who are rich enough to use property as an investment rather than something to live in. The simple fact was that I enjoyed living in the block enough to make my tenure more permanent, and the flat on offer was huge – at seventy-six square metres, at least ten metres bigger than any of the risible private 'starter flats' I had been shown. What I didn't realize at the time was that, having seen the value of their homes explode in a few years, many more of my neighbours were planning to move away to the suburbs and the coast: 'somewhere a bit nicer than here', they always said. When they left, the people who bought their homes were not planning to live in them: rather, their buyers were speculative, often absent, landlords, who were guaranteed healthy returns from Tower Hamlets, a local authority so desperate to supplement its depleted housing stock that it was prepared to pay the market rental rate for flats that had been bought under the Right to Buy policy. There was no logic to it – well, of course, there was, if the net result was that homeless families could be housed in flats rather than squalid bed-and-breakfast accommodation – but, in the space of a couple of years, the effect was to transform the block from a harmonious mini-community into a transient, unsettled place where we no longer knew who many of our neighbours were.

One effect of this change was that, when you saw someone outside the security door trying to get in, it suddenly became far harder to tell whether they were a tenant who had merely lost their keys, or a non-resident angling to get in for other reasons. That may sound vaguely paranoid, but the very reason why blocks of council flats across the country were installed with security doors and intercoms during the 1980s was because stairwells had become vulnerable to muggings, impromptu toilet breaks and the sale and use of drugs. A side-effect of this was that open security doors bred as much fear of crime as there had been actual wrongdoing in the first place.

The town planner Oscar Newman's influential 1972 study *Defensible Space*, and its follow-up, *Creating Defensible Space*, detail how the author's experiences of mapping the incidence of crime on US public-housing projects supported his theory that communal spaces used by large numbers of people would always become prey to anti-social activity. This, he believed, was purely because residents didn't feel as though anonymous stairwells or walkways belonged to them, and so they felt unable to control what went on in them. Once areas of semi-communal and communal space, such as those dim splats of grass you find outside tower blocks, were 'reclaimed' by the residents who used them, the incidence of crime – particularly crimes against people as opposed to property – decreased spectacularly. While many local authorities installed secure entry systems in their council flats to deter unwelcome visitors, the 'reclaiming' of homes in the private sector – with little to fear but the fear of crime itself, seeing as 40 per cent of all crime is committed in 10 per cent of all areas, usually the poorest – along the lines of Newman's theory led to the creation of thousands of gated communities. First in the US and now in the UK, affluent members of both societies have been encouraged to draw electronic and iron boundaries around their wealth.

The fact that the two entrance doors to our block were only ever intended for the use of forty or so tenants had, up to that point, ensured that we all knew each other. We felt proprietorial enough to keep an eye on the occasional unfamiliar face seen in the building. This became impossible once there was a constant stream of new faces to remember, increasing our feelings of vulnerability, whether or not there was hard evidence to support those feelings. The short-term nature of lettings on the estate only added to its sense of instability and lack of community. Little of the ample public space in the area just outside the security door was designated for specific activities, which gave it the atmosphere and appearance of a recently opened landfill site. If the very thought of 'designing out' crime had ever been considered, let alone applied, on this estate, the plan to which it was actually built would never have made it beyond the drawing board.

There was also the small matter of property investors using their newly bought flats in our block as workers' dormitories, installing up to twenty men at a time – Ukrainian, someone said, or 'Bosnias', as my neighbour malapropped – in rows of bunk beds which they occupied on a shift system. The crunch for my neighbour, who moved in fifteen years ago, came when the latter-day Rachmanite applied for planning permission to build another floor on to his flat so that he could fit in another twenty rent-paying shift-sleepers. The landlord's application, unsurprisingly, failed. But while this flagrant over-occupancy was not particularly new in a council ward in which nearly a fifth of households are overcrowded, it seemed to be a symptom of developments that we were unable to influence, still less to control. We may not have been able to do much about London's status as sweatshop of the world, or the wasteful end result of selling off council houses at half-price, but we weren't completely powerless. In fact, we would soon be omnipotent. We were about to be given Housing Choice.

Housing Choice, depending on which way you look at it, is the most empowering thing that has happened to council tenants in their beleaguered history, or a cruel and inaccurate misnomer. The simple facts are these. It was estimated in the year 2000 that 42 per cent of the entire council housing stock – 1.7 million homes – provided sub-standard living conditions. That same year, the government announced that it was to ensure that every council house in the country would be brought up to a self-described 'Decent Standard' by 2010.

Its definition of that standard included the instruction that no dwellings should be damp, cold, draughty, lacking in reasonably modern bathroom or kitchen facilities, or have significant outstanding repairs. There was a snag: councils had, over the years, built up a backlog of yet-to-do repairs and maintenance that would cost £20 billion to implement. The government, baring its teeth, refused to cough up – that would be tantamount to command economics, as well as inflationary – and instead elected to push more local authorities to transfer their housing stock to registered social landlords (RSLs) such as housing associations and long-established entities such as the Peabody Trust. This is where it gets political. RSLs are allowed to borrow private money in order to build new homes and carry out repairs, whereas local authorities aren't. If councils were successful in having the burden of their dilapidated stock removed from their shoulders, it would be at the cost of introducing some element of private finance into what was once entirely public housing.

The government told councils that, in the absence of sufficient funds to repair and maintain their housing stock, they must present their tenants with a choice: they could vote to have their homes transferred to an RSL for refurbishment or even replacement, or to remain tenants of the council and receive nothing. In the case of certain 'high-performing' – that is, solvent and well managed – councils, tenants were given the option of having their housing managed by an arms-length management organization (ALMO), which would ensure that they remained tenants of the council but would have their homes upgraded by a non-profit-making regeneration company. Other estates were earmarked to be part of an experimental PFI (Private Finance Initiative) 'pathfinder' scheme in which regeneration programmes would be funded by private money. In all cases, it would be made clear to tenants that if they chose to vote against transfer, there would be no guarantee that their local authority would ever be able to repair or maintain their homes properly, and their estates would go unimproved. How this could happen concurrently with a drive to upgrade every council house in the country was unclear, but in any case, the government anticipated transferring 200,000 homes a year, or one million over a five-year period, from council to RSL control or management through an ALMO – a figure which, if the policy were continued, would result in the disappearance of all directly run local authority housing by 2015.

On a crude level, Housing Choice seemed more like Hobson's Choice. Of course you'll vote for stock transfer, if it means you'll get double glazing, have your damp-proof course replaced and finally see that ancient obscene graffiti removed from your stairwell. Those who opposed the policy – most vocally, the Defend Council Housing pressure group, which is made up of tenant activists and supported by pro-council-housing Labour MPs including Austin Mitchell and former Health Secretary Frank Dobson – warned that tenants would not only lose their right to a secure tenancy, but that the government had a political agenda to privatize all public housing. That's not strictly the case, as private finance has, so far at least, been of only limited use in funding council-house repair, and neither RSLs nor ALMOs are private companies. Indeed, housing associations are often registered charities. What is important is that opposition to the policy exists, to counter a line of thinking which states comprehensively that council housing – once envisaged as a central pillar of the 1945 welfare state – has failed.

Our own turn to tap another nail into the coffin of council housing came in summer 2002, when a letter was slipped through the door informing us that our estate was approaching Stage 2 of the Housing Choice process. Stage 1 had been a ballot of tenants to decide whether the council should be free to consider transferring its entire social housing stock to an RSL. Leaseholders of former Right to Buy properties had not been permitted to take part. Tenants had voted over-whelmingly in favour of examining the options, having been informed that the borough's queue of repairs would cost £590 million to clear, which it didn't have. (The council's rental income from its housing had decreased so much as a result of Right to Buy purchases that spending on day-to-day estate maintenance would have to be cut still further.) The local authority also warned that the whole transfer process – from examining the credentials of potential RSLs to carrying out the final referendum on whether to transfer stock or to remain with the council – could take up to two years. Most tenants were sanguine: they had waited ten times longer than that for something good to happen.

The language of urban regeneration needs its own diction-ary; it makes you wonder who its chief lexicographer is. Deprived neighbourhoods are called, for the benefit of statisti-cians working for the government and the European Union, 'super output areas'. Central government funding, applied for and delivered in rounds like a game of poverty poker, is called SRB – 'single regeneration budget' – money. My favourite is the 'bus showcase', an SRB-funded series of state-of-the-art bus stops that runs along the main roads leading from Birmingham city centre to the 'super output area' of the Wood. Sometimes the prospect of 'having your say', becoming 'empowered' or, in the case of Birmingham City Council, spending £15 million on promotional material designed to convince your tenants to 'Say yes to stock transfer!', isn't enough to persuade you to vote for change. Although 1.5 million council homes in 120 local authorities have transferred to RSL ownership or ALMO con-trol in the last fifteen years, another thirty-five authorities have experienced the wet fish-slap of democracy as tenants have refused to be parted from the council. While the vocabulary used in local-authority pamphlets is relentlessly positive and forward-looking, not to mention 'inclusive', it hasn't always engineered an equally positive result.

Of the eight estates chosen to be PFI 'pathfinders' – a subtler expression than 'guinea pigs' – the Chalcot Estate in Camden, north London, is among the largest and the highest in profile. In December 2004, Camden Council tenants led a revolt against the three options they were offered, of transfer to an RSL, transfer to an ALMO or staying with the council, which has some of the most deprived wards and worst-maintained estates in London. Activists lobbied for a fourth option of being able to stay with the council while having their estates improved through direct investment from the government. The Chalcot Estate comprises five twenty-two-storey tower blocks overlooking a busy A-road and the West Coast train line that leads out of Euston station. The blocks were built in 1967 with a life expectancy of thirty years. Almost a decade beyond their predicted shelf life, at the time of writing they are in a state of extreme disrepair, housing many elderly and disabled tenants who have to endure winters in which wind, rain and damp whistle through gaps in the single-glazed windowpanes. Both lifts in Blashford, the most dilapidated of the five, are regularly out of service for days at a time, forcing tenants to walk up twenty-two flights of stairs. Tenants were told that they could expect to receive £119 million worth of repairs and redevelopment, including new windows, recladding of the blocks and additional new housing, through PFI. At least, that was the promise until April 2005, when the Treasury rejected the proposal and proposed instead to Camden Council a drastically reduced programme of works worth only £55 million. Quite where the other £60-odd million had gone is open to question: all that is certain is that private funding has proved almost impossible to find for a project as unsexy as council housing.

When I began attending residents' meetings marking Stage 2 – the consultation and design process – of Housing Choice, I wasn't really that dissatisfied with the estate. It was rowdy and noisy at times, but of greater concern was the sense of dragging hopelessness that sat on the walkways outside. It felt grim and forgotten, as well as representing an appalling misuse of valuable space at a time when the government was pleading for house builders to use up brownfield – disused urban – land for affordable housing before encroaching on the green belt. The road that had been paved over in the early 1980s was intended to house a neighbourhood market with a hundred regular stalls. The market never materialized, turning what was once a well-used shopping area into a vacuum that sucks the lifeblood out of the surrounding area. At the time, improving the estate didn't seem to be quite such an urgent issue as it was to become: we simply knew that things needed to change.

Early meetings took the form of a good gripe about the state of the bins, the burnt-out cars that scarred the street to the side of our block, the noise pollution pumped out by the pub, and the desperate state of the shopping area. Some who attended lived in the tower block opposite us, bringing with them a litany of complaints that included drug-dealing in the foyer, security doors falling off their hinges and penetrating damp. It made my expressions of mild discomfort sound like the bored witterings of someone who had tired of slumming it. An older woman needed escorting back to her block after every meeting because her stairwell had become a dope-smoking club for twenty local kids. A disabled man living in a ground-floor flat who came to one meeting announced that he was 'personally insulted' by just about everything that anyone around the table said to him, even though it was all deeply sympathetic to his plight. Each month, we inched further towards an idea of how we all wanted to live: quietly and peacefully, in pleasant surroundings. It didn't seem like too much to ask. In fact, the more we asked for, the more we were encouraged to ask for.

At this stage, leaseholders had the same amount of input as tenants; it was just that we wouldn't have the final vote on whether the estate should remain with the council or transfer to an RSL. After all, the leaseholders had a financial interest in seeing the estate improve. Homes on a refurbished estate a few hundred yards away had risen in value from £35,000 to the local average of £140,000 after they were upgraded inside and out, their owners having been charged a contribution of £10,000 each for the improvements. A neighbour became the steering group chairman, flanked by representatives of the council and an independent consultant who specialized in mediating between all the parties involved in housing transfers.

The process was fascinating, frustrating, but above all democratic. I was the person who had spent by far the fewest number of years living on the estate, sitting next to couples who had raised children and grown old here. Their articulacy made me proud and somewhat in awe of their lightly worn skills. The chairman didn't need telling that he was 'empowered' to lead the group: it seemed to come naturally to him. We discussed the travesty of the rubbish chutes, the broken phone box downstairs and the fact that leaseholders had a mysterious yearly charge for horticulture services when our weed-meadow path had never seen the glinting edge of a municipal hoe. We matched photographs of the high street a hundred years ago with pictures of the same landscape today, to show how a once-thriving area had been turned into a tarmac wasteland. The group believed that there were only two reasons why the area was now a low-level disaster: the paved-over road and the dual carriageway. 'It killed off the whole community,' said an older woman. 'It's dead now compared to how it used to be.' Another blamed the way in which East Enders were moved out to satellite estates in Essex after the war: 'They broke up families and it was never the same.' There was a consensus that the area had not truly felt like a community since it was razed and rebuilt twenty-five years ago. You might be able to pick holes in these kinds of general statements, but it was the fact that people made them month in, month out, that made the consultant town planners and architects, who gradually joined the meetings as we crept through the process, realize that the tenants of this estate were expressing genuine feelings of loss and regret; they weren't merely repeating platitudes. The group was united by a growing belief that a monumental mistake had been made in the design of the estate. It felt disparate and scattered, it made people feel constantly uneasy, and it made people want to leave when once they had wanted to stay.

One March evening, we took a team of architects and master planners around the estate to show them the full horror. Quite by chance, we picked a hellish night: the kids were out in force, dominating the public spaces, criss-crossing through our group on motorbikes, forcing us to part as though welcoming a dictator. Unhappiness stalked us as we picked our way gingerly around flung-open dumpsters, unspecified burnt stuff and malaise-breeding vacuums that were neither public nor private. A representative from a social landlord, whose organization was in the running to take over from the council, came with us, every few paces shaking his head and muttering, 'Whose idea *was* this?' The answer came back, as inevitable as daybreak: someone who didn't have to live here.

It took a year and a half from our first, tentative meeting to realize that, if the estate was to be improved, the only genuinely socially useful option was to flatten most of it and rebuild new homes in its place. In that time, we had met with the master planners nearly a dozen times, but that evening's walk was the first time that they had witnessed what made the estate so difficult to live on in the presence of the people who lived on it. We were here, we knew what it was like, and suddenly, we had the power to change it. We sent them away to come up with the most ambitious redesign of the estate possible, one that included a new health centre, a youth facility and nursery, new housing for rent and to buy, a transformed shopping area and no disused or confused spaces into which anti-social behaviour could seep in the absence of residents' control. This was real power: tenants were not only being consulted, but were – at the risk of lapsing into regeneration speak – designing their own future. It's what should have happened in the 1950s, the 1960s, the 1970s and the 1980s, but didn't, which is precisely how we had come to recommend the demolition of solid buildings that had been built in my short lifetime.

And so it came to pass that I campaigned for my cherished home, my toehold on the property ladder, to be knocked down, only a few years after I'd bought it. Such are the reason-defying consequences of Britain's mistaken refusal to listen to anyone who warned that, if we did not think carefully and act sensitively, we would build new slums to replace the old. I wasn't alone: no member of the steering group seemed overly worried about the stressful nature of being decanted from their old home in order for a new one to be rebuilt, as the collective opinion was that the end result would be worth the disruption. In any case, by the summer of 2003 I had come to hate living on the estate. Word got around that the estate might be knocked down, but because nothing could be confirmed, a sink effect seemed to take hold whereby people simply stopped caring so much about their surroundings. What had been a persistent, but small, knot of resident drunks blossomed into a crowd; the pub started blasting music out through its broken windows; the gangs got louder and more tenacious in their efforts to scare. The council's Homeless Persons Unit paid through the nose for the damp, fungal flat I used to live in next door: a flat it once used to own but now had to pay an absent landlord £800 a month for the privilege of using. A sixteen-year-old girl, drowning in the responsibility of attending to her new-born baby and her screwy violent pinball of a boyfriend, was housed there without obvious support or a telephone, and was left there until one morning he turned up and tried to throw her over the balcony. When he couldn't do that, he tried to strangle her. We wrote to and called the unit repeatedly, over a number of weeks, to ask where they were when she so clearly needed them. (You may ask why we didn't intervene or try to help directly, but you've never met her boyfriend.) My perception of the estate – further damaged by agonizing weeks of trying to avoid bumping into the girl's boyfriend on the stairwell in case he could see in our eyes that we'd grassed him up – changed from thinking that it wasn't perfect but that I could live with it, to actively loathing it. I began to hate leaving the house to walk to the tube station, not because I was worried that something bad might happen, but because it was beginning to make me feel miserable.

I wondered whether something had flipped on that night's walkabout with the master planners, when we first realized that something could be done about a situation we had previously just put up with. It made me think; perhaps too much. Was the estate merely as annoying, as poor and as isolated as it had always been, or had things really got worse? Those of us who planned to move had gone from dreaming vaguely of moving out to somewhere greener, to saying that, as soon as we received our compulsory purchase orders, 'you won't see us for dust'. It was as though the prospect of the whole area changing for the better in the future – or, alternatively, our lives changing for the better by moving out of the area altogether – had made the present seem an awful lot more difficult to put up with. Therein lies the danger of being invited to get your hopes up.

A further year passed, during which we met once a month, had varying versions of the same conversation, and inched forward the argument for drastically changing the estate. Between the steering group, the master planners and the proposed social landlord, we worked out two options from which the council and the Office of the Deputy Prime Minister – since renamed the Department for Communities and Local Government – could choose, according to how much money they felt moved to lend the housing association. The first was little more than a lick-of-paint job, a mere sticking plaster, which had seemed the most we could ask for at the beginning of our meetings, but which, a year later, seemed a vastly unsatisfactory solution to problems that were built into the area like ingrained dirt. Again taking the lead, we stated that we were determined that the RSL should go with the second option of knocking the whole lot down and starting again. The master planners, however, took the view that the same result could be achieved simply by increasing the population density and the social mix of the estate by demolishing selectively and building on the empty spaces. Either way, what had begun as a relatively simple and inexpensive proposal to refurbish and repaint the flats had, as a result of the steering group's tenacity and the fact that we were in charge of directing the process rather than having it directed at us, grown into an extensive and far-reaching redevelopment that would cost more than £20 million to carry out. This caused its own problems: although the planners envisaged knocking down ninety flats, including my own block of twenty, it wanted to built 435 new ones – a net gain of 345 dwellings which could house a minimum of 500 people. That's 500 people who would need to join a doctor's surgery and attend schools, and would need jobs, shops and youth clubs to go to. Our transformation from residents with complaints into active participants held the risk of tipping the whole area even further off-balance, unless the council could be sure that the needs of these additional people could be met.

The government's policy is to increase housing density in urban areas, in order to relieve the outwards pressure on green belt land and prevent the suburban sprawl that has occurred in the post-industrial cities of the United States. (Thoughtful housing design and landscaping techniques can ensure that such areas don't feel crammed or cluttered, but the Campaign to Protect Rural England has accused the then-ODPM of allowing private developments to eat away at the countryside – although it would say that.) Meanwhile, an unimaginative and flimsy rash of new 'affordable' housing is sprawling along the once-polluted banks of the Thames estuary, far from places of work and public transport. The mistakes of the past, it seems, are easy to forget when it is expedient to do so.

I feared that the same could be said of our own plans for the estate. Needless to say, none of us was in possession of a qualification in town-planning, and yet we had somehow – with an architect's help – planned our own, albeit small, town. Perhaps if this had happened in the 1960s, when local authorities collected flats like spare storage tins and decanted their ratepayers like so many broken biscuits, we would not have this job to do, and the slow-unfolding horror story of council housing would not have happened. The scariest thought was that, by assuming that our involvement in the Housing Choice process represented a mandate to speak and act on behalf of every resident on the estate, we were repeating those same mistakes by consigning hundreds of people to temporary homelessness while we turned our own abstract ideas into bricks and mortar. No attempt to involve more tenants – holding open days, giving out balloons and mugs printed with the steering group's logo, knocking on doors, offering to pay for babysitters, posting multilingual newsletters – ever attracted more than one or two additional members. It was said that the leader of Defend Council Housing had told a House of Commons select committee that would-be participants had been told that there was no room left on the steering group, when the reverse was true: we needed and wanted more people to be involved. At around the same time, a mysterious handwritten letter came through every door on the estate saying that if tenants voted yes to Housing Choice, they would lose their home and not have it replaced.

Once the plans had been developed with the master planners, there was nothing more that could be done until the local authority had matched our proposals for increased density on the estate with school places and temporary housing units, and until the Office of the Deputy Prime Minister had approved an application for 'gap funding' that would allow the new social landlord to build the new homes and pay the money back by selling a proportion of them on the open market. We expected to be able to hold the final ballot of tenants, asking them whether they were happy to go ahead with this option or to keep the estate unchanged and in the council's ownership, in April 2005. The date came and went while we sat tight through another summer of pub karaoke nights and mini-motorbike rallies. Having allowed our modest ambitions to escalate into wild fantasies, this extended hiatus felt like purgatory. A Portakabin was set up on one of the walkways of the estate, opening two hours a week in order to give tenants an idea of the stylish kitchens and bathrooms they could expect in their new flats, but also for those involved to dispense the same answer to all those who put a hopeful head around the door: We still haven't heard anything. It's only when housing is managed locally, intensively and accountably that a rudderless estate like ours has any hope of improving. It may not be entirely the fault of local authorities that council housing has failed to do its job properly – if councils had never been subsidized to build highly, quickly and cheaply, and if central government had kept them on a drip-feed of money to repair and maintain their stock, things might have turned out very differently – but the dull sludge of bureaucracy and complacency helped over the years to sever much of the trust that tenants once had in their council landlords.

In March 2006, we finally received an answer: tenants had voted 'yes' to move the estate from council control to a new social landlord, and for much of the estate, including our block, to be demolished and rebuilt. I had never felt so relieved: in a year or two, with any luck, we would be made homeless.

The optimist in me looks around at other housing-transfer schemes that have wound their way through endless drear meetings to reach a stage where everyone gets beautiful, or at least 'Decent Standard', homes. It's a testament to the sheer horridness of many estates that their tenants have, like us, elected to have their own homes destroyed in order that something better might replace them, that crime and anti-social behaviour might be designed out and that overcrowded households might finally be able to offer their children a room of their own. The Old Ford estate, on the north-eastern edge of the borough of Tower Hamlets, is one of the country's most comprehensive regeneration schemes, involving the demolition and rebuilding of 1,500 homes, most of which were crammed into a wall of interlinked tower blocks that ran along the malign Blackwall Tunnel Approach Road. Old Ford was one of the pilot Housing Action Trusts founded under the Conservatives in the late 1980s, which involved the setting up of medium- to

long-term intensive management schemes to take over the running of particularly troubled estates. Again, the flats for rent
have been part-funded by putting some flats up for sale,
making the estate less socially homogenous (though not necessarily any less divided into haves and have-nots), and
ensuring that rents are kept affordable. It's the kind of stuff
that gives the members of Defend Council Housing nightmares, but what they cannot deny is that tenants not only
voted for it, but designed it themselves. The one complaint
that was raised most often in our steering-group meetings was
that 'the council has never listened to us'. In that case, it
would be tempting to ask those who resist stock transfer,
what is so great – and what has ever been so great – about
council housing? Tenants weren't asked whether they'd like to
live in flats, but flats were what they were given. Neither were
they asked whether they minded having their caretakers
removed, or their services cut, but that's what they got. What
they were asked was whether they wanted to buy their homes,
relieving the state of another burden and causing the stock of
social housing in London to reach such dangerously low levels
that only the statutorily homeless have any real chance of
being housed without first waiting for ten years.

I have watched the new Old Ford emerge from the rubble
of the old over the last few years with a mixture of awe and
real, heart-swelling hope for the future. It's attractive – beautiful, even, in places. *It doesn't look like social housing.* I can't
overemphasize how important this is when council housing,
for the most part, can still be divined from 500 paces. The
flats that line the streets off Old Ford Road are built from
sandy brick and are complemented by rows of neat, light
terraced houses with their own front lawns and a road quiet
enough for children to play on. The best advertisement for
the whole project is that children really do play outside, on
the street, getting exercise instead of being locked in on the

fifteenth floor. There is a long row of canalside flats that are indistinguishable from the private ones a few yards along: four storeys high, each with a balcony and french windows looking out over the verdant expanse of Victoria Park. A sheltered-housing complex sits in a wide horseshoe over-looking a large garden with a fountain and good-quality hardwood benches, just around the corner from another brand-new row of terraces brightened by bay windows and skylights. The light colour of the brick is immediately pleas-ing, the white-paned sash windows solid and strong, not tacky. You don't have to search and search to find something nice to look at. It's not as twee as it sounds (and in any case, what's wrong with twee? Sod Modernism, if all it has done is make the people who had it visited upon them unhappy). This is the housing that tenants have chosen for themselves; it's the kind of housing most people would choose for them-selves, given the chance. This is not to say that innovation and imagination should be banished from social housing; only that architects should use both with caution, and that neither should take precedence over the wishes of the people who are going to have to live in the homes they have created.

The 'Three Flats' are undergoing their own transformation, and not before time. Each block has been surrounded with wire fence panels for as long as I've lived around here, giving the estate a feeling of dilapidation and uncertainty. A pro-longed period of consultation with residents revealed that, perhaps surprisingly, and unlike the tenants at Old Ford, they didn't want any of the blocks to be demolished. Rather, they elected to refurbish all three, only demolishing the concrete walkways; and to use the spare land surrounding them to build houses for families currently stranded in unsuitable flats. What the examples of Old Ford and the Three Flats prove is that it can be done, that residents can afford to be ambitious and to have those ambitions realized. If all goes well, our estate will be transformed in the same way. The prospect of our estate staying the way it is – passive, ugly, sinking into itself like every other badly planned, badly managed estate that has ever steamrollered a community – is too miserable to contemplate. For the first time in two or three generations, the political will, the optimism and the money (leaving aside, for now, the question of where the money is coming from) exist to effect a transformation in the living standards of people who have suffered enough from other people's bad decisions. What is happening now has to happen, even if it involves engaging the wrecking ball.

6

Homes Fit for Living In

In Britain, we face a future without council housing, if not without social housing. There are no longer tens of millions of people living in homes provided by the government, with cookers rented from the (nationalized) gas board, and with pans, cups and saucers imprinted with the local authority's name. Most of us own our homes and the things we put inside them. You might argue that we have moved on from a time when mass housing was needed for a mass working class, because the mass working class no longer exists. Most people are not engaged in broadly the same kind of work for broadly the same rates of pay, are not working the same hours with the same holidays, and are not so desperately in need of housing that they have to squat or live with their parents long after they have started families of their own. The facts are that a large majority of people – 72 per cent, and rising all the time – can afford to own their own homes, that very few of those who can afford to buy their homes choose instead to rent from the council, and that very few of those who rent from the council would not rather own their own home. In the years since 1980 we have become a society of homeowners, which is how those people who do rent from councils and social landlords have come to be so marginalized.

Despite the overwhelming culture of property ownership in this country, where casual conversations invariably fall towards prices, interest rates and home improvements, it is only renting from the *council* that carries a stigma of dependence and weakness about it. Those who rent from private landlords are exempt from the national sneer because they usually do so only temporarily, or because they have to move around the country for work. They don't rent because the circumstances of their lives have driven them towards dependence on the state. A flat-renting Englishman can still call his home his castle as long as he doesn't have a corporation rent book and a coin-operated electric meter. Quite why most people are happy to depend on that great state monolith, the NHS, for their wellbeing but are loath to depend on council housing for their shelter is a slippery and complex question. Similarly, a steady 93 per cent of us continue to be educated from the age of four to twenty-one entirely in the hands of the state. Why does mass state provision in health and education continue to thrive and attract ever greater public investment, whilst council housing becomes more fragmented and marginal every year? We are a nation of socialists at heart: we will defend to the death certain tenets of the 1945 welfare state, such as the NHS and free education. We don't consider using the NHS or state schools to be a sign of dependence or weakness, but when it comes to state-provided housing, it seems that we simply can't wait to see the back of such filthy parasitism. I wouldn't dream of taking out private health insurance, or of sending my child to a fee-paying school, but I've had a mortgage since I was twenty-four. It has never once crossed my mind to join the council waiting list, despite living in a city with some of the most expensive housing in the world.

The reasons for this disparity are historical: since the 1940s, with the exception of a few years at the advent of the welfare state, governments and councils have treated housing as a problem that needed to be fixed quickly, rather than as a fundamental part of a healthy, equal society. If public housing were to have the same status as the NHS or the education system, it would have had to have been wholly nationalized in the same way that they were. A second NHS – the National Housing Service – might today be as much a part of the national make-up as the NHS we have got, assuming it would have been treated with equal reverence by state and electorate, and would have received such massive investment. How astonishing to think that it almost happened. The roots of the status of housing as an afterthought to, rather than a pillar of, the welfare state go back to 1945. The brief for housing provision was subsumed into the Ministry of Health, which is how Bevan came to set a high standard for mass council-house building while boasting that he never spent more than 'five minutes a week' on the subject because he was busy creating the NHS. For the most part, local authorities pursued the building of system-built flats in the 1950s largely because they were quicker to build, not because of some one-sided love affair with the clean lines of Modernism. If a dedicated Ministry of Housing had existed, staffed with experts and well resourced, such hasty decisions might never have been made.

At the same time that the Conservatives were building council houses at a rate which Labour never managed to replicate, Harold Macmillan oversaw the rise of a mass affluent class – which included the higher-paid working class – that could comfortably accommodate home ownership, along with the acquisition of a car, a fridge and a television. From the 1950s onwards, the goal of owning your own home was promoted as the ideal outcome for a respectable family, while council housing was built more explicitly for huge-scale slum-clearance purposes rather than as a different-but-equal alternative to paying a mortgage. The vast architectural differences that opened up between private and public housing at the same time caused council housing never again to be regarded as equal, or even desirable. Once word got out that many council estates were becoming awful places to live in, due to bad design, poor planning and remote locations, they became a last resort.

To a great extent, council housing has still managed to serve the nation well. It has put a roof over the head of innumerable people, including my family members, for four or five generations, giving them light and space for the first time and helping to create the circumstances in which I could become, to borrow Neil Kinnock's emotive phrase, 'the first in a thousand generations' of my family to go to university. The same can be said for millions of others, whose grandparents spent their childhoods in cellars and for whom a new council house represented a level of comfort and luxury they could never have imagined enjoying. People are cleaner, taller and healthier now, and although much of that progress can be put down to the NHS and general improvements in public health and nutrition, the building of spacious, warm new homes to replace damp and dark slums formed part of a hard slog towards eroding economic, if not social, inequalities. It cannot be a coincidence that the gap between the highest and lowest incomes in the country reached its narrowest in 1979, the same year in which the largest proportion of the population lived in local-authority housing.

The ensuing twenty-five years have worked in the opposite

direction: the incomes of the richest have been allowed to run away from the rest in the hope that crumbs of their wealth will somehow cascade into the mouths of the poor. At the same time, all but the poorest have been encouraged to buy, rather than rent, their homes in a politically motivated drive towards self-sufficiency, so that those who rely on the state for their shelter can be exposed as losers who cannot provide for themselves. The NHS or the education system have never been seriously threatened by private alternatives: they both cost too much money to run, whereas the nation's housing assets can be micro-managed, unit by unit, by the individual. A house is still the largest and most expensive thing that one person is ever likely to own outright. It would be dogmatic and silly to renationalize the 1.6 million council homes that have been bought under the Right to Buy, especially now that most of us accept or even crave the responsibility of having our own home. If it was going to be done, it should have been done back in 1945. But the mistakes of mass council housing – the need for which has now, to a great extent, passed – cannot be allowed to infect whatever replaces it. There will be a need for affordable social housing as long as property is bought and sold according to demand, and as long as low incomes and wide income disparities exist. Whether it is run by the local authority or by a housing association, it needs to be more thoughtfully placed and designed, more attuned to the needs and desires of the people who will live in it, and above all, more able to provide a liveable and enjoyable alternative to privately owned housing, rather than a miserable sign of failure.

I have a few ideas of my own as to how this might be achieved. My vision of the future is not the result of expertise or in-depth study. Apart from a few years spent pursuing a strange fascination with social housing in all its forms, in

libraries and on self-directed field trips, all I can offer is my
years of lived experience, first on a large peripheral estate,
then on a smaller inner-city estate. My first duty is, once
more, to state the obvious: social inequality is vile. It stunts
and demeans lives; it causes hideous problems for all those
who cannot buy their way out of its effects; and it is unbe-
lievably wasteful. I have spent the last few years trying, along
with others whose living conditions are blighted by bad design,
poor housing management and unaffordable service charges,
to persuade the government to lend the new landlords of my
estate the money to knock down a perfectly sound block of
flats, purely because it was designed without the needs of
the people who must live in it in mind. Such an act will add
more disruption to lives that are already disrupted constantly
by noise, violence and an ugly environment. The only positive
aspect of the estate's demolition is that it will take place with
the support of the residents themselves (which says rather a
lot about their quality of life as it stands). New social housing,
as well as existing estates whose public and semi-public spaces
are to be improved and reassigned around them, must be
designed to take into account the potential for isolation from
the owner-occupying majority. No matter how scattered, or
pepper-potted, council housing is around an area of largely
private housing, it can become cut off from mainstream society as easily as a monolithic overspill estate if its difference –
its social-ness – is emphasized.

An ostensibly minor example of how social housing is
brought to our attention is the way in which large placards
are placed on the site of newly built social housing, or council housing that is being refurbished. They usually feature a
list of organizations that have contributed money to the project – the Single Regeneration Budget, the New Deal, the
European Union, the Housing Corporation – like a giant
finger pointing to the charity cases. It doesn't matter if

Berkeley, or Redrow, or Barratt Homes advertise their wares with giant signs, because there is no social pressure to feel ashamed of moving into a home that you have bought. If, on the other hand, you move into a house or a flat which, according to the huge sign outside it, has been built with money set aside for the poor, and which is rented, not owned, you will instantly have to fight to be recognized as a citizen who has the same rights as a home-owner. That's not to say that people who rent from social landlords *do* have anything to be ashamed of; merely that there is no reason for their housing tenure to be advertised to the world. That is the extent to which owner-occupation has been championed over social renting for the last twenty-five years, and that is why it is so important that the origins of social housing are, for want of a better word, disguised, so that you cannot tell from the outside whether a home is socially rented. Social housing needs to be less distinguishable from private housing, in order to give those who rent a more equal chance in life to those who buy. At present, those who live on council estates, or in postcodes known to contain large swathes of council housing, are routinely refused favourable loan and insurance rates, credit applications and even jobs, on the basis that they're somehow less trustworthy because of the type of home in which they live.

All homes, not just socially rented homes, need to be of good quality, but it matters more when social housing forms a large part of the physical infrastructure of an area. Areas full of private homes tend to have better amenities, including good sports centres, a decent range of shops, clearly demarcated green spaces and a range of transport options. People with their own houses also have their own gardens where children can play and adults can relax. Good-quality homes in the social sector can partly make up for what an estate lacks in other areas. When an estate is both poorly served by its

infrastructure *and* contains bad housing, its potential for pre-
cipitous decline is vastly increased. The Wood, which is so
large that it can be divided into many separate small neighbourhoods, has nice parts and rough parts whose character
and success, or lack of, almost entirely comes down to the
quality of the homes built in them. The homes that are shoddy
and cut off form small ghettoes that bear little resemblance to
the streets full of good solid building.

Those politicians who feared that the rapid bulk-building
of flats in the 1950s and 1960s might lead to the creation of
new slums to replace the old ones were, in too many cases,
exactly right. Old-style cottage estates of large, low-density
semi-detached houses with gardens built in the 1930s are by
no means immune to decline, particularly when they are geo-
graphically isolated and in areas, such as the north-east and
north-west of England, that have suffered the most from deindustrialization. But the most disastrous estates are the ones
where it became immediately clear that the building work was
of poor quality. A population that is constantly trying to
move on because of bad conditions will never settle down and
build the kind of community that is strong enough to with-
stand economic and social shocks. The two most corrosive
effects of poor housing are apathy and transience – when an
estate is populated almost entirely by people who are either
stuck there for the duration, rather than actively wanting to
stay, or who are only there for a few months. People have to
want to stay in order that they can fight for the conditions
they deserve.

No person in this country should have to feel that they live
in a second-class home, which translates into a belief that they
are a second-class citizen with no stake in a society dominated
by property owners. As well as ensuring that social housing is
of equal quality and similar appearance to private housing,
we need those living in socially rented homes to have the same

access to the public infrastructure that is enjoyed by the better-off majority, who can afford to buy their way into the catchment areas of decent schools, to live close to train stations and tube stops, and have the choice of travelling to a large supermarket or walking a short distance to thriving local shops. Secondary schools whose intake comes disproportionately from council estates do less well than those with a broader social mix – not just because their pupils tend to have less well-educated and poorer parents, but also because they lack the means to get out of their area and broaden their horizons. If council estates are to remain the places where the least well-off are concentrated, every possible chance to make up the disadvantages of being poor needs to be concentrated in those areas. This means building children's centres (of which the government plans to build 3,500) and free nurseries, local shopping areas that, if necessary, are subsidised (preferably by taxing the profits of out-of-town supermarkets), and adding a public transport system that is so inexpensive, regular and comprehensive that it doesn't matter if you don't own a car. Amenities which most people would regard as essential to daily life remain bizarrely inaccessible to people living on remote, insular estates where such necessities seem to have been drawn in as an afterthought.

Such problems are beginning to be addressed by the government in the form of the Sure Start programme, which provides education and support for children from birth to age four and their parents, as well as subsidized bus routes and deliveries of fruit and vegetables in the 'food deserts' where local shops have closed due to competition from large supermarket chains (or were never built in the first place). Sure Start, in particular, is an inspired project, but one whose future is already uncertain now that children's centres are to be built all over the country, in affluent as well as poor areas, using the same pot of money that, for now, is concentrated where it is most needed. The government also needs to act to provide at least one well-resourced youth centre for every area containing a high proportion of eleven- to eighteen-year-olds, where young people can go every night for as long as they need to stay out of the house. I grew up on an estate containing nearly 20,000 homes filled with young families, and a negligible number of youth clubs. Again, there are signs that the government is responding to this need, with proposals to turn secondary schools into all-round providers of care and leisure for children after hours. My own estate would be made a better place to live at a stroke if the youth facilities that already exist worked to ensure that everyone who was eligible attended them, and that they wouldn't be thrown out on to the street before they were welcome back home.

The redevelopment of estates whose surface problems – remoteness, graffiti, loitering youths, ugly buildings – are caused by bad design and planning will only work, however, if physical and cosmetic improvements are carried out alongside a serious and prolonged investment in tenants' potential to participate in managing their homes and estates so that they attain a sense of ownership and control. If tenants feel as though the estate is theirs, it doesn't matter whether or not they physically own their home: they will treat it with the same care as they would if their home was something they would one day sell to the highest bidder. All this requires investment of a different kind: an investment in the idea that people who rent are of equal worth to people who own, and that just because they haven't bought a home it doesn't mean that they have done something wrong along the way. It doesn't matter whether it's the local authority, a social landlord or a management organization that works with them, as long as the person in the housing office or on the other end of the phone is attentive and accountable and makes the act of paying rent seem worth the effort.

I don't see any evidence to suggest that a policy of large-scale housing transfers is any more efficient or effective than helping local authorities to do their jobs better by removing the restrictions on what they can spend on repairing and maintaining council housing. Supporters of council housing would argue that in fact the opposite is the case. At least, now, there has been a formal recognition of the fact that much local-authority housing stock was allowed to fall into a state of dire disrepair. A visible effect of the move towards achieving the Decent Homes Standard by 2010 has been the improvements to council or social housing you can see on many estates around the country. Many estates that had been left to rot for twenty years now look fresher, more presentable: most housing in Tower Hamlets has, at the very least, received double glazing in the last five years. Whether these improvements have been carried out by councils using EU money or the Single Regeneration Budget or New Deal for Communities funding, or by stock transfer, matters little as long as something has been done.

The House of Commons Council Housing Group of MPs, led by Austin Mitchell, has claimed that there has not been a single group of council tenants in the country who actively lobbied to have their houses removed from council control before housing-transfer ballots became widespread. While this doesn't explain the enthusiasm of many tenants for transfer – quite apart from aggressive pro-transfer campaigns carried out by councils, a move away from local-authority control has presented thousands of tenants with their first real chance to influence what happens to their homes – it rightly points out that tenants would, in most cases, be quite happy to remain with the council as long as councils maintained their estates properly and treated their tenants with fairness and decency.

As Anne Power and Rebecca Tunstall have written, much

of the serious social and economic polarization that has occurred in the poorest areas of Britain in the last twenty-five years has been caused by deindustrialization and a relative fall in the incomes of the worst-off. That process has been made more acutely painful for people at the bottom of the heap because they have lived on estates that are rotting physically while coming apart socially. The worst estates in Britain don't just suffer from poverty and unemployment but from a sort of social disease, which has caused the people who live on them to be treated as though they are somehow less human, and incapable of acting positively to change their lives and stop being a nuisance to others.

Certainly, there are people whose problems are so severe that it would take sustained support for them to get to the stage where they can take full part in the life of their community, but that is what needs to be done. Anti-social behaviour orders, which seek to ban people from the areas in which they live, are merely a stick with which to beat those who have let nihilism dictate their actions: if it takes intensive rehabilitation, at great expense to the government, so be it. If people don't feel as though they belong, or don't see a point in participating in the unspoken rules of a functioning community, and have to show it by causing misery and havoc wherever they go, there is no obvious benefit in shifting them sideways to somewhere they are likely to feel still more alienated, still more detached from the comforting patterns of normal life. Families that find it impossible to function within the parameters of community life need to be shown how they can do so, and given a sense of routine and continuity wherever possible in the form of resident social workers who, in turn, are well supported by their employers. My bones chilled briefly when I heard the comment made by Frank Field, the Labour MP for Birkenhead, that the small number of 'problem families' in the near-derelict north end of the town ought to be made to live in steel containers underneath the flyover that leads out of the Mersey tunnel. It works in liberal Holland, apparently, where families who have been known to assault their neighbours with baseball bats and Molotov cocktails have been moved to an anti-socialites' ghetto where, one presumes, they can all torture each other to a messy end. An exasperated Field suggests this measure as a way of highlighting how bad things have become in certain benighted communities, but it will not work. Ghettoes do not work. The threat of eviction must exist, not only to protect households whose lives are being blighted by the noise and disruption of others but also so that residents cannot cause havoc in the knowledge that their tenancy is secure. Yet evictions must not be carried out unless there is somewhere for severely dysfunctional families to go where they can be helped to build a semblance of normality into their lives, not to have them further destroyed by being locked in steel cages.

The management of housing by and for tenants is crucial to the success of an estate, whether it is to remain in the charge of the council or be transferred to a social landlord. You need to be able to recognize the people who come and mow the grass verges every few weeks, or the voice of the person you call to ask to have your door repaired or rubbish chute declogged. Things like that don't matter to a homeowner, because they have bought themselves out of the necessity to have a communal bin, and do not have to rely on the council to replace a broken door. The freedom brought about by fragmentation and individualism is no good to the person who needs a unified service, and whose bins, doors and gardens remain communal. There is nothing worse than feeling as though your home is a tiny unit among thousands, which is one of the lasting problems of mass council housing. You need to know that the person who is dealing with your query or problem will not have forgotten who you are the next time you call. More urgently, if those problems are not dealt with as soon as they arise, they will fester to the extent that the social health of the estate – and, by extension, the self-perceived health of the people living on it – will suffer.

Such a high concentration of deprived households exists in my area that the problems can feel insurmountable. A 'healthy living centre' around the corner from me is as attractive, progressive and beneficial an institution as I have seen anywhere in Britain, providing opportunities to better manage one's health, to learn basic skills and to set up social enterprises, but it is hard to believe that it exists in the same square mile as the estates that surround it. The centre works well for the individuals on the estate who use its GPs and childcare facilities, some of whom I know have gone on to take valuable, horizon-broadening courses, but long-term unemployment, persistent poverty and wide cultural and social divides cannot be solved, let alone addressed, by a single institution, no matter how well supported its aims. The fact that it cannot leads back to my initial point, that inequality infects society repeatedly and ever more poisonously until it affects even those who are on the 'right' side of the rich–poor, winner–loser divide. A healthy living centre can ameliorate social isolation and, to an extent, poor health, but it cannot transform overcrowded flats on callously designed estates into places that people feel healthy and contented living in.

That requires total redesign, or at the very least reassignment, of housing types that do not work. Tower blocks and ageing, large-scale tenement blocks do not work when they are crammed full of young families. The East End has a terrible problem of overcrowding because of its young population, and if it is to transform itself into a liveable borough, then these blocks need to be replaced by multi-bedroomed houses, and low-rise flats for those with older children. There is no use double-glazing a fifth-floor two-bedroom flat with no lift and claiming that it is now a suitable place for a family of six to live in. It's not. The desperate pressure on Tower Hamlets' waiting list for larger homes is currently only being addressed on a piecemeal basis, as each estate goes through the painstakingly slow process of Housing Choice with no guarantee that sufficient funding will be available to rebuild larger homes in the numbers that are needed. Just as new homes will not work without a better infrastructure, an infrastructure cannot be imposed on poor-quality homes with the expectation that it will make them good places in which to live.

The national supply of social housing is decreasing every year, as a result of the Right to Buy and selective demolition in areas where demand for housing is low. At the same time, virtually every area of the country has seen the market value of its homes treble in the last seven years, pushing potential buyers on low incomes – service-industry incomes, call-centre incomes, which are barely a tenth of the £200,000 it costs to buy an average property in England – towards an ever-shrinking pool of affordable rented housing. Across the country, there are 1.5 million people on the waiting list for a council or housing-association home: almost exactly the number of homes that have been sold under the Right to Buy since 1980. Many of them will already be housed by their landlord, but in flats or unsuitable temporary housing such as bed-and-breakfast accommodation, and have returned to the list in order to wait for a more appropriate home to become available.

Social housing is not being replaced at the rate it is being lost to the private market, despite various small-scale attempts to increase the proportion of social rented homes built by developers on otherwise private estates, and to allow low earners to buy half-shares of newly built homes until they can afford to take out a full mortgage. This has led to an obscene situation in which local authorities – their housing stock declining as demand is rising – pay buy-to-let property investors the full market rental rate for homes which once belonged to them, in order that they can house people who cannot themselves afford to pay for it.

While the rate of private homes built every year has remained reasonably steady, at around 200,000 to 250,000, since the mid-1980s the rate of new socially rented homes being built has bumped along at under 50,000 a year since its peak in the mid-1970s. The only periods in which more than 200,000 council homes have been built every year were in the early 1950s, when the Conservatives took power and Harold Macmillan launched his house-building crusade, and in the mid-1960s, when Richard Crossman loosened the green belt and allowed overspill estates such as the Wood to be built across the country. The more expensive houses are to buy, the more affordable houses for rent need to be built. Not only that, but the stock which remains in public hands is disproportionately that which was thrown up in haste, only to rot at leisure. Successive governments have shirked the responsibility of matching quantity with quality, which has given tenants the worst of both worlds: bad housing, and not enough of it.

The need for housing that is both affordable and of good quality cannot be met in a half-hearted way. Everyone who has a shred of influence – housing ministers, town planners, architects, building contractors – and who is involved in meeting the demand for affordable housing must unite in order to muster the will to transform the very idea of what housing is for. A house is not an investment, it is somewhere to live: whether you own or rent your home, it has to be good enough for you to actually enjoy living there. I have visited one of the new affordable-housing developments along the Thames Gateway, where lashings of cheap housing (in all senses of the phrase) are being built for sale and rent on a large area of reclaimed land to the east of London. I found a clutter of shoeboxes on the very edge of Barking – itself an edge city, without much identity – ringed by electricity pylons. You arrive at Barking Station and wait for a bus, then change for another. This bus takes you to the terminus, which is at the edge of a council estate on the edge of the town, on the edge of which is the new estate. Soon, everybody will be living on the edges of the edges. These new areas of building replicate the 'doughnut cities' of the 1960s, in which the poorest people were sent to live in high blocks of flats in the very centre of cities and at their very edges, areas which seemed to concentrate their disadvantage.

How do architects working for large construction companies get away with designing flats that no one in their right mind would want to live in for more than a couple of years? As the architecture critic Jonathan Glancey, in a 2004 lecture to the Royal Society of Arts, said of the Thames Gateway developments: 'I wondered . . . whether we're making a bit of a prison for ourselves – whether we're making something altogether more hellish and dangerous. And the question for me is, why is there such a gap between the design talent and true vision in this country and the end result?' The government claims to be doing all the things that need to be done in order to create what it calls 'sustainable communities', but these tiny, flung-out flat-boxes are the very opposite of sustainable. We must build homes that people want to stay in, rather than move away from, preventing roots from forming and adding to the sense that homes are simply places in which to put people according to how much, or little choice they have.

'The really big question,' says Glancey, 'is whether we can escape from the world of liberal economics, of land that's just up for grabs to be bought and done up and flogged off, of housing as consumption units and cities as utilities for consumption.'

He adds: 'We've returned to being a nation of pirates, following a brief and uncharacteristic spell of common sense,
decency and public-spiritedness.' That brief spell he refers to
began over a hundred years ago, the era of the very earliest
council estates, when the Boundary Street flats in the East End
of London and the first garden city at Letchworth were built.
I prefer to think that this period of enlightenment was not
so uncharacteristic after all: remember that Bevan upheld the
ideal of the garden city as late as 1950. I would even go as far
as to say that those who commissioned disastrous tower blocks
and concrete-slab flats in the 1960s had the best of intentions,
as far as giving people a chance to escape dreadful slum conditions goes. But Glancey is right: while demand for housing
still exceeds supply, both buyers and tenants will be held to
ransom by unimaginative builders and developers happy to
put homes on land that should remain condemned.

Wayne Hemingway, the former Red or Dead fashion
designer and a qualified town planner, has developed an 800-
home estate of affordable private housing in Gateshead, and
has also won the commission to design a Thames Gateway
scheme with a large social housing component in Dartford,
Kent. Hemingway, like Glancey, rails against what he calls the
'Wimpeyfication' of Britain, in which identikit homes are
thrown up by the thousand because would-be buyers, who
currently outnumber available homes by two to one, have
little option but to accept what's on offer. Exciting architect-
designed homes remain the preserve of the very rich, who can
afford to have their individuality stamped on the places in
which they live. Mass council housing has never overcome its
reputation for having 'blue front door syndrome', in which
tenants had the choice of any colour as long as it was the one
in the local authority's paint pot. Hemingway's terraced townhouses are spacious and colourful and use wooden panelling
to pick out individual features without damaging the unified,

village-like feel of the whole development. He sees no reason why more of the green belt cannot be used to give people the space they need in which to raise families.

However, there is a bank of 60,000 hectares of brownfield space on which, at current building density levels of thirty-nine homes per hectare, 2.34 million new homes could be built without encroaching on virgin land. At the moment, 67 per cent of new dwellings are being built on brownfield land compared to 57 per cent in 1997, exceeding the government's own target of 60 per cent. Even if the Tudor Walters recommendations of 1919, which encouraged new interwar council homes to be built at a density of no more than twelve per hectare, were to be heeded, 720,000 spacious new houses with gardens could be built, replacing half the number of council homes lost through the Right to Buy.

Low-density housing isn't always desirable from a planning point of view, however: it can be damaging in areas far from city centres, where deregulated bus services are reluctant to go for fear of losing profits, and where shops don't receive enough passing trade to sustain themselves. At the same time, Hemingway believes that the government's drive towards ever-higher housing densities will induce the kind of cabin fever that takes hold in people who live on high-density flatted estates. While I agree that every family deserves a house with a garden, it cannot be at the expense of geographical isolation: peripheral sprawl is no more healthy than inner-city cage rage if it is not accompanied by a balance between access to green, open spaces and ways of getting around cheaply and easily.

My vision – my hope – for the future of social housing is simple. I want it to come to be regarded as an integral part of the national housing stock, and not something that is seen as shameful. I want the desirability of home ownership not to come at the cost of denigrating council housing at every turn. I want the people who manage social housing to be given all the resources they need to maintain the estates that are left in a way that preserves those estates for future generations, so that we don't have to go through an endless cycle of building and knocking down. We may have to accept that the era of mass council housing is over, but that doesn't mean that the housing that replaces it – whether owned by councils, by housing associations or by management organizations – cannot be better and more satisfying than what went before. The Department for Communities and Local Government, which drives the housing policy of this country, has shown that it has listened to the ideas of those tenants who were ignored throughout the 1980s and 1990s: it is committed, on paper at least, to closing the gaps that have grown between planners, architects and builders in the years that have passed since the last great drive to create habitable towns and cities. It may well have noticed that more and more people are moving to the south of England from the north in search of better-paid work, and is seeking to have built as many new houses as possible in the flood-prone, pylon-laced area to the east of London. Here again there are shades of Macmillan's Great Housing Crusade, in the government's apparent prioritization of quantity over quality, and the dominance of kit-form design as a way of allowing mass-market building firms to benefit from public investment. But it must not forget the health of older homes in the north: those estates which suffer not only from population loss but also from a chronic lack of investment, which in turn makes even more people want to leave. It cannot allow an ideological preference for transferring public services to the private sector to get in the way of the fact that tenants need and deserve to have homes of a universally high standard, whether or not they choose to be run by a housing association or by their local authority.

The true test of a successfully housed population will not be when 75, or 85, or 95 per cent are homeowners – a goal which will be revised ever upwards until not a single rented home exists in the country – but when everyone has a home that suits their circumstances, regardless of tenure: affordable, solid enough to last but fluid enough to adapt to the identities and habits of its inhabitants, easily accessible and capable of conferring feelings of security, steadiness, civic pride and self-worth. Only then will the stigma of living in social housing have the slightest chance of withering away.

In the early part of the twentieth century, we had a chance to eradicate a large part of the physical infrastructure of the British class system. We had a chance to house people according to their needs, alongside each other, in communities that did not segregate people according to income or manners. This did not happen; it was a lost opportunity, the effects of which have been as damaging as contemporary observers such as Thomas Sharp and L. E. White, the author of *Tenement Town*, predicted. Having been told that we were in danger of building new slums to replace the old, we have ended up with precisely that. Having been warned that we were creating single-class concentration camps surrounded by invisible barbed wire, we have ended up with many single-class prisons. The way in which many council estates were built – not just in the 1960s, but long before – has actively contributed to the reinforcement of class boundaries, wresting working-class communities away from the old lifelines of work, family and friends and forging a new class of alienated, damaged, highly pressurized people whose links with mainstream society range from incomplete to tenuous. If that is not an indictment of single-class housing in an affluent society, I don't know what is.

Those of us who liked our council homes were given the chance to buy them, turning mass public housing into a fragmented and declining force. Over the last twenty-five years, the right to housing has been supplanted by the Right to Buy housing. As a result of this, we have lost the desire to provide good homes for all, because we now know that only the deserving should have good homes. The rest can go to hell, or be put into containers under the motorway. Rather than fighting to all have council homes built and maintained to an equal standard, we dropped out of the long march towards equality and took a short-cut, house by house. We gave way so easily. Fair enough: we were tired. But can you imagine giving away the NHS like that? We exchanged one right for the other, and most would agree either that the price of individual freedom – polarization, declining social mobility, casual incivility – was worth paying, or that there is no connection between the phenomena.

And yet I still believe in the ideal: not the prefabricated 'utopia' of which the architect Philip Johnson speaks, but in a national housing asset that doesn't pick and choose and divide all those who make use of it. I believe that communities ought not to be stratified by class: not only because the experience of growing up in, then leaving, a class-stratified community was difficult and painful, but also because I'm an optimist. I can't help it: council housing worked, in many ways, for my family. It did everything it was intended to do, apart from make us happy. I could be glib and say that happiness is a new thing, a modern-day expectation that comes from having had our basic need for warmth and shelter fulfilled. The idea of being happy, in addition to being well-housed, clean and healthy, would surely have made our great-grandparents scoff. Well, no, not necessarily. My great-grandparents' generation was the first to be housed in large numbers by the council, and the evidence of Mass-Observation and others shows that, for all the comforts and life improvements that a council home gave them, it couldn't give them that warmth, that closeness, that they had known in the clamorous city. Happiness mattered to them as much as it matters to us. It's just that they didn't feel entitled to it, and now I do.

What differs between the generations, I guess, is the belief that the possibility of a better life is out there, and that it is our right to have access to it. I'm fairly sure that my grandparents couldn't have imagined a much better life than the one they had once they moved into the council house for which they had waited twenty years. My parents were aware that there was another step towards that life, which they achieved by buying a house. My desire for a better life resulted in my escaping the working class almost completely. Almost, I say: the chip on one of my shoulders is balanced by a large lump of escapee guilt on the other. There is also the small fact that I still live on a council estate, albeit as a homeowner. One day soon, I will move away from here. I've done my time. I want some peace and quiet, and a pretty home. The people who move here in my place will, I hope, find a much better environment in which to live, once the planners and the builders have undone the work of their predecessors. Until socially mixed – and fully integrated – communities are the norm, rather than the exception, that is the only choice on offer.

The estate where I grew up, wrote a *Birmingham Post* reporter in 1971, 'is a town of strangers. [The] Wood, where there is a town itching to be born, but is prevented because they haven't delivered the blood yet, the community spirit, and where the wind gathers in rude pockets around the corners of the precincts. (Why are these new, straight, square precincts always so windy?)'

The empty town of strangers gave me space and light, but it didn't give me a chance to see what life could be like outside it. You cannot know what that was like unless you grew up inside it. Breaking out of it was like breaking out of prison. For all its careful planning and proximity to the city and the country, the estate was ringed by that invisible, impenetrable force field: the wall in the head. That may say as much for the closed ranks of the working class as it does for the failures of town-planning. But I know that I will never scale another wall quite so high.

Notes

Introduction

The quote attributed to Leonard Downie Jr, former executive editor of the *Washington Post*, comes from 'Embattled London', a piece he wrote in 1972 while on secondment from the *Post* as a fellow with the Alicia Patterson Foundation. As you might expect from the title, he writes mainly about slum clearance in London, but compares the Wood – not particularly favourably – with the contemporary Thamesmead estate in south-east London. Of the former, he adds: 'Because there is no day care for children of working mothers, many children wear their house keys on strings around their necks in school and wander by themselves through the project with nothing to do until parents return home at night. Vandalism and teenage gang activities have become enormous problems in the six years since the project was begun.' The piece is accompanied by some choice photographs of Brobdignagian high-rise blocks towering over the East End terraces they were replacing.

Talking of Pot Noodles, Barry Austin – the fifty-stone man believed to be the fattest in Britain, and star of documentaries on Sky One and Five – lives on the Wood. The *Observer* reported in September 2005 that he was about to embark on a diet that would reduce his daily calorie intake from 29,000 to 1,500, and, in so doing, the size of his liver – currently 'black and covered in fat' – from 8lb to a more healthy 3lb. There is a slight chance I'm imagining this, but in the days when he could still move unaided, he often used to get the same bus as the one I caught home from school; he was recognizable not only by his bulk but by his unusually high speaking voice.

With regard to the public view of council tenants as 'scum', the novelist V. S. Naipaul seems especially taken with this idea, describing council estates in a BBC World Service interview as 'a slave growth, parasitic growths on the main body' of British society, and writing in his 2004 novel *Magic Seeds* about a vision of council-estate culture in which criminality, promiscuity and dishonesty are the norm.

I first found out about Cutteslowe through the BBC Radio 4 documentary *The Cutteslowe Walls*, broadcast on 10 November 2004, which led me to Peter Collison's 1963 book *Cutteslowe Walls: A Study in Social Class* (Faber & Faber, 1963).

Information regarding interviews conducted to sift 'rough' families from 'respectable' ones when allocating council housing in the interwar period came from Dr Peter Scott of Reading University's paper *Visible and Invisible*

Walls: Suburbanisation and Social Filtering in Working-Class Communities in Interwar Britain.

The statistics comparing life expectancies in north and south Solihull came from a study that was carried out by the borough in 2001 in an attempt to secure regeneration funding from the European Union. It was reading about these figures in the 6 April 2001 edition of the *Solihull Times* that made me want to write this book.

Chapter 1: This Must Be the Place

Richard Crossman's abridged *Diaries of a Cabinet Minister 1964–70* (Hamish Hamilton, 1979), edited by Anthony Howard, were very useful for this chapter, as was Michael Young and Peter Willmott's *Family and Kinship in East London* (Pelican, 1962).

Sir Frank Price, former Lord Mayor of Birmingham, is quoted in Professor Carl Chinn's book *Homes for People: Council Housing and Urban Renewal in Birmingham 1849–1999* (Brewin, 1999).

The local-history archives of Solihull Central Library and Birmingham Central Library contained, among other invaluable papers, master-plans and newspaper cuttings, a working paper written by a researcher at the University of Birmingham in 1968 detailing the reasons for building the Wood in the size and form it took.

The line 'the type of memories that turn your bones to glass' comes from the song 'Cold Blooded Old Times' by Bill Callahan, who records under the name Smog.

Chapter 2: The End of the Slums

The link between relative poverty, social immobility and premature death is so strong as to be pretty much irrefutable, argues the epidemiologist Michael Marmot in his book *Status Syndrome* (Bloomsbury, 2004).

As well as the 2001 updated edition of Peter Hall's *Cities of Tomorrow* (Blackwell), I read and found endlessly interesting Hall's mammoth book *Cities in Civilisation* (Weidenfeld & Nicholson, 1999).

Another informal name for Lea Village, as the historian of working-class life Carl Chinn wrote in the Birmingham *Evening Mail* in July 2002, was 'World's End'. He added that Birmingham's 50,000th interwar council house was built there.

The reference to Philip Ward-Jackson's translation of the term 'the Viennese thirst for ornament' is from a 2004 lecture given by Ward-Jackson, former Conway Librarian at the Courtauld Institute of Art, titled 'Pioneering Art for the Community: Vienna and London 1930–1960'.

Homes Fit for Heroes, a book that compiles Bill Brandt's wartime photographs for the Bournville Village Trust, was produced by Dewi Lewis Publishing in conjunction with Birmingham Library Services and the University of Birmingham in 2004.

I know very little about the book *Tenement Town*, except that it was written in 1937 by an author called L. E. White. It can be found in the library of the Bartlett School of Architecture, University College, London.

I could have spent the rest of my life cooped up happily in the Special Collections area of the University of Sussex Library, where the Mass-Observation archive is kept. The Mass-Observation book *People's Homes* (John Murray, 1943) is slightly more widely available, namely at academic libraries specializing in architecture and town-planning.

Nicholas Timmins' book *Five Giants* is a bible for anyone who is remotely interested in the welfare state – its successes and failures – and post-war British society.

The descriptions of the interior of a Lansbury Estate home are given in a brochure called 'The 1951 Furnished Flat, Lansbury Estate, Poplar', which was produced by the London Co-Operative Society to coincide with the Festival of Britain's Living Architecture exhibition.

The Lorna Sage book referred to is *Bad Blood* (Fourth Estate, 2000).

Anne Power, Professor of Social Policy at the London School of Economics, is the author of many key long-term studies of social housing estates in Britain and Europe. Her report with Rebecca Tunstall is titled *Swimming Against the Tide: Polarisation or Progress on 20 Unpopular Estates 1980–1995* (Joseph Rowntree Foundation, 1994).

Karel Teige wrote *The Minimum Dwelling* in Czech in 1931, but an English translation was only produced for the first time in 2002, by the MIT Press.

I give thanks to Professor Peter Hennessy, whose book *Never Again: Britain 1945–1951* (Jonathan Cape, 1992) not only alerted me to possible reasons for the popularity of prefabs, but was my staple reading diet while studying for A levels in Politics and History. He later became my extraordinarily patient and understanding tutor in Contemporary British History at Queen Mary, University of London.

Chapter 3: Slums in the Sky

Chris Holmes' quote about housing poverty is taken from his 2003 report *Housing, Equality and Choice*, written when he was a visiting research fellow at the Institute for Public Policy Research.

In a piece written for the *Observer* on 25 September 2005, Professor Danny Dorling of Sheffield University reports: 'Most children growing up in the tower blocks of London and Birmingham – the majority of children "living in the sky" in Britain – are black.'

The information given in the graph on house-building between 1949 and 2002 comes from the Office of the Deputy Prime Minister.

At the retired architect's house I was shown a set of five books comprising Le Corbusier's *Oeuvre Complète* from 1910 to 1952 (Erlenback-Zurich: Les Editions D'Architecture, 1955).

Crossman's successor as Housing Minister, Bob Mellish, was said by his former private secretary Brian Sedgemore to 'always symbolically pull the chain in a loo' when visiting the construction site of a new tower block. 'As he did this he said to me one day, "Brian, we are building slums in the sky"' (letter to the *Guardian*, 10 April 2006).

The full title of Professor Patrick Dunleavy's indispensable book is *The Politics of Mass Housing in Britain, 1945–75: A Study of Corporate Power and Professional Influence in the Welfare State* (Oxford University Press, 1981).

Nigel Warburton's book is called *Ernö Goldfinger: The Life of an Architect* (Routledge, 2003).

Walter Segal, who died in 1985, was a popularizer of self-building, particularly using environmentally sustainable techniques. The Walter Segal Self Build Trust encourages small-scale community builds throughout the country. I have quoted from his essay 'The Housing Crisis in Western Europe: Britain – Assessment and Options', which can be found in the volume *Architecture for People: Explorations in a New Human Environment* (Holt Rinehart Winston, 1980).

The Open University series *From Here to Modernity*, shown on BBC2 in 2001, gave me an illuminating introduction to the most important – whether loved or hated – Modernist buildings in Britain, including Park Hill, Trellick Tower and Ronan Point.

For the section about Park Hill's regeneration, I found useful the Office of the Deputy Prime Minister's *Government Response to ODPM Housing, Planning, Local Government and the Regions Committee Report on the Role of Historic Buildings in Urban Regeneration* (HMSO), presented to Parliament in November 2004.

Sheffield City Council's then Executive Director of Housing, now Executive Director of Neighbourhoods, Joanne Roney, is quoted in a *Guardian* report from July 2003 titled 'History of Conflict'. I do read newspapers other than the *Guardian*, by the way – it's just that their weekly *Society* supplement features the most pertinent and comprehensive reporting on issues of social housing and regeneration.

Dr Phil Jones of the University of Birmingham is the author of many papers on post-war high-rise building. In particular, I read his papers 'The Suburban High Flat in the Post-war Reconstruction of Birmingham, 1945–71', 'Bigger Is Better?: Local Authority Housing and the Strange Attraction of High-rise, 1945–70', 'A Room with a View: Post-war Suburban High-rise Housing in Birmingham, UK' and 'The Place of Design in English High-rise Flats During the Post-war Period', the last of which I have quoted from.

Anne Power's book *Estates on the Edge* (Macmillan, 1993) gives a comprehensive account of events on Broadwater Farm in the 1970s and 1980s from the point of view of housing management and sustaining social cohesion on council estates.

The Joseph Rowntree Foundation's 1994 report *Lessons from Hulme* was helpful for the Crescents part of the chapter.

Shrinking Cities, an exhibition held at the KW Institute for Contemporary Art in Berlin in September 2004, contained several informative and entertaining contributions to do with the post-industrial status of Manchester and Liverpool, including Newbetter's *Remember Tomorrow: Hulme as Urban Myth*, which took the form of a mural pasted with the wildly dissimilar testimonies of residents of the Crescents in the 1980s and mocked-up glossy magazine covers suggesting that the estate's reinvention as a 'des res' was imminent.

Arthur Marwick's *The Penguin Social History of Britain: British Society Since 1945* (Penguin, 3rd edn, 1996) offers a convincing, if slightly depressing, view of British life in the years leading up to the election of Margaret Thatcher in 1979.

Space is the Machine: A Configurational Theory of Architecture by Bill Hillier was published by Cambridge University Press in 1996.

Jason Cowley's comments on Harlow are from his essay 'Down Town', published in the *Guardian* in August 2002.

Chapter 4: The Wall in the Head

The *Staggers*, for those unfamiliar with arcane Fleet Street slang, is the political magazine the *New Statesman*.

Shortly before I left home, Richard came to visit me at my parents' house so he could pilfer my CD collection while seeing for himself this possibly mythical mammoth council estate of north Solihull. As we walked along the giant arching bridge that leads over the dual carriageway to the bingo hall at the shopping precinct, he groaned: 'I can't believe this actually exists.' We went back to mine and listened to The Smiths.

The article 'Ghetto Miasma – Enough to Make You Sick?', written by Helen Epstein, was published in the *New York Times Magazine* on 12 October 2003.

ACORN is, according to its website, 'the leading geodemographic tool used to identify and understand the UK population and the demand for products and services'. In other words, it helps companies to avoid the bother of trying to sell rich people's stuff to poor people.

A Joseph Rowntree Foundation *Findings* paper, dated September 2005 and subtitled 'The Relationship Between Poverty, Affluence and Area', also highlights the disparities in health, wealth and experience both between and within social groups.

The section about food poverty and food 'deserts' was deeply informed by the Demos pamphlet *Inconvenience Food: The Struggle to Eat Well on a Low Income*, written by Tim Lang in 2002.

The November 2005 exchange between Matthieu Kassovitz and Nicolas Sarkozy can be followed, in French, on the former's website: www.matthieukassovitz.com/blog.

Chapter 5: Begin Afresh

For this chapter I read the report of the inquiry into 'Support for the "Fourth Option" in Council Housing' produced by the House of Commons Council Housing Group in 2004.

Readers interested in knowing more about housing in Tower Hamlets might like to read Geoff Dench, Kate Gavron and Michael Young's book *The New East End* (Profile, 2006), a sequel of sorts to Young and Willmott's *Family and Kinship in East London*. Because it concentrates more on the effects of council-housing allocation, rather than the physical and environmental attributes of the housing stock, I felt that discussing it in the main text would open a whole new can of worms and so mention it here instead. Another reason for doing this is that the issue of white East Enders and families of Bangladeshi origin competing for a limited stock of housing, while having some wider resonance, is peculiar to Tower Hamlets. The issue of stock transfer, on the other hand, which I discuss with reference to Tower Hamlets in this chapter, is relevant to social housing nationwide.

A film about the failure of PFI on the Chalcot Estate, *Tower Blocked*, was made by community worker Paul Perkins in 2005. A clip can be viewed on the *Guardian* website www.societyguardian.co.uk.

Chapter 6: Homes Fit for Living In

The 1999 Demos report by Ben Jupp entitled *Living Together: Community Life on Mixed Tenure Estates* was very useful in trying to work out whether placing public and private housing together really works, why it does when it does, and why it doesn't when it doesn't. The aforementioned IPPR report by Chris Holmes does the same.

Frank Field's suggestion of sending disruptive families to live in steel containers 'under the motorway flyover' was reported in the *Daily Mirror* on 21 June 2005.

Jonathan Glancey's lecture to the Royal Society of Arts in London was called 'The Re-generation Game: What's Really Happening to Our Cities?' and took place on 27 October 2004.

The Staiths South Bank complex designed by Wayne and Gerardine Hemingway, ironically, was built and marketed by Wimpey Homes.

NORTHERN COLLEGE LIBRARY

BARNSLEY S75 3ET

Acknowledgements

First, my overwhelming thanks go to Matt Weiland, who somehow knew exactly what kind of book I wanted to write without my being able to explain it to him coherently. To Caroline Dawnay, for agreeing to be my agent on the basis of a few scribbly scraps. To Gail Lynch and Ian Jack, who were crucial champions at a time when I felt like putting it all in the bin, as was Sukhdev Sandhu, without whose encouragement I wouldn't have got even that far. Also to Andrew Martin for his advice in the book's putative stages. To my parents, for their immeasurable contribution, to Richard for sticking with me, and to all my wonderful friends, from whom I gain and learn more than I ever knew there was to gain and learn in the first place. To my teachers Jude Humphries, Ian Meacheam and Ken Bird, for their wisdom and support, and to my fellow steering group members, for theirs. To Nicci Tucker and Tom Booth, for reading this book in the draft stages and being kind enough not to laugh and use it as a firelighter, and to the anonymous expert readers who alerted me to some real howlers. Any others I take full responsibility for. To anyone who told me that a book about council estates sounded like a good idea, even if it sounded like the worst idea ever.

And to James, who is everything.

NORTHERN COLLEGE LIBRARY

BARNSLEY S75 3ET